D1191060

17-17

DE PROPRIETATIBUS LITTERARUM

edenda curat

C.H. VAN SCHOONEVELD

Indiana University

Series Practica, 110

NARRATIVE AND DRAMA

*Essays in Modern Italian Literature
from Verga to Pasolini*

by

Olga Ragusa

1976
MOUTON
THE HAGUE · PARIS

ISBN 90 279 3474 6

Printed in the Netherlands

FOREWORD

The essays collected in this volume are a contribution to the meager list of works of criticism in English on modern Italian literature. They are not, however, introductory surveys of an author's work but explorations of specific literary-historical and critical problems. As such they are characteristically oriented to questions of methodology.

"Stendhal, Tomasi di Lampedusa, and the Novel" is concerned essentially with trying to find a more comprehensive description than "historical novel" for Il gattopardo. "Narrative vs Stylistic Structure in I Malavoglia" reexamines a passage in that novel, which has played a particularly important role in the history of Verga criticism. "Pirandello and Verga" considers relationships between the two writers in terms of affinity rather than influence. "Pirandello's La patente: Play and Story" analyzes the transformation of narrative into drama in a play that stands at the confluence between Pirandello's Sicilian and European experiences. The essay on Svevo's Con la penna d'oro assesses limitations in his production as a playwright. "Alberto Moravia: Voyeurism and Storytelling" centers around the novel, L'attenzione, and the collection of short stories, L'automa. The final essay, the only one that can in some ways be considered introductory, presents the novels of Carlo Emilio Gadda and of Pier Paolo Pasolini in relation to more extreme examples of experimentalism in contemporary Italian fiction. Throughout, an effort has been made to blend close reading of the text with placing works within their broad historico-cultural contexts.

Acknowledgement is made to the editors of The Southern Review, Romanic Review, Comparative Literature Studies and Le parole e le idee, as well as to the Toronto University Press, Indiana University Press and the University of Tulsa Press for their kind permission to use material previously published.

TABLE OF CONTENTS

STENDHAL, TOMASI DI LAMPEDUSA, AND THE NOVEL

In the flood of critical appraisals that followed the publication of Il gattopardo in 1958, surprisingly scant attention was paid to Lampedusa's analysis of the work of a fellow novelist, Stendhal. His lectures on Stendhal, part of a series of "lessons" he held privately for a small group of students and friends in Palermo, were published while the Gattopardo controversy was still at its fiercest. (1) Yet they engaged the attention only of Louis Aragon, who made use of them in an article for Les Lettres françaises. (2) This article was almost immediately republished in Italian translation in Rinascita, journal of the Communist leader Togliatti. (3) A few months later, Aragon's remarks were made the subject of illuminating comment in a survey of French criticism of Il gattopardo, one of several articles defending the novel to appear in 1959-60 in Luigi Russo's leftist review Belfagor. (4) The writer of that article came to the conclusion that Aragon's was the only truly critical analysis of Il gattopardo to have come out in France.

This critic's statement could easily have been extended to cover Italy as well. As in France so in Italy, the early commentators on the novel concentrated mainly on its ideological content, analyzing that content in its historical reconstruction or in the theme of universal decay and death that accompanies and underscores what appears to be the author's disenchanted and pessimistic view of the benefits brought to Sicily by Garibaldi's conquest or, if you wish, liberation. Though much lip service was paid to the artistic merits of the work, both by those who shared Lampedusa's dolorous fascination with the past and by those who rejected it and yet admired the effectiveness of isolated episodes and the richness of the stylistic texture, no one analyzed these merits in terms of the "craft of fiction", a craft with whose theoretical principles Lampedusa was, as we will see, remarkably well acquainted.

This was true even of Aragon, who characterized Lampedusa's discussion of the technical aspects of the novel as that of "un homme du siècle qui a connu Proust, Joyce, Virginia Woolf", (5) but who went no further. Aragon's shock of recognition came not from discovering in Lampedusa a man completely up to date on the twentieth-century question du roman but rather from discovering in Lampedusa's reading of La Chartreuse de Parme confirmation for his own (Aragon's) contention that critics had erred in equating the intention behind Lampedusa's portrayal of the historico-political reality of post-Risorgimento Italy with the judgments overtly expressed by the protagonist, Don Fabrizio. (6) Aragon argued that just as Stendhal, according to Lampedusa, had set out to represent an infernal world of sinister but historically accurate intrigues and cruelties but had ended up instead with "the most adorable Dantesque Purgatory", (7) so Lampedusa may have proposed to describe "une sorte de Purgatoire de l'aristocratie sicilienne" but, "raté son coup", had come up instead with a novel which is "l'image de la perdition de cette aristocratie, l'image consciente, politique, de cette perdition, comme pouvait seul la décrire un homme qui avait fait de sa classe une critique impitoyable, une critique de gauche."(8) Thus, Aragon's momentary attention to "Lezioni su Stendhal" bore no further fruit but led back to the principal point of dispute: Lampedusa's conscious or unconscious ideological involvement.

It is my purpose, instead, to examine the "lessons" on Stendhal for the light they shed not on Lampedusa's ideological position but on his understanding and practice of novelistic techniques. (9) Many of the moot points on which critics ran afoul, many of the contradictory assertions that muddled their evaluation of Il gattopardo, and many sterile discussions of the precise genre or sub-genre to which the novel should be assigned are clarified or nullified in the light of Lampedusa's own affirmations. Aragon was of course correct in using Lampedusa's "merveilleuse explication, cette explication juste de la Chartreuse de Parme", as he calls it, as the key to a more penetrating reading of Il gattopardo. He was correct in pointing out that like the painter who lends his own traits to the subject whose portrait he is painting, so Lampedusa, in speaking of Stendhal, was actually speaking of himself. But Aragon was not really interested in Lampedusa's work as such. He was interested in drawing a lesson from it, in using it to show how through the conflict between an author's overt opinion and his latent involvement, a purportedly "reactionary" work can actually and almost inevitably become "revolutionary". As one critic put it, Aragon's role in the Gattopardo polemic was but one skirmish in his anti-Stalinism of the 1960's, one aspect of his participation in the "cultural thaw" of those years. (10)

In my own approach to the Gattopardo controversy and to the relevance of "Lezioni su Stendhal" to it, I shall begin by looking at the literary climate in Italy at the time of the novel's publication. The appearance of the first reviews of Il gattopardo coincided with the first discussions in Italy of nouveau roman. Though single works of Robbe-Grillet, Sarraute, and Beckett had received some notice earlier, (11) it was only in April 1959 that the concept of nouveau roman was introduced on a large scale and with polemical intent by the Milanese avant-garde periodical Il Verri. (12) In addition to the translation of Robbe-Grillet's basic "Une Voie pour le roman futur", (13) this issue contained articles on Robbe-Grillet, Butor, and Beckett, accompanied by excerpts from their works in Italian translation. (14)

The following February (1960) Il Verri published a number devoted
to the Italian novel. The outstanding contribution to this issue was
Renato Barilli's "Cahier de doléances sull'ultima narrative italiana".
(15) Barilli took an extremely negative view of practically all of post-
World War II Italian narrative literature (neorealism), finding it
below the level of acceptability for a reading public that had come to
expect - or should have come to expect - something better or, at any
rate, something different. In Pratolini, Cassola, Bassani, Pasolini,
and others, Barilli found, in spite of obvious surface differences,
the same "unimaginative and unconditional adherence to common
sense", the same spineless conformism to the underlying modes of
experience accepted by the public at large. Barilli allowed the writers
he mentioned their "progressive" position in the social and political
arenas, but he accused them of having done nothing to promote a
deeper kind of change, change involving the very structures of experience: "the manner of conceiving time and space, of perceiving objects,
of identifying and naming sentiments, of articulating the syntax of
propositions". All of this - this thorough subversion - Barilli continued, had to some extent been achieved by writers such as Joyce,
Kafka, and Proust in the early part of the century, and their innovations were being continued outside of Italy in the work of the "new"
novelists or "experimentalists". (16)

The problem of the Italian novel - with or without respect to the
state of the novel elsewhere - had of course been discussed before.
In the years immediately preceding talk of the nouveau roman, for
instance, the periodical Ulisse had published a special number (1956-
57) devoted to the "fate" of the novel: "Le sorti del romanzo." Con-
tributors ranged from Goffredo Bellonci, man of letters and founder
of the Strega Prize, to Mario Praz, dean of Italian Anglicists, and to
the novelist and cultural activist, Pier Paolo Pasolini. Among the
problems discussed were: realism in contemporary narrative writing;
the relationship between the novel and history, between the novel and
society, the novel and science, the novel, the theater and the motion
picture; and the Catholic novel in France, England, and Italy. Answers
were sought to questions such as: What is the state of Italian narrative literature today? Is there really a conflict between content and
form? If so, what shape does it take? Though a wide variety of
opinions was expressed, and one participant (Luigi Bartolini) went so
far as to deny the existence of novels of any kind in Italy, no one
seemed aware of imminent and drastic changes either in the types of
novels being written or in the theoretical premises on which they
were based. The feeling of crisis, however, was present prominently only two years later in a questionnaire on the Italian novel sponsored by the review Nuovi argomenti (May-August 1959), of which
Moravia was coeditor. Here, in the questions if not always in the
answers, there is definite evidence that a deep break in the tradition
was felt to have taken place.

It is not my purpose to examine the merits of the case: whether, that is, the Italian novel was in 1959 in a worse crisis than before, whether the indigenous Italian "experimental" novels that were later written on the model of nouveau roman came up to "international standards", and whether Italian literature through them indeed caught up with the achievements of Joyce and Kafka. (17) Strains of a familiar plaint are heard in all this: a long Italian habit of self-denigration, which at one time played itself out almost completely in comparisons with the French cultural situation and which was now extended to include the Anglo-Saxon and Germanic worlds as well. For the purpose at hand, it is sufficient to point out that it was into this atmosphere of insecurity, self-criticism, and doubt that the immediate and phenomenal popular success of Il gattopardo burst like a scandal. (18) The enthusiasm with which the book was read appeared to give the lie to the then current apocalyptic predictions that the nineteenth-century type of novel, the novel par excellence, was dead. To the journalistic critic who was or wished to be up to date, Lampedusa seemed at best a latecomer who had by accident written a best seller. At worst, he was the undeserving beneficiary of a wily advertising campaign conducted by that favorite of the literary establishment, Giorgio Bassani, who had known how to capitalize on the timeliness of the book's theme in the year of the centennial celebration of Italian unity. (19) With greater objectivity, a critic like Leone Piccioni described Il gattopardo simply as an example of "horizontal" (i.e., following the chronology of events) storytelling, which appeared at a time when the public was turning to "vertical" (i.e., digressive or in depth) narration. (20)

Of course critics and reviewers had difficulty with Il gattopardo. It both suggested and eluded a variety of classifications. As a historical novel it inevitably called to mind I promessi sposi. But nothing in it echoed Manzoni's quiet confidence in Providence nor his controlled distance from his characters. As a "regional" novel it was immediately connected with the work of the Sicilian writers of the turn of the century, Verga and de Roberto especially. (21) But its overt lyricism was at odds with their programmatic desire for impersonality and objectivity. As a post-World War II novel it jarred because of its florid writing and its sympathetic portrayal of a defeated and discredited class. As a "Proustian" novel it was too firmly anchored in history, too much concerned with the non-psychological determinants of action and experience. (22) Montale, in reviewing it for Il giorno (9 June 1959), called it the book of a "grand seigneur", one of the last representatives of a dying if not already defunct class. It occurred to almost no one that it was also, and perhaps primarily, the book of a great connoisseur of the twentieth-century theory of the novel. (23)

It is true that Bassani in his preface had remarked that Lampedusa should "probably" be related to "several great English writers of the

first half of the century (Forster, for example) with whom he must
have been familiar". (24) But Bassani made the connection because,
as he said, these writers were in essence essayists and poets rather
than novelists, and not, as he might have said equally well, because
they had a distinctive approach to fiction. Francesco Orlando, the
young student for whose benefit Lampedusa began his teaching activities in 1953, wrote in his reminiscences of the years of almost daily
association with the novelist that he appeared to be unacquainted with
critics and works of criticism after Croce, that he was not up to date
on more modern developments. (25) It is my contention, instead, that
he was very much up to date but that the kind of interest in the "craft
of fiction" which his "Lezioni su Stendhal" reveals had not yet reached
Italy. (26) It may be argued that when that kind of interest finally did
reach Italy, it could have only an academic resonance; that by then
the "experimental" novel had definitively supplanted the last offshoots
of the great realistic tradition; and that the Gattopardo case was
therefore sealed. Whatever the reasons, "Lezioni su Stendhal" as a
key to Il gattopardo was, in spite of occasional references to it, overlooked, and it was overlooked, I would claim, because of unfamiliarity
or insufficient familiarity on the part of Italian critics with the
Jamesian tradition of criticism in the novel. (27)

By one of those strange and recurrent accidents in historical development, Il gattopardo was written both before and after its time. For
that reason it has no proper and easy place in the commonly accepted
schemes of the history of the European novel. In the context of twentieth-century Italian literature, Lampedusa was original precisely
because he looked back, because he belonged to a tradition that had
in a sense run its course but had at the same time never had a full
impact on Italian literature. (28) It is no wonder that avant-garde
critics in 1959 and 1960 misunderstood him. They were busy celebrating the demise of neorealism. The Marxists, on the other hand,
were attracted by the work but read it as a historical document, a
socio-political indictment of the "heroic" period of modern Italian
history. Neither the Marxists nor the avant-garde were capable of
capturing the full intention of Lampedusa's understatement. In
"Lezioni su Stendhal", however, Lampedusa left the necessary clues
for a more proper and comprehensive interpretation of his work.

Lampedusa deals with the whole of Stendhal's production, convinced
that all Stendhal's works, including the so-called minor ones, bear
the mark of an exceptional personality, a personality able to give
new life even to what appeared to be outworn and no longer valid
genres. Thus he describes Les Promenades dans Rome as a unique
travel book that ranks as a literary work of art and De l'amour as an
extraordinary "physiologie" that belongs with the best in literature.
But if his attention to the early Vies, the Histoire de la peinture en

Italie, and Racine et Shakespeare (12-17); to Rome, Naples et
Florence, Mémoires d'un touriste, and Promenades dans Rome (17-
20, 36-37); to De l'amour (20-22); to the Chroniques italiennes and
Armance (22-26, 37-38); to the unfinished Lucien Leuwen and Lamiel
(44-47); and to the many posthumous and unpublished fragments (47-
49) - if this attention reveals Lampedusa's thorough acquaintance
with the corpus of Stendhal's work, it is to the two masterpieces that
he devotes the substance and particular acumen of his analysis. Le
Rouge et le noir and La Chartreuse de Parme are presented first
together as "works of absolute first rank" (3-12) and are then discussed separately under the section heading "L'Heure des
cuirassiers" (26-36 for Le Rouge, 38-44 for La Chartreuse). Since
this study is concerned mainly not with Lampedusa as critic of
Stendhal but with Lampedusa as novelist, I propose to focus only on
those passages of "Lezioni su Stendhal" in which he formulates general rules of narrative technique and applies them to Stendhal or
where he uses Stendhal as a point of departure to discuss the art of
fiction.

In light of the kind of criticism to which Il gattopardo was later
subjected, Lampedusa's single most significant statement comes at
the very beginning of the essay, when he writes that Stendhal's two
masterpieces possess a quality that the minor works for all their
excellence do not. That quality is manysidedness (poliedricità), (29)
the distinguishing feature of works of absolute first rank. For,
Lampedusa says, if Le Rouge and La Chartreuse can from one point
of view be considered (1) historical novels, they can also be considered (2) the "lyrical" outpouring of their author's sentiments, (3)
psychological case studies, (4) lessons in a certain kind of morality,
and (5) models of the most difficult of styles, the style of extreme
conciseness (estrema abbreviazione). Let us discuss each of these
points.

Inasmuch as Il gattopardo was generally recognized to be first and
foremost a historical novel, we should note the meaning Lampedusa
gives to the term. He ignores Scott and the novel of archeological
reconstruction of the past altogether. Instead, he speaks of "novels
that have become historical for us", that portray objectively
(oggettivazione) a period that was contemporary for their author but
has become so remote for the reader that he can know it only through
art. Thus it is possible for Lampedusa to speak of both Balzac and
Stendhal, chroniclers of their own times, as historical novelists. But
with the difference, he is quick to add, that for him Stendhal achieved
in the five hundred pages of Le Rouge et le noir what Balzac failed to
achieve in "twenty volumes". For it is not completeness of documentation that counts for Lampedusa, but something else. To paraphrase
and compress his words, what counts is the miraculous intuition of
"la couleur du temps": "in them (the five hundred pages of Le Rouge

et le noir) there is everything: the motives, the impulses, the oppo-
sitions, the cultural richness, the time lags (gli sfasamenti), the
creakings (gli scricchiolii), the sense of a dawn, the 'couleur du
temps' of that vital crossroads of French history" (4). And echoing
a feeling often expressed by critics with regard to I promessi sposi,
he adds that other works of the period, even memoirs, bring only
confirmation of Stendhal's "miraculous intuitions". Further, extending his remarks from Le Rouge et le noir to La Chartreuse de Parme,
he sees in this second novel a "tenderly ironic evocation" of pre-
Risorgimento Italy, a period, according to him, almost completely
ignored by writers, except for Byron in his correspondence and for
some brilliant hints (felici bagliori) in the novels of Mme de Staël.
"The dearth of documents with which to reconstruct human experience
is staggering" (la carenza di documenti umani è sbalorditiva), he
states, putting into those few words the searing recollection of the
millions of lives that have passed on earth without leaving a trace of
their existence. (30) Thus, this brief passage on the historical novel
contains what we might call Lampedusa's definition of its subject
matter and a rapid but powerful hint of the pietas out of which it is
born.

We can treat the next three points as a unit. Lampedusa connects
the lyrical quality of Stendhal's work, his psychological penetration,
and the ethical doctrine that his novels imply and others of his works
openly display with Stendhal's sense of himself and with the projection of that self into his fictional creations. Thus, Sorel is the man
the ambitious Stendhal actually was; del Dongo, the noble, wealthy,
beloved man he would have wished to be. Through both, Stendhal
speaks directly; that is, lyrically. The other characters, those who
are neither the author himself nor stand-ins for him, are given life
not so much by his feelings as by his intelligence: Stendhal's much-
admired psychological knowledge. The Epicurean, hedonistic ethic
that paradoxically attributes greater satisfaction to the pursuit of
pleasure than to its attainment and enjoyment impels Stendhal's
characters as it impelled him. These points, though Lampedusa does
not present them as such, might be summarized as his comment on
the autobiographical aspects of Stendhal's novels.

This leaves us with the fifth point: Stendhal's style, the "mortar
that binds together the different stones and assures the durability of
the edifice" (8). It is here that we encounter the first unmistakable
sign that Lampedusa's reading of Stendhal is that of the craftsman or
potential craftsman interested in the writing of fiction. His reading
is not simply that of the enthusiastic reader who finds himself extra-
ordinarily well attuned to a favorite writer's portrayal of experience,
nor is it that of the cultivated and educated reader who is at home in
the critical literature that deals with his subject. Lampedusa makes
a point of separating himself from the average reader, whose main

concern in a novel is plot. He specifically warns that Stendhal's works must be read with the proper attention and not merely to find out what happens in the story. He does not fix his gaze on the world created by Stendhal - though that world is completely "real" to him, as witness his rounded views of the characters Julien and Fabrice, Mme de Rênal and Sanseverina, of the "twin figures" of M. de Rênal and Count Mosca, the "absurd and attractive" Ferrante Palla, the "wooden" General Fabio Conti, the "myriad mean priests and plotters" (the descriptive epithets are all Lampedusa's). Rather, his attention is on Stendhal in the act of creating that world. And just as he emphasized Stendhal's involvement in his characters, playing down his much vaunted objectivity, so he now chooses as the perspective from which to examine his style not the traditional view of the "style du Code Civil" but Jean Prévost's "style de l'improvisateur". (31) Not that he ignores the "style du Code Civil" completely, for he does mention Stendhal's disdain "pour les phrases" and his remarkable talent for economy. In the latter connection, he cites three well-known instances of quasi-miraculous understatement: Manzoni's famous remark about the Monaca di Monza, "La sventurata rispose"; Stendhal's no less famous "Aucune résistance ne fut opposée"; and the semicolon that contains Julien's night of love with Mathilde.

To observe Lampedusa most intently absorbed in watching the writer at work we must follow his discussion of the "style de l'improvisateur" in some detail. The apparent spontaneity of Stendhal's style, he says (citing Prévost), was achieved by Stendhal's habit of "internal" composition or (in Proust's words, which he quotes) by his ability to "raturer à l'avance". He devotes considerable attention to an analysis of this process, reconstructing Stendhal's efforts to reduce to the page the data supplied by experience. With extraordinary sensitivity to the genetic moment of the process, Lampedusa points out that Stendhal aimed at eliminating everything but the "essential" from the sensations of experience themselves, and not merely from their notation on the page. (32) Thus Stendhal's text "appears fluent, impetuous, improvised, while it was actually the fruit of long and minute elaboration" (10). The elaboration, he then carefully notes, took place not on the page, "where only words can be elaborated on, but in the heat of the sensation itself, with the infallible instinct which tends to render thoughts clear before we formulate them. (They become muddy later, in writing.)". It is instructive to juxtapose this passage to Orlando's recollection that in 1956 Lampedusa read him Il gattopardo from what he described as a first draft. Orlando notes that this draft was so free of erasures, corrections, and insertions that he doubted that it was indeed a first attempt: "If the author spoke the truth, we must conclude that the novel was written in a state of veritable literary grace."(33)

But with a deeper and more ascetic understanding of the process of
literary creation, Lampedusa shows in "Lezioni su Stendhal" that it
is not a miracle that accounts for a "miraculous" work of art, but the
tireless and intense effort required to give form to the chaos of experience. In Stendhal, Lampedusa says, this effort took place contin-
uously in the mind, as memories were sifted down to offer up their
essential and irreducible nuclei. (34) The result was that extraordinary "writing in two columns, composed in equal measure of a first
series of sensations expressed and transmitted, and of a second
series transmitted only through an accentuated silence intended to
make the attentive reader prick up his ears" (11). Lampedusa describes this technique of suggestion as characteristic of Stendhal,
but it is of course no less characteristic of Lampedusa himself, of
whose novel it can be said that in spite of its success as a best seller
it is dedicated, as is the Chartreuse, "To the happy few."

When Lampedusa returns to the subject of the two novels the second
time in "Lezioni" (26), he moves at once to place the discussion
within a broader frame of reference. He no longer focuses on the
characteristics of Stendhal's works (the five points just considered)
but on the more general questions of narrative technique. While the
earlier set of remarks is therefore useful as a key to the affinities
that draw Il gattopardo and the novels of Stendhal together, (35) this
second set serves to confirm the impression of technical control, of
conscious craftsmanship (36) that accompanies a careful reading of the
novel. Lampedusa's "reading" of Stendhal and his acquaintance with
the tools for critical analysis of narrative technique converge to
throw the formal - as against the ideological - aspects of Il gattopardo
into strong relief. (37)
   Lampedusa starts out by recognizing the uselessness of repeating
praise of Stendhal's gifts as a poet, a psychologist, and an "evoker"
of milieus. (38) But if there is little point in repeating what has already
been said and about which there is general agreement, he continues,
there is every reason for turning to the why (il perchè) of Stendhal's
greatness - for examining, that is, his technique of expression. "In
art", Lampedusa states axiomatically, "the possibility of communicating is everything" (27). And again later: "In art the 'technique of
execution' is everything, for the artist is nothing more than a fellow
(tizio) who knows how to express himself" (34). In the case of the
novel the specific problems of expression are (1) the treatment of
time, (2) the concretization of the narrative situation (concretizzare
la narrazione), (3) the suggestion of milieu, and (4) the treatment of
dialogue. Although Lampedusa lists the problems in this order, he
does not discuss them thus. For as soon as he is forced to touch
upon (5) the position of the narrator, it becomes obvious that the
central and crucial consideration, the pivot around which all else

revolves, is "point of view", a term he does not use but a concept he describes perceptively and at length.

We can omit the details of Lampedusa's exposition of these five points, except to note a few significant observations. In connection with the first point, he mentions specifically as tools of suggestion to indicate the expansion of narrative time (rallentamenti nel ritmo della narrazione): reference to the succession of the seasons (Tolstoy's method in "the immortal chapters" (28) telling of the progressive estrangement of Anna and Wronski); the use of the imperfect tense; observations on physical changes; and the celebration of anniversaries. With respect to the fifth point, the position of the narrator, he speaks of the three expedients by which the old writers (not further identified) placated their scruples on omniscience: the epistolary form; first-person narrative in which the protagonist knows his own inner life; and first-person narrative in which he is presumed to be endowed with the power of interpreting his own thoughts and also those of the other characters.

Lampedusa warns that passing time must be suggested or alluded to incidentally, almost secretly (di sfuggita e quasi di nascosto), for time in a novel is not the time of a "train schedule" (28), and that first-person narrative in which the protagonist also knows the inner life of other characters is fraught with dangers that only a genius like Proust can brave with impunity. As for Stendhal, he "chose the quickest and proudest way: to simplify, we may call it the way of having God tell the story. In the garb of a deity, Stendhal knows the most hidden thoughts of every character, pointing them out to the reader who shares in his omniscience. Stendhal leaves nothing in shadow, except what he chooses not to say in order to heighten the emotion" (29).(39)

This whole passage is as important as the discussion of Stendhal's style to which we referred earlier. Both statements are crucial for a proper understanding of Il gattopardo: the first directs attention to Lampedusa's use of understatement, the second is a clue to the reason that inclined him to third-person narrative. Together they bring into relief the role of the reader, a point to which Lampedusa refers specifically: "This technique (Stendhal's telling of the story as though he were God) of almost unbelievable subtlety results in the complete fusion of author, character, and reader. The latter is no longer an outsider (estraneo) who watches the action but almost always one of the protagonists of the action itself" (30).(40)

The remaining three technical problems dealing with expression are concerned essentially with the concretization of the action, with turning theme into plot. Here Lampedusa's most significant remark has to do with the treatment of dialogue. In Stendhal, he points out, "there is not one instance of a famous dialogue" (33). This he attributes to the fact that Stendhal avoided the "error of so many novelists (including some of the greatest!) who reveal a character's inner life through what he says". In real life, Lampedusa continues, "verbal revelation" almost never occurs: we understand people through "their actions, their glances, their stammering, the entwining of their fingers, their silences or their sudden speech, the color of their cheeks, the rhythm of their step" (33). Thus, Lampedusa illustrates, Stendhal reports not Julien's words in refusing to marry Elisa, but their gist. This permits him to interject his own implied comments so as "to rectify what has been said", to unmask the intention that words so often hide or misrepresent - "words which are always the chaste or impudent masks of a person's inmost being" (34). (41)

It follows quite naturally that as the usefulness of direct discourse is discounted, the importance of stream of consciousness (monologo interiore, as Lampedusa calls it) increases. Stendhal's recourse to stream of consciousness in order to reveal the motives behind an action differs, according to Lampedusa, from use of the same technique in Proust, Joyce, and Virginia Woolf. (42) This is because Le Rouge et le noir is not only "a lyrical effusion and a novel of psychological analysis" but also a portrait of its time and a story filled with deeds and actions. In such a story (i.e., in a historical novel), stream of consciousness can never become an end in itself but must remain subordinated to the narrative intentions of the storyteller. "The action of Ulysses", says Lampedusa, "lasts twenty-four hours and is a simple, ordinary action; yet its reading takes at least five times as long, in spite of Joyce's magnificent efforts at concentration. But his efforts are directed toward verbal concentration. Stendhal's instead aim at obtaining a concentration of the substance (concentrazione sostanziale) of the psychological moments. Of each of these he has kept only the essential, and only in a second moment did he subject it to the distillation of his style, one of the most agile (svelto) in existence. The 'interior monologues' of Stendhal's characters are extremely brief: just a few lines. The transitions between them and the rest of the story are handled with a few indirect expressions, forming a kind of gentle slope that connects the two kinds of exposition" (31).

The relatively few passages from Lampedusa's "Lezioni su Stendhal" on which I have based these remarks were selected for the strong light they shed on Lampedusa's conscious art in Il gattopardo and have been rearranged in such a way as to form a kind of statement on the poetics of the novel. In conclusion, I wish to call attention to one final point: Lampedusa's conviction, which may at first seem paradoxical, that much of the negative criticism leveled at Le Rouge et le noir upon its publication must be attributed to Stendhal's technical achievement (potenza di tecnica). The accusation of moral indifference, the view that Stendhal had actually written an apologia of Julien's ruthless opportunism, derives, according to Lampedusa, not from the inherent depravity of the "monstrous" Julien but from the ability with which he is portrayed: "In comparison with Dorian Gray, Lafcadio, Morel, and even the Reverend Slope, Julien is a little angel . . . . Insignificant rogues like Julien can be found by the thousands in life and by the dozens in literature. But he is one of the very few who has been described with a technique such as to render all his (after all, banal) evil sunlike (solare, i.e., all-encompassing) for the reader . . . . We are not dealing with a monster but with a character who is monstrously alive" (35).

Readers of Le Rouge et le noir, Lampedusa continues, have also been disturbed by Julien's death, which seems to them unmotivated psychologically, slovenly in execution, and consequently an artistic failure. Again, on the strength of his own critical analysis, Lampedusa differs from this opinion. For him, the ending of the book is one of its greatest merits. It is not only the logical conclusion of the basic narrative situation but also proof of Stendhal's fundamental honesty as a writer, for his interest in Julien had come to an end the moment Julien had achieved the goal of his quest, the moment his pursuit of happiness had been satisfied. Stendhal's haste to kill off the character once he had no further use for him results for Lampedusa in "an ending without equal, tragically suggestive" (36). Finally, Lampedusa comes back to a reflection that runs like a leitmotiv through much of "Lezioni su Stendhal": the uselessness of trying to explain beauty and artistic achievement to those who have insufficient sensitivity to perceive them. In this, of course, he no more than echoes Stendhal, who had resigned himself to being misunderstood in his own time and had looked into the future for readers who would finally penetrate his intention - his craft - and proclaim him a master.

Except for three articles published in 1926-27, (43) Lampedusa's extant works belong to the brief span of time between his return in the summer of 1954 from a literary gathering in northern Italy and his death in July 1957. (44) Of the short pieces collected in 1961 in the volume Racconti, "Il mattino di un mezzadro" (presumably the first chapter of a new novel to be entitled I gattini ciechi) and "I luoghi della mia prima infanzia" are related to the subject matter of Il gattopardo, while "La gioia e la Legge" and "Lighea" are autonomous short stories. Bassani, in his preface to Il gattopardo, gave "between 1955 and 1956" as the period during which the novel was written, but in an interview published later he changed the first date to 1954 so that it coincides with Lampedusa's return from the meeting at San Pellegrino Terme, where his cousin Lucio Piccolo had won recognition for a volume of poetry and where he himself had come into contact "with the writing of the 1950's" (Bassani, Banti, Vittorini, Cassola, and others). (45) Orlando reported that he began his daily readings of the manuscript at Lampedusa's request "in one of the early months of 1956". (46)

Three distinct drafts of the novel have been preserved: a hand-written one (1955-56), the one read by Orlando; a typewritten one (1956), copied by Orlando and corrected by Lampedusa; and a long-hand copy of the latter (1957), made by Lampedusa himself and bearing on the frontispiece the words Il gattopardo (completo). It was the typewritten copy that was submitted to Mondadori, Einaudi, and Feltrinelli, and (with the addition of two chapters) served as the basis for the printed text when Bassani accepted the work for publication by Feltrinelli. However, after type had already been set and the proofs were about to be read, Bassani also obtained the long-hand copy and incorporated some of its variants into the printed text. He later summarized his work of revision in these terms: "Everything new in the manuscript copy I put into the book or, if you like, nothing new in the 1957 version fails to be there. "(47) In addition, he "corrected or supplied" punctuation.

The matter would probably have rested there if, in examining the possibility of making a critical edition of the by then famous work, Carlo Muscetta had not some years later reopened the question of the two manuscripts by suggesting melodramatically that readers had not been supplied with the genuine and authentic product. (48) A new controversy stirred the Italian literary world and led to the publication of a second edition of the novel. (49) Its foreword, by Gioacchino Lanza Tomasi, Lampedusa's adopted son, rehearsed once again the history of publication and described at length and in detail the divergences between the 1957 manuscript and the first edition. (50) These divergences, however illuminating, do not concern us here. As a matter of fact, of the very considerable mass of background material now available on the conception and execution of the novel, a small part only is relevant to the rereading of Il gattopardo in the light of "Lezioni su Stendhal" that interests us here.

There is, first, the information that was supplied by Lampedusa's widow with respect to the novel's long period of incubation. Bassani quotes her as saying that "twenty-five years ago (Lampedusa) announced his intention of writing an historical novel set in Sicily at the time of Garibaldi's landing at Marsala and revolving around the figure of his paternal great-grandfather, the astronomer Giulio di Lampedusa. He was constantly thinking of it, but he never actually sat down to write it. "(51) Secondly, there is Gioacchino Lanza Tomasi's recollection of the original tripartite division of the novel, each division marked by the lapse of twenty-five years: 1860, Garibaldi's landing at Marsala; 1885, the death of the prince (in the final version of the novel the episode was moved to 1883, but the actual date of the great-grandfather's death was 1885); 1910, "the end of everything. "(52)

While the princess's words bear witness to the fact that, if the book was in the end the product of intense and regular application, (53) it had actually been in the making for a quarter of a century; Lanza Tomasi's call attention to the equally significant fact that the last chapter, considered superfluous and unsuccessful by the majority of critics, who all read the novel as the story of its protagonist, was from the beginning part of the overall scheme. (54) As far as the other chapter found perplexing by critics (the present chapter 5) is concerned, though not part of the original plan, it too belongs to Lampedusa's own vision of his work as it appears in the 1959 Il gattopardo (completo). (55) The inequalities and disproportions perceived by many critics no doubt exist. According to Lanza Tomasi's report, the three Donnafugata chapters (about half of the book as we have it today), not to speak of the scene at the ball and the chapter on Father Pirrone at San Cono, were not part of the original conception, (56) a state of affairs that must inevitably have left traces in the novel. But rather than speak of disproportions and inequalities, most frequently attributed to Lampedusa's presumed inexperience or to the fact that his completion and revision of the novel might be supposed to have been cut short by death, it would seem more profitable to take the book as it is, in the very form in which it won popular success, and to examine it along the lines suggested by Lampedusa's own statements on narrative technique. Only after considering such matters as Lampedusa's (1) treatment of time, (2) his presentation of milieu, (3) the point of view from which he tells the story, and (4) his handling of dialogue should such other questions be examined, as (5) the type of novel it can primarily be said to be, (6) the nature of its message and (7) its style.

Rather than attempt the comprehensive analysis just outlined, I shall single out two problem areas to which critics have returned time and again: the relevance or discrepancy of chapter 5, and the significance, appropriateness, or incongruence of chapter 8. Though ultimately the judgments made depend on one's view of the overall form or structure of the work, these two chapters present sufficiently differentiated problems to permit us to consider them as separate and independent case studies. Because it is more closely and obviously related to the novel's ideological content, chapter 5 has received the greater share of attention. Chapter 8, instead, has been rapidly dismissed as an unfortunate afterthought on the part of the author, who was presumably torn between a biographically centered and a cyclical concept of the historical novel.

Chapter 5 is the first chapter of the novel in which the prince does not occupy center stage. (57) At its end, when Father Pirrone returns to Palermo, the hierarchy is reestablished and the prince again becomes the major god of his household. During the two-day visit to

his native village, however, Father Pirrone is given the opportunity
to talk and act on his own initiative: his reflections on the political
changes taking place echo the prince's colloquy with Chevalley; his
arrangement of a marriage for his niece parallels the prince's
"swallowing of a toad" in the latter's negotiations for the marriage
of Tancredi. Father Pirrone's visit marks an anniversary, that of
his father's death fifteen years before. Lampedusa's retrospective
look at the priest's family background - something he had not been
able to do when the character was first introduced - is thus deftly
justified, and the introductory pages in which don Gaetano's business
activities and Father Pirrone's childhood and youth are rapidly recalled show no signs of artifice or strain.

The sense of the unchanging continuity of life and of the momentary surface disturbance brought by the recent "liberation" of Sicily
(chapter 5 is dated February 1861, a mere three months after the
preceding one) is expressed by two "objective correlatives", mirror
images of identical objects that function in the prince's milieu: the
dog Romeo, "great-great-grandson" of a dog that had romped with
the boy Saverio, and the tricolor cockade that Father Pirrone's
nephew Carmelo "had had the bad taste" of putting in his cap as a
sign of rejoicing. The chapter forms a diptych: Father Pirrone
answers the old herbalist's question about the reactions of the nobil-
ity to the revolution that is undermining its privileges; and Father
Pirrone smoothes over a revengeful seduction and one brother's
"dirty trick" on another, by convincing his sister to give her
daughter the proper dowry. With understated irony, Lampedusa
reduces Father Pirrone's audience to one sleeping man, no doubt
intending to show thereby that truth can be revealed only when there
is no chance of its being heard: "now [that no one was listening] he
could talk freely, without fear of being misunderstood, and he talked
so as to fix in the concrete pattern of phrases the ideas that were
dimly milling about in his mind" (232). More overtly, Lampedusa
calls attention to the parallelism between the love antics of the rus-
tics Angelina and Santino and Angelica's and Tancredi's retracing
of the stops on the carte du tendre, by remarking on the residue of
unpleasant impressions that his visit has left in Father Pirrone:
"that brutal love affair whose culmination had come during Saint
Martin's Summer (November 1860 was also the time of Angelica's
and Tancredi's exploration of the abandoned rooms at Donnafugata),
that miserable half of an almond grove grabbed back by means of a
premeditated courtship, showed him the rustic, sordid side of other
happenings that he had recently witnessed" (246). But before we
reach this explicit statement at the very end of the chapter, the
sophisticated reader has been free to draw his own conclusions from
the careful balancing of mood and event, of characters and comments.

We have seen already that chapter 5 is one of the two chapters that were not part of the original manuscript read by Bassani. Bassani came upon the chapter later, in the longhand version, and decided to use it in spite of the princess's objection. "I found that it was essential to the structure of the novel. This sort of descent to hell is a fundamental clue to understanding Fabrizio and Sicily", he was quoted as saying in the 1970 interview. The princess, instead, would have preferred to keep the chapter, together with the scene of the ball, to which she had herself called Bassani's attention, for inclusion in a possible publication of Lampedusa's shorter pieces. But she may of course also have been influenced by what Lanza Tomasi remembers of Lampedusa's own hesitation about the chapter, which displeased him because, contrary to his usual practice, it was "explicit" rather than "implicit", providing a kind of "gloss" to the prince's behavior rather than permitting it to express itself simply through the narration of events. (58) It is interesting to note once again that Lampedusa's judgment as reported here is based on a consideration of technique, on an awareness of the importance of the choice of point of view in storytelling. But it is equally interesting to note that he seems to have shared with Bassani, at this point at least, the conviction that the prince is after all the one and only center of the novel.

Simonetta Salvestroni, whose two articles in Filologia e letteratura and whose full-length study of Lampedusa are among the few really perceptive discussions of Il gattopardo, advances a different hypothesis, and buttresses it with a rare, if not unique, reference to "Lezioni su Stendhal". (59) By asking herself how Lampedusa succeeded in giving movement and complexity to what is essentially a static situation, she discovered elements of a thoroughly worked-out pattern in which scenes of bitterness and pessimism alternate with others which mark a recovery of serenity. Chapter 5 thus counterbalances the taste of ashes left by the prince's encounter with Chevalley at the end of chapter 4, and lightens the atmosphere before the depressing observations in chapter 6 on the decline of his class and on the inevitable sinking of all men into old age and death, made by the prince during the festivities at the ball of the Ponteleones. The passage which she quotes from "Lezioni su Stendhal" reads as follows: "But in the course of a novel, especially if it is composed of tense psychological probing and of a hurried action, moments of pause must be provided for the reader. Obviously, it always takes less time to read a novel than to write it, and even if the author does not feel the need to pause for himself, he must not forget that the reader needs it. If the reader fails to find these oases in which to rest, he will close the book at the least appropriate moment and reopen it when the accumulated energy has evaporated. Every great author of long works has provided these breathing spaces: Homer, with his interpolated episodes; Dante, always; Ariosto, with his rough technique, breaking a story off at its high point to turn to other inventions (fanfaluche) destined to be trimmed in their turn; Cervantes and Mme de Lafayette, by inserting secondary stories; Richardson and Thackeray, by speaking themselves in lieu of their characters."

Thus, for Simonetta Salvestroni chapter 5 is not only a pendant to and a parody of the main story but also a break in the narrative, a determined turning away from the main character and the lesser characters disposed about him in the guise of satellites. Or to put it in Lampedusa's own terms, chapter 5 is a major device for the expansion of narrative time, for creating what he called "rallentamenti nel ritmo della narrazione".

These, then, are some of the thematic and formal reasons that can be adduced to support the idea that chapter 5 is an integral part of the novel and that Lampedusa might perhaps have changed parts of it but would not have abandoned it altogether. (60) Of course, these reasons become apparent only after we discard the preconceived notion that the unity of Il gattopardo depends on the continuous presence of the protagonist on stage. How deeply rooted this notion is (a notion the title of the book itself does not help dispel) can be seen in the fact that although chapter 6 was, like chapter 5, an afterthought, and felt by Bassani to be stylistically inferior to the rest of the novel, it was never seriously considered de trop: the presence of the prince was enough to mute any nascent negative impressions. And yet, not only the book's original tripartite plan and the report that Lampedusa once planned to call it Ultime luci (61) ("Last Lights", a theatrical, cinematic allusion that would not have been inappropriate, although far less economical and striking than "The Leopard") but especially its inclusion of another chapter that does without the prince - these facts should have alerted the critics that they might possibly have overlooked something.

Chapter 8 takes place twenty-seven years after the death of the prince and fifty after the opening pages of the book. Of the Salina family only the girls survive: Carolina, Caterina, Concetta, and Chiara, their married sister in Naples, of whom there had been no mention earlier. Angelica, too, whose forty-year marriage to Tancredi "had erased all traces of the Donnafugata accent and manners" (315), is in her seventies. Like chapter 5, chapter 8 moves between two main episodes: the official inspection of the private chapel at Villa Salina, in accordance with the new regulations of the Papal Curia, and the visit to Concetta of Tassoni, erstwhile comrade-in-arms of Tancredi and now an aged senator. Like chapter 5 but with greater force of impact, chapter 8 ends with the new experiences of the two days (13-14 May) whose events it recounts echoing through the psyche of its protagonist, this time however with the grand conclusiveness of the final chords of a heroic symphony. The word Fine, centered on the last page of the 1957 manuscript, is corroboration of the completo we read on the title page. In omitting the word, the English edition respects a publisher's sensitivity to the quaintness of its use in a modern novel but betrays Lampedusa's own intention of emphasizing the fully conscious aspect of his technique of composition.

If chapter 5 is in some respects, as we have seen, an anniversary chapter, chapter 8 is almost exclusively so. There is first of all and most obviously the celebration being planned to mark the 1860 conquest, or liberation, of Palermo. It is an occasion for which visitors are expected to arrive from all parts of Italy and in which the Salinas are to participate in an official capacity. Angelica is a member of the Board of Patrons, and the young Fabrizio will march down Via Libertà in frock coat as part of the parade. "Don't you think that's a first-rate idea? A Salina will render homage to Garibaldi. It will be a fusion of the old and new Sicily", Angelica says to Concetta (314), thus underlining for the last time one of the principal public themes of the novel.

Equally obvious is the parallelism of the dates, May 1860 and May 1910, that stand at the beginning of the first and last chapters respectively: not only do they state the fifty-year lapse, but none of the other six chapters takes place in the month of May. A closer look reveals that the day of the month corresponds as well. In chapter 1, which is filled with allusions to the beleaguered state of Sicily between the uprising of 4 April in Palermo and Garibaldi's landing at Marsala on 11 May, the precise date 13 May appears in the course of a landscape description made from the vantage point of the prince's observatory (53). It is stated incidentally, almost in passing: "di sfuggita e quasi di nascosto", as we have already quoted Lampedusa as writing apropos the treatment of time in the novel. In chapter 8 we find the precise date 14 May spelled out during the description of the cardinal's visit to the Salina household to make arrangements for the required examination of the relics (324). As in chapter 1, the date enters surreptitiously and elusively while the reader's attention is engaged elsewhere.

What is particularly significant about 13-14 May, however, is that it is not the date of the fall of Palermo (27 May, presumably the day for which the celebrations to commemorate the exploits of Garibaldi's Thousand are being planned) but a date with a private meaning in the history of the Salina family. Yet the proximity of the two dates and Lampedusa's skilful interweaving and blending of references to historical and individual destiny muddy the waters sufficiently to make the novel's concealment or disclosure of meaning entirely dependent on the reader's capacity of penetration. And this in spite of the fact that there is a moment in the account of Tassoni's visit to Concetta at which the author intervenes with his own statement of the perspective from which the episode should be read. Of Concetta's youthful love for Tancredi, Lampedusa writes at this point: "But as someone who recovered from smallpox fifty years before still bears the marks of the illness upon his face although he may have forgotten its pain, so she bore in her present tormented life the scars of her by now historical disappointment, historical indeed to the point that its fiftieth anniversary was now being officially celebrated" (319-20, italics mine).

For chapter 8 is Concetta's chapter. Just as Father Pirrone was finally allowed to speak and act on his own in chapter 5, so in chapter 8 is the spotlight finally and unequivocally on the prince's daughter. That she has become both an unappealing and a pathetic figure, "fat and imposing in her stiff black moiré . . . with contemptuous eyes and an expression of resentment above her nose" (304), must not blind us to this fact. In spite of the fanfare of political celebrations and in spite of the feeling of nausea Lampedusa so ably imparts to the reader through his reflection on the fate of the Church, religion, and taste in the Italy of democracy, (62) this is the great "family" chapter of the book, the point at which the historical novel most clearly makes way for the deep psychological insights of the bourgeois novel. It is the chapter of leave-taking, the enforced discarding of the objects of a naive and superstitious piety that clutter the Salina chapel, and the voluntary rejection of the "mummified memories" (311) that make Concetta's room a place of torture to her. At the end, when "the little heap of moth-eaten fur" (311) that had been Bendicò forty-five years before, turns from "the only memory of [Concetta's] past that did not awaken painful feelings in her" (312) to the only thing left in the utter emptying out of all her feelings (63) still capable of evoking a shadow of uneasiness in her, and she orders it thrown out, we have truly reached that "end of everything" we had not reached at the prince's deathbed. Thus, Concetta and not Tancredi, nor yet the blooming Angelica, is revealed to be the figure most closely related to the prince and second in importance only to him for a full explication of the novel's meaning.

And indeed, in retrospect, it becomes obvious that in spite of the central group - the giant prince; the gay, self-affirming, opportunistic Tancredi; the opulently beautiful and confident Angelica - in whom the fictional elements of the story find expression, Concetta has actually never been far from Lampedusa's focus of interest. With repeated insistence but at the same time extraordinary discreetness he has directed the reader's attention to her time and again.

She appears first in chapter 1, with what will become characteristic understatement, when in the course of a flashback her father remembers an audience granted him by Ferdinand II: the king's godchild, she is the only one of the prince's offspring to be mentioned by name (27). Her second appearance in chapter 1 is at the Salinas' midday table: the prince surmises that she is anxious about Tancredi, who has just left to join the invaders, and Lampedusa quotes him as thinking,

"They would make a fine couple. But I fear Tancredi will have to aim higher, by which of course I mean lower" (58).

Against the background of the prince's rediscovery of the perennially unchanged attractions of Donnafugata and his perception of some alas! altered social and economic circumstances, chapters 2 and 3 recount his betrayal of his daughter in favor of Angelica and Concetta's own double rejection of Tancredi: the first time at the dinner table when he tells a vulgar soldier's tale about the forcing of a convent (101-3), the second during the Salinas' visit to the Convent of the Holy Spirit (107). Concetta's realization of what has happened fails to reach the level of consciousness at this point, but in the final paragraph of chapter 3, when she is the only one who does not look up when her father crosses the girls' sitting room and she does not <u>hear</u> "the vigorous, rapid steps that announce his arrival thirty feet <u>away</u>" (160), Lampedusa has created one of those "accentuated silences intended to make the attentive reader prick up his ears", a silence which surely places this episode next to Manzoni's "La sventurata rispose" and Stendhal's "Aucune résistance ne fut opposée", cited in "Lezioni su Stendhal" as instances of quasi-miraculous understatement.

The many pages devoted in chapter 4 to Chevalley's visit to Donnafugata and those that follow Tancredi and Angelica in their voyage of erotic discovery through the maze of used and abandoned apartments of the palace - these pages have diverted all critical attention from the rest of the chapter. The public themes of the historical novel, which reach their acme in the long monologue in which the prince rejects the Piedmontese envoy's invitation to participate in the new government of united Italy by becoming a member of its senate, and the love theme of the romance, whose high point of optimistic life-affirmation is placed in the <u>hortus conclusus</u> of a magic place where time stands still, have overshadowed other aspects of the story being told. The chapter, which takes place only one month after the preceding one, shows the situation that has crystallized after Angelica's engagement to Tancredi. Remorseful over his abandonment of Concetta, Tancredi brings a young fellow officer, the Lombard Cavriaghi, on a visit to Donnafugata: he hopes that Concetta may follow his own example and let self-interest and common sense rule her heart. But Concetta is deaf to Cavriaghi's wooing: "she looked at the sentimental little count with icy eyes, in whose depths one could even read a bit of contempt" (195).

It is no surprise then to find Concetta again in chapter 7, unmarried and forty. (64) Already on the way toward assuming the position of leadership in the family ("hegemony", Lampedusa calls it not without a touch of irony), a position which will later earn her the nickname of "La Grande Catherine" from one of her nephews (304), it is she who has accompanied her father to consult a specialist in Naples and it is she who insists that a priest be called to his deathbed. In the prince's balance sheet of his life, in which the "happy moments" are no more than "golden specks" on the "immense ash-heap of liabilities" (294), Concetta figures as having provided him with the satisfaction of having one day discovered her beauty and character to be those of "a true Salina" (296). But with another deft, almost imperceptible touch, Lampedusa notes what it cost her to be a true Salina: she is the only one of those gathered at the prince's bedside – his son Francesco Paolo, his daughter Carolina, Tancredi, and Fabrizietto, but not Angelica – who does not weep (297). It is a step in that process of petrification of feeling that had begun with the repeated numbing "transitions from a secret, warm world to an open, frozen one" (175) and that had made it possible for her to live with the pain of the double betrayal of her father and Tancredi. (65)

Thus chapter 8, which has been judged by most critics as the application of an unimaginative and overworked device for finishing off the novel by calling attention to its cyclical aspect, is the celebration of that member of the Salina family who has been most obviously sacrificed to the inexorable laws of historical development which, according to sound naturalistic doctrine, entrust the future to the "fittest". Beside the prince, oversized protagonist whose physical presence and philosophical reflections fill the pages until his death, Lampedusa has placed a quiet, cruelly overshadowed figure whose inner life actually explodes in the space he has created around her. The final chapter recapitulates her story, as Senator Tassoni unwittingly brings her a message from the long-since-dead Tancredi, "transmitted across that morass of time the dead can so rarely ford" (317). And together with the recapitulation comes also the interpretation: in rapid succession, insights born of depth psychology show Concetta that "there had been no enemies, but one single adversary, herself" (320). (66) Throughout, Lampedusa's sympathy, which in the course of the novel had so often been on the prince's side, is unmistakably on Concetta's: hers is the story of "the desperate" (320). That she may not be every reader's idea of a "heroine" is quite another matter: neither Lucia in I promessi sposi nor Mena in I Malavoglia, the other two great understated heroines of Italian literature, has had a particularly good press.

At the end of "Lezioni su Stendhal" Lampedusa turns for a last time to a comparative evaluation of Stendhal's two masterpieces. He remarks wryly that his listeners were troubled by his having at one time singled out Le Rouge et le noir for the highest praise, while he had more recently assigned that place of preeminence to La Chartreuse: "it is true that I changed my mind. My irrepressible historiographical tendencies had misled me; as an aesthetic document of an historical period Le Rouge et le noir is of greater merit. From a lyrical, artistic, and human point of view it is La Chartreuse that

excels" (49). These two aspects of the type of novel with which
Lampedusa was concerned, aspects which find their separate and equal
embodiment in his view of Stendhal's two masterpieces, are the inseparable poles around which his own Il gattopardo finds its unity.

(1973)

NOTES

1. Giuseppe Tomasi di Lampedusa, "Lezioni su Stendhal", Paragone,
9, no. 112 (April 1959), 3-49. Hereafter referred to parenthetically in
text.
2. Louis Aragon, "Le Guépard et la Chartreuse", Les Lettres
françaises, 18-24 February 1960, 1 and 8. Aragon read "Lezioni su
Stendhal" in the selective translation that appeared in Stendhal Club, 2,
no. 6 (January 1960), 155-68, as "Notes sur Stendhal". The French
translation is divided into two parts. The first part, "Le Rouge et le
noir", starts with page 27 of the original Paragone article and omits
the long theoretical digression (27-29) in which Lampedusa broadens
the discussion of narrative time by referring to other novels, War and
Peace and Anna Karenina especially. The translation resumes on page
29 with the passage analyzing Stendhal's treatment of time in Le Rouge
et le noir; occasional brief omissions up to page 36 are indicated in the
customary fashion. The second part in Stendhal Club, "La Chartreuse
de Parme", covers pp. 38-44 of the original, omitting a number of remarks the unidentified translator must have deemed irrelevant to the
discussion of Stendhal. As is to be expected, these are often the very
remarks most valuable for an understanding of Lampedusa's intentions
in his own novel.
3. Louis Aragon, "Il Gattopardo e la Certosa", Rinascita, 17, no. 3
(March 1960), 223-26. It is not my purpose here to discuss the official
opinion of the Italian Communist Party with respect to Il gattopardo,
and I am therefore making no mention of other articles that appeared
in Rinascita.
4. Ivos Margoni, "Il gattopardo in Francia", Belfagor, 17, no. 3
(March 1960), 531-43. Other articles appearing in Belfagor were Luigi
Blasucci's review of Il gattopardo, 14, No. 1 (January 1959), 117-21;
Luigi Russo's "Analisi del Gattopardo", 15, no. 5 (September 1960),
513-30, and his "I luoghi del Gattopardo", 16, no. 1 (January 1961),
90; and the review article by Giuseppe Stammati, "Gattopardeschi e
no", 15, no. 2 (March 1960), 160-70. Later, again in the pages of
Belfagor, Gaetano Trombatore took his cue from the novel for his
"Considerazioni sulla narrativa siciliana", 9, no. 1 (January 1965),
1-10; and Gualtiero Todini contributed a good summary of Lampedusa's
total production, with discriminating assessments of the criticism to

which it gave rise, "Giuseppe Tomasi di Lampedusa", 25, no. 2
(March 1970), 163-84.
5. Aragon, "Le Guépard et la Chartreuse", 1. The three names were
mentioned by Lampedusa himself in one of the passages that appeared
in Stendhal Club.
6. Aragon had stated this view in an earlier article, "Un Grand Fauve
se lève: Le Guépard", Les Lettres françaises, 17-23 December 1959,
where he wrote: "Un livre n'est pas achevé par son auteur, il l'est par
le lecteur, par la philosophie du lecteur. Voilà pourquoi je m'étonne
qu'on ne semble pas comprendre que Le Guépard étant un fait, il s'agit
de savoir l'interpréter, selon ce qu'on pense, et non selon ce qu'en
penserait l'agnosticisme sicilien, ou même une certaine dégénérescence
de la pensée critique, fort caractéristique d'un déclin de classe, qui
n'est plus celui de l'aristocratie . . . . Ils ont vaincu, ces garibaldiens.
Le 'cocu' n'aura pas été Garibaldi. La victoire des 'Piémontais' n'aura
pas été une occupation comme une autre mais l'unité italienne. Le
mouvement de l'histoire s'est emparé de la Sicile au point d'effondrer
les plafonds des Ponteleone avec une bombe américaine . . . . Le
sens que prendra l'œuvre de Giuseppe Tomasi di Lampedusa ne saurait
être que celui de l'histoire. Les individus peuvent bien être agnostique,
l'œuvre de leurs mains et de leur cœur leur échappe, elle entre dans
le grand brassement des choses réelles, s'y inscrit, devient objet de
connaissance. Et Le Guépard ne dira pas à l'avenir l'immobilisme
sicilien, mais le mouvement des hommes que, comme don Fabrice,
Giuseppe Tomasi saluait, à sa façon, et peut-être et certainement au
de là de ce qu'un don Fabrice a pu voir."
7. To understand the analogy it is necessary to quote Lampedusa
("Lezioni su Stendhal", 39-40) more fully: "tutti noi conosciamo ed
amiamo il Purgatorio dantesco. Quanti di noi però hanno riflettuto che
esso rappresenta un luogo di pena, che in esso le anime soffrono dei
tormenti paragonabili a quelli infernali? Ogni lettore, credo, voglio
sperare, giunge all'ultimo canto con l'impressione di aver attraversato
una regione di pacata serenità, sempre illuminata da un benigno sole.
Così non è, liste dei tormenti alla mano. Così è per la maggior parte
dei lettori, in virtù dell'arte di Dante. So benissimo che Ernesto IV è
un immondo personaggio, delineato ricalcando le figure di Francesco
di Modena, di Francesco I d'Austria e del giovane Carlo-Alberto; so
che di 'fiscali Rassi' la terra (e l'inferno) sono pieni, so che la Torre
di Parma è un luogo di supplizio degno del Piranesi e del resto desunta
tanto dalla realtà di Rubiera che dalle narrazioni di Pellico e Maroncelli
circa lo Spielberg, mi rendo conto che il conte Mosca è un perfetto
ritratto di quei ministri e ministrucoli, assolutamente egoisti e privi
di scrupoli, copia ridotta e peggiorata del loro grande modello
Metternich, mi accorgo di quanti tradimenti, pastille avvelenate e
colpi di pugnale è tessuta la trama del romanzo; dirò di più, so
benissimo che Stendhal voleva indignare il lettore contro tali uomini e

tali metodi. Lo so, ma affermo che non me ne importa niente; in quanto a me, Stendhal ha fallito il colpo: voleva dipingere l'Inferno, ha creato il più adorabile Purgatorio dantesco" (italics mine).

8. Aragon, "Le Guépard et la Chartreuse", 8. Note especially the passage italicized in note 7 above, which shows Lampedusa's awareness of the two levels of latent involvement and overt statement in La Chartreuse de Parme: the society Stendhal describes is the object both of his reprehension and of his nostalgia, though obviously not for the same reasons. It is also amusing to note Aragon's brand of widespread rhetoric: "une critique impitoyable" can only be "une critique de gauche."

9. Since 1959 numerous studies have looked at the literary rather than ideological aspects of Il gattopardo: Stanley G. Eskin, "Animal Imagery in Il gattopardo", Italica, 39 (1962), 189-94; Jeffrey Meyers, "Symbol and Structure in The Leopard", Italian Quarterly, 9, 34-35 (1965), 50-70; John Gilbert, "The Metamorphosis of the Gods in Il gattopardo", Modern Language Notes, 81 (1966), 22-31; Augustus Pallota, "Il gattopardo: A Theme-Structure Analysis", Italica, 43 (1966), 57-65; Arthur Evans and Catherine Evans, "Salina and Svelto: The Symbolism of Change in Il gattopardo", Wisconsin Studies in Contemporary Literature, 4 (1963), 298-304; Simonetta Salvestroni, "Analisi del Gattopardo" and "La struttura e lo stile del Gattopardo", Filologia e letteratura, 17 (1971), 101-28 and 209-37. But in spite of occasional references to "Lezioni su Stendhal", none of these has followed the advice of Michel David, La psicoanalisi nella cultura italiana (Turin, 1966), 541: "Lezioni su Stendhal dovrebbero essere il punto di partenza necessario per ogni studio del Gattopardo"), or of Furio Felcini, "Giuseppe Tomasi di Lampedusa", in Letteratura italiana. I contemporanei, III (Milan, 1969), 261: "A comprendere le intime ragioni strutturali e stilistiche dell'opera maggiore . . . si rivelano utilissime le pagine delle Lezioni su Stendhal, in cui par lecito intravvedere, per trasparenti allusioni, un suggerimento e una guida alla lettura del Gattopardo." In her full-length study, Tomasi di Lampedusa (Florence, 1973), of which pp. 17-24 deal with the "Lezioni", Simonetta Salvestroni says specifically that in his analysis of Stendhal Lampedusa described the novel he would have wanted to write, not the one he succeeded in writing (20). Giancarlo Buzzi, Invito alla lettura di Tomasi di Lampedusa (Milan, 1972-73) devotes a chapter to "Lezioni su Stendhal e la poetica di Lampedusa". Buzzi's purpose in examining the essay is in some respects broader than mine and leads him to explore the reasons for which Stendhal's poetics did not achieve the same results in Lampedusa's work. Lampedusa, according to Buzzi, does not succeed in being objective because he identifies with one character only. The conclusion, it seems to me, is debatable.

10. Margoni, "Il gattopardo in Francia", (see note 4 above), 538.

11. On Robbe-Grillet, see Sergio Solmi, Nuovi argomenti, 23-24
(1957), 101-04, and Arnaldo Pizzorusso, Letteratura, 6, 31-32 (1958)
180-85. On Sarraute, see Guido Neri, Il contemporaneo, 29 June 1957,
3. On Beckett, see Nino Frank, Il mondo, 7, 40 (4 October 1955), 10.
Note also the article by Guido Neri, "Sperimentalismo nella giovane
narrativa francese", Il contemporaneo, 1, 5-6 (August 1958), 27-38,
which makes use of the current Italian equivalent, "experimentalism",
for the expression "nouveau roman".
12. In resuming publication after the war, the Almanacco letterario
Bompiani devoted a section of its 1959 number to " Le punte dell' avanguardia" (261-74). This included brief articles on the Italian experimentalists, the French "nouveau roman", German literature in
the "year zero", the British "angry men", American "hipsters", and
electronic music. The section was separate from and in addition to
the usual annual reports on literary and artistic developments in different European countries. Since the Almanacco Bompiani for any
given year is issued in the last months of the preceding year, its
attention to "nouveau roman" preceded Il Verri's and it should be
given this credit.
13. Later issued in book form as Una via per il romanzo futuro: Gli
scritti teorici, trans. and introd. Renato Barilli (Milan, 1961).
14. Renato Barilli, "La narrativa di Alain Robbe-Grillet"; Edoardo
Sanguineti, "Butor, 'une machine mentale' "; Sandro Bajini, "Beckett
o l'emblema totale".
15. Barilli's "Cahier de doléances" is now included in his La barriera
del naturalismo (Milan, 1964).
16. For Barilli's position see also his "Le strutture del romanzo", in
Gruppo 63 (Milan, 1964). By and large, Angelo Guglielmi shares
Barilli's views: see "Avanguardia e sperimentalismo", in Gruppo 63;
now also in Avanguardia e sperimentalismo (Milan, 1964).
17. Edoardo Sanguineti's Capriccio italiano (Milan, 1963) was the experimental novel that created the greatest furor in Italy. Raffaele La
Capria's Ferito a morte (Milan, 1961), which could well be called an
experimental novel in the same sense, preceded the days of nouveau
roman. For other experimental narrators, see the Gruppo 63 anthology
and Vent'anni d'impazienza: Antologia della narrativa italiana dal '46
ad oggi, ed. Angelo Guglielmi (Milan, 1965), which latter provides a
historical overview. For a statement regarding the problem of Italian
literature "catching up" with the great European innovators of the
early part of the century, see Barilli's "Le strutture del romanzo".
A word should perhaps also be said about the earlier group of essentially linguistic experimenters (P. P. Pasolini and his collaborators
in the periodical Officina), but inasmuch as they belong to a different
moment in the development of the new avant-garde, their relation to
the Gattopardo polemic would require separate treatment. On some of
these points, see my own "Gadda, Pasolini, and Experimentalism:

Form or Ideology?'' included in this volume.
18. A good part of the novel's initial success must be attributed to the circumstances of its publication. As the posthumous work of an unknown writer, it had a very special appeal for the popular imagination catered to by mass publications such as the illustrated weeklies. For a sketch of the critical reception, see Felcini's "Giuseppe Tomasi di Lampedusa" (note 9 above), 261-64.
19. Reflection on the essence of Bassani's own work would indicate that it was not commercialism that prompted his evaluation of Il gattopardo. "Bassani è anche egli un notomista dei vinti", Gioacchino Lanza Tomasi writes in his introduction to the second edition, Il gattopardo (completo): Edizione conforme al manoscritto del 1957 (Milan, December 1969).
20. Leone Piccioni, La narrativa italiana tra romanzo e racconti (Milan, 1959), 132-34; the essay is now part of Piccioni's Pazienza e impazienza (Florence, 1968). The "in-depth" as opposed to "chronology of events" characterization of Lampedusa's storytelling technique receives important corroboration in David's seminal work, La psicoanalisi nella cultura italiana (note 9 above), though from a psychological rather than "formal" point of view.
21. Tom O'Neill, " Lampedusa and De Roberto", Italica, 47 (1970), 170-82.
22. In his anthology, Letteratura dell'Italia unita, 1861-1968 (Florence, 1968), Gianfranco Contini with considerable acumen places Lampedusa among the "Solariani", the writers most closely associated with the literary ideals of the review Solaria (1926-1936). In thus removing Il gattopardo from the cultural contexts of the period in which it was published and returning it to the time of its conception, Contini emphasizes the Proustian elements of the novel: psychological analysis, memory, "le temps retrouvé". In this sense the publication of the book in 1958 was anachronistic because it came too late.
23. I have been unable to see Pietro Citati's review in Il punto, 24 January 1959. According to Barilli (La barriera del naturalismo, 203), Citati sees in Lampedusa a Proustian writer, "a keen connoisseur of twentieth-century techniques". Barilli himself discounts the importance of technical devices in Il gattopardo, although he does note (209) the presence of certain "modern" features: introspective analysis, the casual treatment of time, cynical and ironic commentary. Instead, he emphasizes the regionalistic aspects of the novel which he sees as a kind of continuation of I vicerè. For a very brief indication on Proust as against De Roberto in the formation of Lampedusa, see Arnaldo Bocelli, "Tomasi di Lampedusa", Enciclopedia italiana, appendix III (1961).
24. Giorgio Bassani, introd., Il gattopardo (Milan, 1958), 12. It is interesting to note that E. M. Forster wrote the introduction to Lampedusa's Two Stories and a Memory, trans. A. Colquhoun (New

York, 1962). Forster also reviewed Il gattopardo in the Spectator, 13 May 1960.

25. Francesco Orlando, Ricordo di Lampedusa (Milan, 1963), 57. Orlando mentions one exception, Georges Poulet's La Distance intérieure (Paris, 1952). Everything we know of Lampedusa's cultural formation tends to prove Orlando wrong on this point. But what does he actually mean by "after Croce"? Many of the works with which Lampedusa was acquainted did indeed find their way to Italy only "after Croce", but Lampedusa's range was cosmopolitan, not limited by what was available in Italian translation only.

26. One of the earliest presentations of the "craft of fiction" to the Italian reading public that I know of was made by Remo Ceserani in Almanacco letterario Bompiani, 1966. In an article bearing the deceptive title "Manuali americani sulla narrative", Ceserani reviewed specialized works on fiction, scholarly periodicals, and textbooks, using them to illustrate the theoretical premises of the vast bulk of American fiction written in the first half of the twentieth century. If we were to inquire why Italian interest in this area of criticism was so late in developing, we would have to point to Croce's opposition to the concept of literary genre in criticism, and more inclusively to the idealistic and romantic devaluation of technique in art; on this last point specifically, see Marina Forni Mizzau, Tecniche narrative e romanzo contemporaneo (Milan, 1965). While Croce was both a "close" reader and a defender of "pure" poetry, he shied away from the rhetorical kind of criticism that had such an important role in discussions of the novel in Anglo-Saxon countries. However, when the history of Italian theories of the novel is someday written, much significant and unexpected material will come to light. As far as the period between the two wars is concerned - seminal years for the contemporary Italian novel - it is sufficient to turn from academic to what was once called "militant" criticism, or from Croce and the Croceans to a "cultural free lancer" (the epithet is Montale's) such as Giacomo Debenedetti, to enter into a radically different formative environment. In contrast to the vast majority of the critics of his time, Debenedetti had a very strong interest in the novel, so much so that in the latter part of his life, when he had turned to university teaching, he devoted six courses to the twentieth-century novel. His lecture notes are available in Giacomo Debenedetti, Il romanzo del Novecento (Milan, 1971). For an analysis of Debenedetti's literary activities, see Francesco Mattesini, La critica letteraria di Giacomo Debenedetti (Milan, 1969). There are some interesting observations in David's La psicoanalisi nella letteratura italiana, 322-25 especially, although David is concerned primarily with the Freudian component of Debenedetti's culture. On Il romanzo del Novecento and on the related collection of essays, Il personaggio uomo (Milan, 1970), see Marco Forti, "Debenedetti postumo 'in valuta oro'", Paragone, April

1971, 82-93. For a good rapid survey of the situation of narrative literature in Italy in the twentieth century, see Valerio Volpini, Prosa e narrativa dei contemporanei dalla "Voce" all'Avanguardia (Rome, 1967).
27. Henry James was of course not unknown in Italy. But interest in
him as a critic and theorist first appeared in the post-War years and
was strictly limited to academic circles. Agostino Lombardo, founder in 1955 of the journal Studi americani, translated and introduced
James's prefaces to his novels, Le prefazioni (Venice, 1956), a collection first gathered together by R. P. Blackmur in the anthology,
The Art of the Novel (1947). Lombardo also published L'arte del
romanzo (Milan, 1959), James's critical essays on other writers. In
reviewing Le prefazioni in Il mondo (18 September 1956), Salvatore
Rosati, another Anglicist, regretted that in his preface Lombardo had
not gone deeper into an evaluation of the contemporary significance of
James, but concluded that his essay was "tra quanto di più compiuto,
penetrante, e impegnativo si è scritto in Italia sul grande romanziere
americano". In order to reconstruct James's reputation in Italy, a
series of articles written by Emilio Cecchi for La Tribuna in 1921 and
1922 is of fundamental importance; some of these articles were later
collected in Cecchi's Scrittori inglesi e americani, 2 vols. (Milan,
1962 and 1964) and Aiuola di Francia (Milan, 1969). In considering the
failure of Italian critics to evaluate Proust properly, for instance,
Cecchi at one point writes: "la gran questione è che l'Italia, rispetto
alla conoscenza degli scrittori stranieri si divide essenzialmente in
due tribù: la tribù, poco numerosa, degli entusiasti, degli eterni
catecumeni, sempre a bocca aperta aspettando che ci caschi dentro
qualcosa; e costoro si arrabbian come maladetti [sic], se vi azzardate
ad avvertirli che invece di un fico hanno inghiottito una buccia, o anche
peggio; 2a la tribù degli ignoranti: e naturalmente comprende i critici
più numerosi, i quali si accorgeranno di Proust, o di Meredith, o di
James, sì e no fra trent'anni" ("Libri nuovi e usati", La Tribuna, 7
July 1922). But if we look closer at exactly what Cecchi felt that Italian
critics ignored, we find that he is not concerned with James the theo-
retician of the novel but with James the psychological analyst: " Mai
era stato dato all'uomo interno un écorché più crudo ed esasperante"
(10 November 1922). In placing Proust within the tradition of narrative
literature, Cecchi suggested a historical perspective that transcends
linguistic and national barriers: because Meredith and James were
virtually unknown to French as well as to Italian readers, says Cecchi,
a huge gap seemed to exist between the last group of great French
novelists (Balzac, Flaubert, the Goncourts) and Proust. This gap,
Cecchi insists, was filled by the work of Meredith and, above all,
James. But again, it is the "esperienze psicologiche e stilistiche che
appunto s'intendono sotto i nomi d'un Meredith e d'un James" that
Cecchi has in mind, and not those other techniques that "Lezioni su
Stendhal" shows Lampedusa to have been acquainted with. One final

fact may be referred to as emblematic of the situation: E. M. Forster's Aspects of the Novel was not translated into Italian until 1963, as Aspetti del romanzo (Milan) and with an unsigned preface by none other than Debenedetti.
28. Note 22 above shows how the publication of Il gattopardo in 1958 was anachronistic in the sense that it came too late; note 26, instead, shows how it was anachronistic because it came too early. For a good statement of the equivocations and ambiguities that accompanied the publication, see Furio Felcini's "Giuseppe Tomasi di Lampedusa" (note 9 above), 252-53, and his "Dieci anni del Gattopardo: Bilancio e prospettive", Cultura e scuola, 25 (1968), 55-66.
29. Lampedusa, "Lezioni su Stendhal", 4. For the sake of continuity in my exposition I have translated all quotations, but because of Lampedusa's exceptionally vivid lexical choices, I have sometimes included the original Italian expression.
30. Readers of Manzoni are well acquainted with the expression of that sentiment and with his repeated efforts to find a narrative form (history? the historical tragedy? the historical novel?) in which the inner life of historical personages can be expressed. In the Discorso storico sopra alcuni punti della storia longobardica (1822), which belongs to the most important period of his activity, for instance, he writes: "Un'immensa moltitudine d'uomini, una serie di generazioni, che passa sulla terra, inosservata, senza lasciarci traccia, è un tristo ma importante fenomeno" (end of ch. 2). The various stages of the introduction to I promessi sposi offer further documentation on this point. As far as Lampedusa himself is concerned, he writes in "I luoghi della mia prima infanzia" (Giuseppe Tomasi di Lampedusa, Racconti, Milan, 1961, 104) that all men should be required at a certain point in their lives to write their memoirs: "il materiale che si sarebbe accumulato dopo tre o quattro generazioni avrebbe un valore inestimabile: molti problemi psicologici e storici che assillano l'umanità sarebbero risolti. Non esistono memorie, per quanto scritte da personaggi insignificanti, che non racchiudano valori sociali e pittoreschi di prim'ordine."
31. Jean Prévost, La Création chez Stendhal: Essai sur le métier d'écrire et la psychologie de l'écrivain (Paris, 1951). Prévost distinguishes between two classes of writers (23): "Du point de vue de la technique, on peut distinguer les prosateurs, surtout les romanciers, en deux grandes classes. Les uns se consacrent en artisans à leurs œuvres, se sacrifient à elles, tâchent que cette œuvre vaille mieux qu'eux, la mettent au-dessus d'eux par des recommencements acharnés. Les autres, au lieu de travailler sans cesse leurs manuscrits, travaillent sur eux-mêmes, raturent le vif, s'affinent par la culture et par l'expérience, s'exercent à tous propos, fût-ce par des badinages ou par des œuvres inégales, et deviennent enfin capables d'improviser. Chacune de leurs pages, fût-elle dictée en quelques

minutes et échappée de leurs mains sans ratures, peut résumer
autant de travail que la page de l'artisan minutieux; mais c'est un
travail plus lointain. Le Voltaire de Ferney, Stendhal, Gobineau,
Gérard de Nerval sont des exemples de cette sorte d'hommes, qui
peuvent exprimer en quelques pages écrites à la diable les longs
progrès et les affinements de leur esprit." Lampedusa's admiration
for Prévost is unqualified: "È necessario leggere (quando si sia
conosciuta l'intera opera di Stendhal) il magnifico libro di Prévost"
(10), but a careful comparison of Lampedusa's and Prévost's for-
mulations of similar ideas convinces me that Lampedusa is not para-
phrasing Prévost but is either taking Prévost as a point of departure
for some of his own observations or, more probably, has found corroboration in Prévost for some of his own intuitions about Stendhal.
This can be seen, for instance, in the passage on the manner of
suggesting milieu (see note 38 below), which echoes Prévost's observations on description in Stendhal (257). Lampedusa's debt to
Prévost would deserve further study.
32. On Henri Brulard, which he reread in 1955, Lampedusa writes:
"Vi è una immediatezza di sensazioni, una evidente sincerità, un
ammirevole sforzo per spazzar via gli strati successivi dei ricordi
e giungere al fondo. E quale lucidità di stile! E quale ammasso di
impressioni tanto più comuni! Vorrei cercare di fare lo stesso" ("I
luoghi della mia prima infanzia" [note 30 above], 103; italics mine).
Attention to this passage is also called by Felcini ("Giuseppe Tomasi
di Lampedusa", 255), whose use of the minor works to throw light
on Il gattopardo is extremely successful.
33. Orlando, Ricordo di Lampedusa (note 25 above), 80.
34. On this point see the perceptive remarks of David, La psicoanalisi
nella letteratura italiana (note 9 above), 541.
35. Jeffrey Meyers, "The Influence of the Chartreuse de Parme on Il
gattopardo", Italica, 44 (1967), 314-35. Meyers finds the influence in
the theme of the evasion from reality through reverie, the significance
of astronomy, the meaning of the prison cell and the observatory, the
feeling of the futility of political strife, and the scenes of the audience
with the Bourbon king that recall a similar scene with the prince of
Parma. A more comprehensive comparison of the two novels remains
to be done.
36. Lampedusa uses the image of taking a clock apart to describe the
type of analysis to which he is subjecting Stendhal: "È come smontare
un orologio: osservando nel loro giusto ordine le mollette, le ruote
dentate, gli scatti, le viti ed i perni vi renderete conto di come
avvenga il movimento. Potrete anche provarvi a rimontare l'orologio
e questo si metterà a camminare se . . . se avrete un vostro tempo
da far segnare alle lancette. Questa però è una condizione che
nessuno potrà aiutarvi ad adempiere. O c'è o non c'è" ("Lezioni su
Stendhal", 27). The metaphor describes to perfection Lampedusa's

critical self-awareness: his analysis of narrative technique will be vindicated when he finds his own "time" to tell.

37. However, Lampedusa's reading of La Chartreuse (see especially 42) shows how form can point up ideology.

38. Lampedusa emphasizes the importance of "men, institutions, and customs" rather than "landscapes and buildings" for defining milieu but finds it difficult to identify the specific techniques used by Stendhal: "Stendhal non dispone della minuzia necessaria a descrivere edifici e mobili con la meticolosità da regista cinematografico dalla quale talvolta Balzac ha saputo estrarre grandiosi effetti poetici. Però questi mobili e questi edifici egli li suggerisce, non so davvero come, nella maggior parte dei casi; quando Julien penetra nella camera di M. me de Rênal alla sua uscita dal seminario, il senso di oscurità, di afa, di rinchiuso e di cattivo odore è reso inequivocabilmente, come, però, non lo so" (32). There seems to be some confusion, perhaps of a semantic nature or the result of compression, in Lampedusa's discussion of milieu. Anyway, it seems to be no accident that the French translator of the passage for Stendhal Club substituted the word "atmosphère" for the "ambiente" of the original, rather than use "milieu".

39. A reminiscence and restatement of Flaubert's famous words "L'auteur, dans son œuvre, doit être comme Dieu dans l'univers, présent partout et visible nulle part"; see the Correspondance (Paris, 1922), I, 486. It is interesting to note that Lampedusa uses the word "onniveggenza" to express the idea of omniscience, thus underlining the "seeing" in "knowing".

40. On the collaboration between author, protagonist, and reader, see also Lampedusa's remark on Stendhal's first use in Rome, Naples, et Florence of the technique to achieve it ("Lezioni su Stendhal", 19).

41. For an excellent stylistic analysis of Il gattopardo, one that shows how Lampedusa himself used words exactly to this end, see Salvestroni's "La struttura e lo stile del Gattopardo" (note 9 above), 227-37.

42. The distinction between the concepts of stream of consciousness and interior monologue (the first a fairly recent manner of psychological interpretation, the second an old literary technique for rendering the content of the psyche) is now rather well established. However, confusion in terminology persists, and it is because of this confusion that Lampedusa makes a connection between Stendhal, Proust, Joyce, and Virginia Woolf on this point. Again, a consideration of the situation of Italian criticism in the area of the novel is relevant here: Debenedetti, for instance, discusses the concepts of stream of consciousness and interior monologue at length (Il romanzo del Novecento [note 26 above], 594-616), basing himself on Wellek and Warren's Theory of Literature, which was translated into Italian in 1956.

43. The three articles, which appeared in the Genoese review Le opere e i giorni, are on Paul Morand, W. B. Yeats, and Friedrich Gundolf's Caesar: Geschichte seines Ruhms. See Giuseppe Quatriglio,

"Le radici del Gattopardo", Giornale di Sicilia (Palermo), 2 April
1970, and Piero Meli, "Gli scritti critici di Lampedusa giovane",
Le ragioni critiche, 9 (1973), 239-53.
44. Lampedusa's literary activities, this time in the form of "lessons"
on English literature from the Anglo-Saxon period to T. S. Eliot and
Christopher Fry, had actually begun even before his visit to San
Pellegrino Terme. In the French series of "lessons" Bassani reports
having seen notes on Mérimée and Flaubert in addition to those on
Stendhal.
45. "Siamo tutti Siciliani", Giornale di Sicilia, 13 January 1970. The
article, consisting of the interview with Bassani, was translated for
Newsletter, Istituto Italiano di Cultura (New York), no. 23 (April
1970), 10-11 and 14-15.
46. Orlando, Ricordo di Lampedusa (note 25 above), 80.
47. "Siamo tutti siciliani."
48. Carlo Muscetta, "Saggio di correzioni del Gattopardo completo",
Mimesis (Catania) 1 (1968), 119-27.
49. This was the edition referred to in note 19 above. Hereafter cited
simply as Il gattopardo (completo).
50. Lanza Tomasi mentions "thousands" of divergences, mostly irrelevant or of minor importance: the use of "Don Fabrizio" for "Il
Principe", inversions in word order, omissions of occasional parenthetical or redundant expressions, the alternating use of capitals and
small letters in titles such as "Don Fabrizio" and "don Calogero",
adjustments in figures or distances for greater precision, elimination
of an occasional word borrowed from some technical jargon, a different criterion for punctuation (Lampedusa favored the use of semi-
colons to separate independent sentences that are all part of the same
thought unit, and he used commas to mark pauses rather than to set
off logical and grammatical units). The two more substantial changes
consist of omissions in the description of the bathing room at Donnafugata and of additions to the enumeration of the furnishings of the
"torture" apartment in chapter 4. Antonio Dipace, Questione delle
varianti del "Gattopardo" (Latina, 1971), contains a detailed comparison of the various materials. On Dipace's book, see the review
by Ornella Moroni, Italianistica, II (1973), 403-5.
51. Bassani, introd., Il gattopardo (see note 24 above), 11. Henceforth all page references to this first edition will be cited in the text,
the translations being the present writer's.
52. Lampedusa, Il gattopardo (completo), x.
53. Early readers were not a little intrigued by the report that
Lampedusa wrote the book at his club in Palermo, the Circolo Bellini,
to which he would go with clocklike regularity every day early in the
morning, remaining there until three in the afternoon.
54. What was not part of the original scheme, aside from the three
Donnafugata chapters, were chapters 5 and 6.

55. The chapter at the ball, too, is in the 1957 manuscript, although Bassani actually received it separately from the princess to add to the 1956 typescript he had. This chronological detail regarding its provenance may have influenced Bassani in his judgment of its inferiority to the rest of the book.

56. It is important to note that the original conception already included a section devoted to the time after the prince's death.

57. The only other places in the novel where the prince does not occupy center stage are in the Angelica / Tancredi "love cyclone" of chapter 4 (also criticized by some for being tangential), and in chapter 8.

58. Lanza Tomasi, introd., Il gattopardo (completo), xii–xiii. Orlando's Ricordo di Lampedusa (note 25 above), 46–58, contains an illuminating discussion of Lampedusa's understanding of explicit as against implicit or understated art, and of "fat" as against "thin" writers. Paradoxically, the very implicitness or allusiveness Lampedusa strove for is found irritatingly obvious, "slick", and "trivial" by Andor Gomme in his "Irony and The Leopard", Oxford Review, no. 6 (1967), 23–35.

59. "Lezioni su Stendhal", 31. I have gone back to the original source for the quotation, which appears in an inexplicably garbled version in Salvestroni's "La struttura e lo stile del Gattopardo" (note 9 above), 218.

60. The reason I feel justified in making this statement is that Lanza Tomasi's comment on the explicitness of chapter 5 concerns, strictly speaking, only "the apology of an aristocrat made by Father Pirrone to the sleeping herbalist". The chapter, as we have seen, has other dimensions beside the ideological one.

61. Felcini, "Giuseppe Tomasi di Lampedusa" (note 9 above), 251.

62. Among the themes that link chapters 1 and 8, the religious one, concretized in customs of worship within the family setting, is particularly strong. Tightly interwoven with it is the theme of the decadence of taste, again concretized, this time in the art objects that surround the scenes of worship: the pre-Revolutionary mythological figures that decorated the walls, ceiling, and floor in the drawing room of chapter I have given way in chapter 8 to a painting of the Tranquillo Cremona school, variously interpreted as representing the Madonna of the Letter or a girl reading a letter from her lover. The relationship between the sacred and the profane persists, but its "objective correlative" is now a typical example of the bourgeois taste of the great age of liberalism.

63. The process is described by Lampedusa by degrees. It reaches its high point in the sentence: "Her father's portrait was just a few square inches of canvas, the green chests [in which her trousseau had been stored fifty years before] just a few cubic feet of wood" (326).

64. Between chapter 4 and chapter 6 Concetta appears only once, during the ball. The significant reference to her, underlining the betrayal theme, occurs while the prince is dancing with Angelica: "He felt a twinge at his heart: he was thinking of the proud and defeated eyes of Concetta. But it was a brief pain: at every turn [of the waltz] a year fell from his shoulders" (271).

65. Her mother had also abandoned Concetta; see 123-24.

66. It is curious to note that David (La psicoanalisi nella cultura italiana, 539-44), who carefully lists and evaluates Lampedusa's use of the technical vocabulary of psychoanalysis, should have failed to remark the obvious psychoanalytical character of Concetta's gaining of insight.

NARRATIVE VS STYLISTIC STRUCTURE IN I MALAVOGLIA

Of the seven essays constituting Il Verga maggiore (1) four appeared in
Cecchetti's somewhat ambiguously entitled Leopardi e Verga (1962),
two in Luigi Russo's review Belfagor (1962 and 1963), and one is new.
Of the earlier essays "Le traduzioni verghiane di D. H. Lawrence" is
in part superseded by Arnim Arnold's "Genius with a Dictionary: Re-
evaluating D. H. Lawrence's Translations" (Comparative Literature
Studies, V [1968], 389-402). Cecchetti's study of Lawrence's Verga
translations, written while he himself was translating Verga for the
anthology The She-Wolf and Other Stories (1958) and perhaps conceived originally as a justification for the need of a fresh translation,
reveals a touch of the typical insensitivity of the scholar vis-à-vis the
artist and the irritation of the native speaker vis-à-vis the foreigner
who dares to approach a work in his language without "serious preparation" (196). Lawrence is reproached among graver faults for not
having consulted earlier translations of Verga and not having checked
back through his own translations for uniformity and consistency. (2)
In contrast to the Lawrence essay, the other five studies published
previously continue to be considered generally valuable contributions
to Verga studies, and in focusing exclusively on Verga's major works
they do indeed form a kind of unity. (3)

By far the most important essay of the book is "Il 'carro' e il 'mare
amaro'." It deals with Verga's unquestioned masterpiece and is thought
of as central by Cecchetti himself, both because its discussion of the
stylistic structure of I Malavoglia serves as a point of convergence for
the other essays and because in it Cecchetti's method of criticism is
more clearly displayed than elsewhere. In concentrating upon the final
paragraphs of Chapter II Cecchetti follows in the footsteps of Günther
(1928), Devoto (1954), and Spitzer (1956), whose various analyses of
Verga's narrative technique were to a large extent based on this same
passage. But feeling that his predecessors failed to relate the passage to the rest of the novel, Cecchetti proposes to show that only in
the context of the whole can its full import be appreciated and only
thus the artistic perfection of the work demonstrated. Cecchetti's
attention to the passage thus aims not at the study of a delimited
sample of Verga's style but at a broader consideration of the whole of
I Malavoglia. Methodologically the approach is suggested and justified
by Spitzer's claim that in I Malavoglia, style indirect libre was used
for the first time not for occasional passages only but for an entire
novel. (4)

In order to broaden his base of operations Cecchetti extends the
passage beyond the cut-off point used by the earlier critics - the cru-

cial così pensava Mena sul ballatoio aspettando il nonno - to include Padron 'Ntoni's final remark, Chi ha il cuor contento sempre canta, and the concluding words of the chapter:

> Le stelle ammiccavano più forte, quasi s'accendessero, e i Tre Re scintillavano sui fariglioni con le braccia in croce, come Sant'Andrea. Il mare russava in fondo alla stradicciuola, adagio, adagio, e a lunghi intervalli si udiva il rumore di qualche carro che passava nel buio, sobbalzando sui sassi, e andava pel mondo il quale è tanto grande che se uno potesse camminare sempre, giorno e notte, non arriverebbe mai, e c'era pure della gente che andava pel mondo a quell'ora, e non sapeva nulla di compar Alfio, né della Provvidenza che era in mare, né della festa dei Morti; - così pensava Mena sul ballatoio aspettando il nonno.
>
> Il nonno s'affaciò ancora due o tre volte sul ballatoio, prima di chiudere l'uscio, a guardare le stelle che luccicavano più del dovere, e poi borbottò: "Mare amaro!"
>
> Rocco Spatu si sgolava sulla porta dell'osteria davanti al lumicino. - "Chi ha il cuor contento sempre canta" - conchiuse padron 'Ntoni. (5)

The stars were beckoning more brightly, as though caught on fire, and the Three Kings were glittering above the Fariglioni, with their arms outstretched like Saint Andrew on the cross. The sea was snoring softly at the foot of the lane, and at long intervals the sound of a cart could be heard passing in the dark, jerking over the stones, and it was going about the world which is so big that even if you were to walk and walk, night and day, without ever stopping, you'd never reach the end of it, and yet there were people going about the world at that hour, and they knew nothing of Compare Alfio, nor of the Provvidenza which was out at sea, nor of the Feast of the Dead; - this is what Mena was thinking on the gallery as she was waiting for her grandfather.

Before closing up for the night, the grandfather came out on the gallery again two or three times to look at the stars that were glittering more than they should, and then he muttered: "Bitter sea!"

Rocco Spatu was shouting himself hoarse at the tavern door in front of the light. - "He whose heart is happy can always sing" - concluded Padron 'Ntoni.

Cecchetti defines the whole passage as "a kind of double inner monologue" through which Verga penetrates and expresses the inner reality, the states of mind, of his two protagonists. In the cart (carro) which Mena, according to Cecchetti, hears passing in the night and in the threatening storm (mare amaro) which Padron 'Ntoni "reads" in the peculiar glittering of the stars, Cecchetti isolates the recurrent signs or keynotes which in a manner not dissimilar from musical leitmotifs (6) identify the two characters throughout, telling their two distinct stories: Mena's doomed love for Alfio and Padron 'Ntoni's equally doomed struggle for the survival of his family. The major part of Cecchetti's essay is therefore devoted to an analysis of the occurrences of the two motifs, or, as he puts it generalizing, of significant words: "a precise web of images, of symbol-words - the only thing that connects all the events in the consciousness of the characters without a break in continuity" (113). For Cecchetti, then, the structure of the novel is struttura espressiva which, as a matter of fact, he claims to be the only kind of structure possible: "There cannot be various kinds of structure: the only structure possible is the one that resides in words" (113). In making this comprehensive and perhaps indefensible statement Cecchetti is obviously prompted by an orientation which puts a premium on "poetry" and encourages critical analysis based on the strict distinction in any given work or group of works between "what is poetry" and "what is not poetry". Thus, finally, I Malavoglia becomes for Cecchetti not an example of narrative writing (narrazione) but a hybrid romanzo-poema. (7)

The formula romanzo-poema brings us to two fundamental problems in Verga studies and poses the further question of how well Cecchetti was served when he chose the passage already dissected by his predecessors as the starting point for his own argument. Of the two problems the first concerns what most frequently, though often imprecisely, is referred to as Verga's style; the second deals with the apparent irreconcilability between two "manners" or phases in the corpus of Verga's work. The stylistic problem originally caused Verga to be rejected because of his dialectal and often incorrect language. It has been completely restated and thereby satisfactorily solved, however, by critics who like Cecchetti see style and technique as the two sides of the same coin. The second problem has been formulated by the majority of critics and apparently solved by them in positing a dividing line between an early manner and a later one and explaining the reappearance in some of the later works of themes prevalent in the early ones as a falling off of creative vigor. This in spite of the strongest evidence to the contrary. (8) In delimiting a major as against a minor Verga, Cecchetti implicitly accepts the majority position, although by ignoring the "other" Verga completely he has no cause to enter into the matter of chronology. (9) As far as the choice of passage is concerned, Cecchetti himself recognizes that once the basic fact of the "poetic" structure of I Malavoglia - its quality of romanzo-poema - is accepted, many other passages could have served his same purpose. The choice of the particular one must therefore be attributed to the authority of the earlier critics and to the fact that their attention to it resulted in giving a name to an inescapable characteristic of Verga's narrative technique.

There is controversy about the precise nature of this characteristic. Verga himself spoke of impersonality - and thereby began to muddle the issue. In the introductory passage to the short story L'amante di Gramigna he envisioned a novel in which the hand of the artist would be invisible: ". . . the work of art will seem to have produced itself, to have matured and grown spontaneously like a fact of nature, without maintaining any point of contact with its author, any blemish of original sin". More particularly with reference to I Malavoglia critics have used the term "choral": the point of view from which the story is told being not the omniscient narrator's but that of both the major and minor characters through whose words the narrator tells the story in a kind of unique collective stream of consciousness or sustained narrated monologue. (10)

In this respect the passage under consideration is of the utmost interest because, regardless of the terminology applied to it, it fuses aspects of narrative that in traditional storytelling are kept. separate. Specifically, the landscape indications with which it begins - the glittering stars, the slow "snoring" of the sea, the sound of a cart now and then bouncing on the stones - are imperceptibly, so it seems, drawn into the consciousness of Mena so that the paragraph which refers to her ends with the author's outright summary statement: - così pensava Mena sul ballatoio aspettando il nonno.

The exact point of transition between setting and stream of consciousness is open to doubt. For Günther, according to Spitzer, it would seem to occur in the second e of the polysyndetic sentence Il mare russava . . . . (11) This clause tells of carts (or of a cart) moving along the roads of a measureless world - e andava pel mondo il quale è tanto grande, che se uno potesse camminare e camminare sempre, giorno e notte, non arriverebbe mai - and points back, always according to Spitzer's reading of Günther, to the udire of the immediately preceding segment of the sentence - e a lunghi intervalli si udiva il rumore di qualche carro che passava nel buio - in which the reader's and Mena's perceptions of the sounds of the bouncing cart(s) can be said to be joined.

For Spitzer, instead, the whole passage from the very first sentence - Le stelle ammiccavano sempre più forte, quasi s'accendessero e i 'Tre Re' scintillavano sui fariglioni colle braccia in croce, come Sant'Andrea - is determined by Mena's filtering consciousness. The specific points cited by Spitzer in support of his position are the twinkling stars, which echo Mena's actual words to Alfio reported in direct address in the passage immediately preceding, and anthropomorphic expressions such as the one likening the constellation of the Three Kings (perhaps Orion) to the representation of the martyrdom of Saint Andrew, or the one picturing the heaving sea as a man asleep and snoring. For Spitzer, these expressions are all Mena's although of course insofar as Mena is herself one of the villagers she speaks no differently than they and in the use of similitudes and personifications her stream of consciousness is similar to what theirs would be.

Cecchetti feels that Spitzer's analysis generates confusion at this point because if the whole passage is erlebte Rede (which Cecchetti agrees it is) it cannot at the same time be the expression of the collective soul of the villagers: for Cecchetti, style indirect libre "implies something absolutely subjective" (112). (12)

As controversial as the exact point of transition to erlebte Rede, is the value to be assigned to the parenthetical così pensava Mena. Cecchetti warns the reader against seeing a possible parallel between it and Manzoni's comment at the close of the Addio, monti: Di tal genere, se non tali appunto, erano i pensieri di Lucia . . . [Of this kind, though not exactly thus, were Lucia's thoughts . . .]. Emphasizing the contrast between Manzoni's logical, rationally articulated discourse and Verga's emotional one, "with the sentence wandering from one thing to the next, in a manner similar to Mena's state of mind" (80), Cecchetti concludes that Verga's così, in contrast to Manzoni's, is to be read as meaning that Mena's thoughts were indeed those and none other and that Verga reported them "as faithfully as possible, without rearranging them in a logical pattern" (81).

Spitzer's argument makes no reference to Manzoni, is more subtle than Cecchetti's, and takes into consideration the formal tension set up by the storyteller in the process of telling the story rather than his desire to vindicate the verisimilitude of what he has told. Thus Spitzer starts out by recognizing the modern reader's malaise when he comes upon the così pensava Mena for, Spitzer argues, the reader's familiarity with style indirect libre would make such a comment superfluous even if it were meant to underline the fact that the whole passage and not only the section beginning with the second e after Il mare russava . . . is erlebte Rede. For Spitzer, the reader - or the critic - must not pause after the così pensava Mena but must continue to the end of what Verga wrote, sul ballatoio aspettando il nonno. Read thus, the sentence points both back to the dialogue between Alfio and Mena immediately preceding (rispose Mena, la quale era rimasta sul ballatoio ad aspettare il nonno), and ahead to Il nonno s'affaciò ancora due o tre volte sul ballatoio, the sentence which leads directly into Padron 'Ntoni's concluding two comments at the end of the chapter. In brief, to explain the presence of the così pensava Mena . . . Spitzer invokes a "rhythmic-epic principle", similar to Homer's use of formulaic verse repetitions. Thus Spitzer comes close to seeing a dominatingly narrative structure in I Malavoglia. Given his basic orientation, however, he veers away from an analysis conceived in terms of genre back to esthetic considerations, and his discussion of the passage ends by his viewing the "rhythmic principles" exclusively as those of the thought processes of the chorus and of the erlebte Rede of the individual.

This conclusion, indeed, is already implicit in the qualifying adverbial clause of his definition of the "rhythmic-epic principle": "the author's habit of introducing certain repetitions in the speech of his characters, as though their nature (and Nature's) obeyed some inner rhythm". (13)

I should like to argue now in favor of the narrative structure of I Malavoglia (I Malavoglia as narrazione rather than romanzo-poema) and try to show how the very passage in question can be read more accurately when we bear in mind that Verga is not only, as Cecchetti puts it, "digging down" into the psyche of his protagonists but that he is also telling a story. To do this we must not forget that the concluding paragraphs of Chapter II cannot be separated from what preceded them in their genetic development - and that this is especially so if we accept Cecchetti's characterization of Verga's style as alogical, allusive, and analogical. The immediate precedent of the finale of Chapter II is obviously the chapter itself. Chapter I, similarly an immediate precedent, presents a somewhat different problem in defining Verga's narrative technique and we shall return to it briefly later. Apart from the novel the most important precedent, the one most closely connected to its substance, is the short story Fantasticheria.

Cecchetti's reading of the passage in question as the double stream of consciousness of Mena and Padron 'Ntoni and his concomitant purpose in relating the passage to the rest of the novel prompt him to look ahead in the story. He is thus particularly successful in following the ramifications of the carro image within the overall descending parabola of Mena's love for Alfio. Spitzer, instead, looks back. We have already seen this in connection with the evidence he adduces for making the twinkling stars part of Mena's erlebte Rede and in his "rhythmic-epic" justification of the così pensava Mena . . . . Thus Spitzer is able to call attention to the fact that mention of the carts passing in the night (according to Günther, part of the passage in which we hear "the beating of Mena's heart") is actually a throwback to an earlier passage very close to the beginning of the chapter. In this passage, Compar Cipolla, one of the minor characters, is speaking:

> - Notte e giorno, c'è sempre gente che va attorno pel mondo, - osservò poi compare Cipolla.
> E adesso che non si vedeva più nè mare nè campagna, sembrava che non ci fosse al mondo altro che Trezza, e ognuno pensava dove potevano andare quei carri a quell'ora. (Spitzer's italics)

> -Night and day, there are always people going around in the world, - then observed Compare Cipolla.
> And now that one could no longer see the sea and the countryside, it seemed as though there were nothing in the world beside Trezza, and everyone was wondering where those carts might be going at that hour.

Preoccupied with erlebte Rede and, unlike Cecchetti, not particularly interested in the carro image, Spitzer must have been so struck by that pensava, which parallels the pensava applied to Mena, (14) that he quite overlooked or ignored the sentence immediately preceding Compare Cipolla's direct address: Sulla strada si udivano passare lentamente dei carri [On the street one heard carts going slowly by]. The sentence is also overlooked by Cecchetti who, as we have seen, is looking ahead in the novel and who is concerned primarily with the resonance those carri have (or as is more accurate for Cecchetti, that carro has) in Mena's consciousness.

The overlooked sentence, however, is extremely important. Just as important is the second occurrence of carro in Chapter II, this one also prior to the much discussed passage and likewise overlooked by both Spitzer and Cecchetti. As in the instance cited by Spitzer but not by Cecchetti, mention of the carro in this case is also connected with the "chorus" rather than with the protagonists. The village women are discussing Alfio Mosca, il quale [who], writes Verga in reporting Zuppidda's comment on Vespa's supposed rejection of Alfio as a possible husband, non possedeva altro che un carro da asino: "carro, cataletto" dice il proverbio [owned nothing but a donkey cart: "cart, coffin", says the proverb]. This occurrence of carro is one of the many hints of disaster to come scattered throughout the novel: in the main passage under discussion the feeling of foreboding is epitomized in Padron 'Ntoni's exclamation Mare amaro! and in Mena's thinking of the festa dei Morti as a time terminus of special significance for her. Cecchetti could easily have found a place in his theory of struttura espressiva for the image of carro changed to cataletto (stretcher, bier) although as it occurs it is not part of Mena's or Padron 'Ntoni's streams of consciousness. Being a proverb, however, it can be assumed to belong as much to Mena's and Padron 'Ntoni's folk wisdom as to that of the other villagers. The first of the overlooked sentences, on the other hand, could not be fitted into Cecchetti's argument. As a matter of fact, its occurrence casts considerable doubt on the correctness of his reading qualche carro as "the cart which is naturally Alfio's" (84). Had Spitzer included the sentence in his discussion, he would probably have related it to the "rhythmic-epic principle", though he might have had to modify its definition even further.

What happens if we take the overlooked sentence - Sulla strada si udivano passare lentamente dei carri - out of the "precise web of images, of symbol-words" of which Cecchetti writes and place it instead in the context of Fantasticheria, the short story where i carri che passavano per via at Aci-Trezza are first mentioned? As is well known, Fantasticheria is a kind of ur-Malavoglia which contains the story of the novel in embryo. There are even some details later omitted, such as the reference to the "desperate and sombre courage" with which Bastianazzo, Padron 'Ntoni's son and Mena's father, meets his death by drowning. (15) It is not possible to discuss fully here the light which <u>Fantasticheria</u> throws on <u>I Malavoglia</u>. For the present purpose we shall have to be content with pointing out that whatever we find in <u>Fantasticheria</u> is related genetically to the later work and is proof of the long process of elaboration which the novel underwent. (16) I am speaking here not vaguely of Verga's total development as a writer (which would naturally have to be a part of a really exhaustive study of his narrative technique in <u>I Malavoglia</u>), but quite specifically of the link between <u>Fantasticheria</u> and <u>I Malavoglia</u>. Generally, when critics have spoken of the link they have been concerned with what Luigi Russo calls the "polemical genesis" of the novel, (17) revealed, among other sources, by Verga's formulation in <u>Fantasticheria</u> of his social message involving the moral superiority of the poor. No critic, as far as I know, has examined <u>Fantasticheria</u> as an example of Verga's storytelling technique. In the chapter "Aspetti della prosa di <u>Vita dei campi</u>", Cecchetti himself is silent on <u>Fantasticheria</u>, implying thereby, I suppose, that it does not belong to Verga's major works. This opinion is of course shared by all critics who subscribe to the dichotomous view of the Verga <u>corpus</u>, who decry autobiographical intrusions into a work of art, and who feel so ill at ease at the presence of "mundane" elements in Verga's life and art that they would like to suppress them, and indeed do suppress them in their discussion of his work. But the fact remains that Verga belonged not to the peasantry but to the upper class and that he wrote about that class throughout his career, so much so that the last volume of the series of which <u>I Malavoglia</u> is the first was to have been <u>L'uomo di lusso</u>, a novel with a protagonist racked by aristocratic vanity and political ambition.

The two features that indispose Verga critics, the presence of autobiographical elements and the social world of elegance and privilege, are both part of <u>Fantasticheria</u>. For, in striking contrast to the novel, in <u>Fantasticheria</u> the story of the fishermen-family is framed within a second story, that of the narrator's visit to Aci-Trezza years before in the company of a capricious woman to whom he is now writing of their experiences there. Yet, in spite of any hypothetical autobiographical reminiscences that it might contain, the frame story must be regarded in narrative terms as a fiction. This fiction gives Verga a number of possibilities which he does not have in the novel. There is, most significantly, a first-person narrator who can - indeed must - express directly what is in his mind. (18) Moreover, the narrator has an interlocutor and her reactions during the visit to Aci-Trezza are used as a foil to his own. In addition, the narrator's reactions are given even further depth by the process of reflection which has taken place in him since the original visit, reflections prompted in part by additional knowledge gained in later visits of which he now writes to the woman. All this enables him (the narrator / Verga) to be more

effectively persuasive in trying to convince the reader that he (or she)
should have greater understanding and sympathy for the primitive
fishermen whose attachment to home and family is so different from
the sophisticated cosmopolitan notions of the woman. I cannot here
enter into a discussion of the compassionate witness/impassive observer duality in Verga, (19) nor yet consider whether and to what
extent the woman companion on the narrator's visit to Aci-Trezza is
a projection of Verga's alter ego rather than a partner of flesh and
blood. Having established the basic importance of Fantasticheria not
only as other critics have done with regard to the nature of Verga's
ideological involvement but also with regard to a more comprehensive
view of his narrative technique, I must return instead to those carri
che passavano per via in the Aci-Trezza of Fantasticheria and try to
see what light they throw on the qualche carro che passava nel buio of
the famous passage in I Malavoglia.
   I propose initially that the first mention of passing carts in Chapter
II - Sulla via si udivano passare lentamente dei carri - is simply part
of the description of the setting of this chapter. By contrast to Chapter
I, which is essentially "summary narrative" with only an occasional
"immediate scene" (such as the one at the railroad station when the
younger 'Ntoni is leaving for his military training), Chapter II is all
"immediate scene". (20) It is Saturday evening in the village and except
for the inevitable household tasks all work and other every day occu-
pations have been interrupted. The overall scene can, if one wishes,
be subdivided into subordinate scenes so that the scene of the men
sitting on the church steps, for instance, could be viewed as a counterpoint to the scene of the women busy in their homes and participating
in the general conversation from their thresholds and windows. But
there are features of the setting common to the chapter as a whole.
As is well known, Verga was extremely chary of landscape indications,
(21) the magnificent descriptions of the shimmering sea under the sun
in Chapter VI and of the fearsome storm in Chapter X being quite exceptional. As far as Chapter II is concerned, unless some further detail has escaped my attention, nothing is said of the natural setting
except for the glittering stars, the "snoring" sea, and the sound of the
carts bouncing on the stones. There is much more in Fantasticheria,
including a sunrise which the two protagonists watch from the fariglioni, those legendary rocks cast by Polyphemus after the fleeing
Ulysses, and which are treated in I Malavoglia as no more than place
names so that, in contrast to their use in the short story, they can in
no sense be considered as part of the landscape description in the
novel. It might be claimed that in the Malavoglia passage under discussion Verga does not describe the passing carts but that he evokes
them through the sound they make. In Fantasticheria too he does not
describe them but evokes them, this time through the woman's remembered gesture of boredom in counting them: La mattina del terzo

giorno, stanca di vedere eternamente del verde e dell'azzurro, e di contare i carri che passavano per via . . . [On the morning of the third day, tired of always seeing that green and blue, and of counting the carts that were passing on the road . . .]. But though the udire and the vedere of the respective passages create distance, the carri in both instances are not in anyone's consciousness but are part of external reality. The most that could be said is that the narrator(22) is aware of their presence and that he communicates this awareness to the reader. But this only brings us to the well-known ambiguity of realism in art and does not change my contention that the carri of Fantasticheria prove that at least the first mention of carri in Chapter II has nothing to do with erlebte Rede. This conclusion, moreover, was already implicit in Spitzer's slip (Freudian?) in failing to notice the sentence - Sulla via si udivano passare lentamente dei carri - in spite of its being so close to the passage he cited.

The second occurrence of carro (carro this time, not carri) in Chapter II can be related to the first only if it is taken out of context. The relationship in other words is only apparent. We have seen how the carro, cataletto image of the proverb spoken by the "chorus" belongs to the metaphorical web of the novel, being but one of the intimations of disaster scattered throughout. The proverb is cited immediately following mention of Alfio's carro da asino, the donkey cart by which he makes a living. It is this donkey cart, whose repeated presence both explicit and implicit in Mena's thoughts Cecchetti has traced so perceptively, coupled with Spitzer's almost unilateral emphasis on erlebte Rede, that undoubtedly led Cecchetti to confuse the qualche carro of the second segment of the polysyndetic sentence Il mare russava . . . with il carro dell'asino, the "sign" of Alfio's presence in the novel. But the qualche carro is obviously not Alfio's carro da asino but simply a further attenuation of i carri of Fantasticheria and of dei carri in the first mention of Chapter II. Cecchetti writes: "The carro that passed in the dark (note the indefinite singular qualche carro rather than carri, because in Mena's emotional life it is always the same cart) is naturally Alfio's, and it will return again and again throughout the whole novel, as here, or as carro dell'asino, or simply as asino" (84). However, although the invariable adjective qualche is, grammatically speaking, followed by a singular noun, it has a plural meaning, being the equivalent of alcuno/alcuni (some). With respect to i carri, therefore, both dei carri and qualche carro are partitives; however, dei carri implies a considerable number, qualche carro only a few. Between the dei carri of the beginning of Chapter II and the qualche carro of the end, night has fallen on the village: Un'ora di notte! - osservò Padron Cipolla [One hour at night! - observed Padron Cipolla] - and others of the villagers have already said good night to one another and returned home. The attenuation of dei to qualche is in perfect keeping with the dying down of activity in preparation for bed time. Thus the qualche carro is simply an echo of the dei carri of Sulla strada si udivano passare lentamente dei carri (and beyond that of the i carri of Fantasticheria). It is easy to see, however, how Cecchetti mistook the qualche carro for Alfio's carro dell'asino.

This is a mistake that Günther would not have made, and which indeed he did not make. We have seen how Spitzer's reading of Günther places the transition between setting and stream of consciousness in the second e of the sentence Il mare russava... and how as a consequence the whole paragraph is determined for him by Mena's filtering consciousness. But as I read Günther, there is little to justify Spitzer's conclusion. The point is sufficiently important to warrant quotation in full of the original statement. (23) Under the chapter heading, "Einzelne Beispiele erlebter Rede", Günther first cites the passage (omitting the part of the first sentence that follows s'accendessero) and then comments:

Dieses Beispiel enthält einen feinen Übergang von imperfektivischer Zustandsschilderung in imperfektivische erlebte Rede: die Darstellung einer stimmungsmässigen Schau gleitet unmerklich hinüber in die erlebte Wiedergabe von Gedanken. Mitten im Satze geschieht ein kleiner Perspektivenwechsel: ganz still beginnt plötzlich ein menschliches Herz hinter den Indikativen zu schlagen, und deren Bedeutung rückt aus dem sinneswirklichen Wert dargestellter Wahrnehmungen hinein in den engen Kreis eines subjektiven Gedankens, aber hinein auch in das Universum einer Seele. Und so umfasst denn eine grammatische Form das Aussen und das Innen und verschwistert sie. Der Dichter hört das Brausen des Meeres und das Geräusch eines rollenden Karrens in der Nacht, und er hört zugleich auch die Stimme eines Herzens, und beide sind für ihn Offenbarungen der grossen Natur, des All und Einen, des ewigen Geistes, der in Allem wohnt. Der ächzende Karren, der in der Nacht auf holperigem Wege dahinrollt und nie ans Ziel der Welt gelangt, und das Meer, das unaufhörlich und beängstigend und nutzlos brandet, und der Mensch in seiner Einsamkeit, sie alle sind in das Mysterium des Daseins verwoben, über allen schwebt eine unerklärliche Schicksalsmacht. In dieser erlebten Rede liegt ein ganzes Bekenntnis ausgedrückt: das Bewusstsein von der Immanenz alles Seins, von der Einheit von Natur und Geist. Das pantheistische Gefühl aber ist beschwert von einem pessimistishen Fatalitätsglauben.

The significant sentence for my argument is of course the central one with its unequivocal assertion that it is Verga who hears the surging

of the sea and the creaking of the cart in the night and that it is he who
at the same time hears the beating of a human heart. We are here at
the point where the two problems we spoke of earlier - that of the
transition between setting and stream of consciousness and that of the
value to be assigned to the così pensava Mena - intersect and where
both further interlock with the larger problem of the structure of I
Malavoglia. Moved by Günther's truly magnificent recreation of the
pantheistic mood of the passage, Spitzer comments: "The interpenetration of style and poetic atmosphere in this passage could not be
described better." He then goes on to an analysis of the "choral" quality of Mena's consciousness which explains for him the successful
achievement of that interpenetration, and coming full circle he ends
by applying Günther's insight into the dominant pantheistic mood of the
passage to the specific setting of the novel: "it is the collective soul of
Trezza that at that moment feels man's solitude in the universe". One
wonders how his analysis might have been modified had he not omitted
another (Freudian?) slip - in his quotation and translation of Günther
the crucial und er hört zugleich auch die Stimme eines Herzens, thus
making the beide of the immediately following phrase apply to the
surging of the sea and the creaking of the cart, instead of to the surging of the sea and the creaking of the cart as one unit of the beide, and
the beating of the human heart as the second. (24) Cecchetti, on the
other hand, stops with the first third of Günther's observation, thus
emphasizing the grammatical basis for Günther's definition of erlebte
Rede. (25) In contrast to Spitzer, as we have seen, he then insists on
the individuality of the feeling expressed, divorcing Mena's subjectivity from that of the other villagers. Both Spitzer and Cecchetti -
although Spitzer less so, as has already been pointed out in connection
with his positing a "rhythmic-epic principle" for Verga's storytelling -
undercut the concept of authorship. In doing so they are of course in
a sense simply pushing Verga's stated desire for impersonality and
objectivity to its logical conclusion.

My question now is whether this diminished concept of authorship is
a necessary prerequisite for establishing that "this passage" (as
Spitzer puts it) or "Mena's monologue" (as with no more ado Cecchetti
substitutes) "represents perhaps one of the high points of Italian prose
narrative". (26) Having, I believe, demonstrated satisfactorily that the
qualche carro is not to be mistaken for Alfio's carro dell'asino and
that the cart is therefore not inevitably in Mena's mind as Cecchetti
assumed he had proved, we can proceed to ask whether Spitzer was
right - in spite of his obvious error in attributing his own reading to
Günther - in feeling that the point of transition between setting and
stream of consciousness occurs in the second e after Il mare russava
. . . . There can be no doubt that the rendition of the idea of the vastness of the world with the image of someone walking day and night
without ever arriving is in no way equivalent to the immediately pre-

ceding descriptions of the sea and carts. (27) Moreover, what is added
by the third and fourth e of the sentence is directly derived from that
specific characterization of the vastness of the world. In other words,
our polysyndetic sentence falls quite naturally into two parts:

Il mare russava in fondo all stradicciuola, adagio, adagio, e
a lunghi intervalli si udiva il rumore di qualche carro che
passava nel buio, sobbalzando sui sassi,//
e andava pel mondo il quale è tanto grande che se uno potesse
camminare sempre, giorno e notte, non arriverebbe mai, e
c'era pure della gente che andava pel mondo a quell'ora, e
non sapeva nulla di compar Alfio, né della Provvidenza che
era in mare, né della festa dei Morti.

To answer the question, however, of what part of the passage is in
Mena's mind - that is, how much of it is stream of consciousness and
how much of it is narrative - we shall have to return to a passage cited
earlier and which I would like to repeat here without Spitzer's editori-
alizing and in a slightly more complete version:

Sulla strada si udivano passare lentamente dei carri.
- Notte e giorno c'è sempre gente che va attorno per il
mondo, - osservò poi compare Cipolla.
E adesso che non si vedeva più nè mare nè campagna,
sembrava che non ci fosse al mondo altro che Trezza,
e ognuno pensava dove potevano andare quei carri a quel-
l'ora
- Prima di mezzanotte la Provvidenza avrà girato il Capo
dei Mulini - disse padron 'Ntoni, - e il vento fresco non
le darà più noia.

On the street one heard carts going by slowly.
- Night and day, there are always people going around in
the world, - then observed Compare Cipolla.
And now that one could no longer see the sea and the countryside, it seemed as though there were nothing in the world
beside Trezza, and everyone was wondering where those
carts might be going at that hour.
- By midnight the Provvidenza will have gone around Capo
dei Mulini - said - Padron 'Ntoni, and this brisk wind will no
longer bother it.

We have already commented on the light which this passage throws on
the first part of the polysyndetic sentence. If we now look at the second part, we note that in the later passage two facts are referred to
which do not appear in the earlier one: the existence of Compare Alfio

and the forthcoming festa dei Morti. About both of these the reader
has learned something in the course of Chapter II, after the narrative
passage just quoted. Both are inextricably connected with Mena's
most intimate feelings, feelings which she has shared with no one -
although there may be ground for supposing that she has intimated
them to Alfio. Strictly speaking, then, it is only in the final segment
of the sentence that we are given the content of Mena's consciousness,
what belongs to her and no one else. The "snoring" sea is definitely
part of the external setting and so are the rattling carts passing in the
night. The wondering of where the carts are going is common to
ognuno: it is still part of the author's description of the world of
Trezza. Concern for what will happen to the Provvidenza is primarily
Padron 'Ntoni's but is shared by Mena as a member of his family,
whose future depends on its economic status. If it is Mena's heart
that is heard beating in this passage, then it is heard beating as such
only at the very end, immediately prior to Verga's stepping back to
conclude the sentence with - così pensava Mena sul ballatoio aspettando il nonno.

If my analysis is correct at this point, then the question that must
follow concerns the significance of the juxtaposition. In other words,
of what nature and how strong is Verga's assertion in the word così?
Is it to be interpreted, as Cecchetti claims, as marking a situation
completely different from Manzoni's similar authorial intervention
at the end of the Addio, monti passage? "That così pensava Mena",
writes Spitzer, "is situated on a crossroad on which the rhythmic
principles of choral thought and of individual erlebte Rede meet", but
in a footnote he expresses reservations about his own statement by
making room at that crossroads for the author himself.(28) And indeed, for all Verga's desire to eclipse himself from the telling of the
story, he is present there.

However, it would be my claim that his presence is revealed not
only in the parenthetic statement with which the paragraph ends but in
the whole passage that leads up to the ending, and specifically in the
mention of the cart. In one sense, of course, the paragraph recapitulates and summarizes the chapter, a common enough procedure in
storytelling. In I promessi sposi the Addio, monti similarly recapitulates and summarizes, in its case the first eight chapters of the book,
a fact which acquires all its significance for the narrative technique
with which we are concerned when we remember that the novel was
originally divided into Books and that Book I ended at this point. In
another sense, however, the manner of the summary of the Malavoglia
passage adds something, or perhaps it would be more exact to say
brings out something which was in essence there already: it surrounds
the facts of the story with an aura. The same aura, of course, is given
by Lucia's filtering consciousness to the landscape of Lake Como which
had at the beginning of I promessi sposi been described in topographic

and geologic terms only.

But exactly where does the aura begin? There can be no question that it begins in the second e: "a small change in perspective", Günther calls it. The passing of the cart, from its first muted appearance in Fantasticheria, triggers something in Verga's imagination. In the first two instances discussed, this something is controlled by the author and pushed back into objectivity: in Fantasticheria the woman counts the carts as they pass by; in the first passage of Chapter II Compar Cipolla wonders where the carts may be going. Here, instead, mention of the cart leads into the second part of the sentence, which is characterized by its overwhelming questioning and wondering until it smooths out into the three names with which it concludes: Alfio, the Provvidenza, and the festa dei Morti. As these are referred to, we are back in the factual, plot world of I Malavoglia: Verga looks ahead to the story he is to tell. He is aware, however, that he had momentarily lost hold, that subjective lyricism had disturbed his role of impassive observer, and in order to re-erect the barrier he makes the strong assertion, - così pensava Mena. (29) This assertion would not have been necessary if we had indeed been in Mena's mind all the time, if it had indeed been her heart and hers alone which we heard beating. (30)

Manzoni's statement at a parallel point in his story is, as Cecchetti correctly feels, quite different, but it should be obvious by now that I would assign other reasons than Cecchetti's to explain that difference. For Manzoni's statement is not different from Verga's as far as narrative exigencies are concerned: it, too, is intended to correct an erroneous impression or a question which the author feels his telling of the story might have induced in the reader. It is, however, different in its tone which is not assertive but descriptive: Di tal genere, se non tali appunto erano i pensieri di Lucia . . . . The difference in tone is a direct reflection of each author's perception of his distance from the subject at that particular point in his narrative. Manzoni's distance, the typical distance of the omniscient author, is constant throughout the novel. His occasional authorial interventions, while they appear to span the distance, actually maintain it. He is fully conscious of the control he exercises over plot and characters and he writes for a reader whom he assumes endowed with the ability to read critically and to question what he reads. It is a reader who must be convinced of a truth through logic rather than be propelled into an attitude through sentiment. Verga's position instead is ambiguous and uncertain. The distance of the impassive observer-author must be achieved paradoxically, through the author's total identification with his characters. In a technique which would have the story tell itself, no dividing line is possible between what is exclusively the author's and what is his characters'. Thus, while the characters, as one critic puts it, are often muscling their way into

what should be the author's exclusive domain, the author also on occasion introduces himself into what should be the exclusive domain of
a character. (31) It is my claim that the appearance of the carro image
in the passage we have been discussing is one instance of the occurrence of the latter, and that Verga's subliminal awareness of what
has happened brings him to the assertion at the end. I would thus conclude that while Cecchetti's analysis continues the discussion of the
two crucial Verga problems cited earlier and while his attention to
the Malavoglia passage invites a second and most needed look at what
both Spitzer and Günther have written, he fails to answer adequately
the questions he has himself raised. His failure to do so can, I believe, be attributed to his insufficient awareness on a theoretical
level of the narrative structure of Verga's works. (32)

Though Dorothee Böhm(33) approaches Verga from a quite different
direction than Cecchetti, her study contributes to an understanding
of some of the problems we have been discussing. Guided by
Heidegger's postulation that man's view of time is the clue to his
view of himself and the world and by Emil Staiger's application of
Heidegger's thought to literary criticism, she aims at a comprehensive definition of Verga's forma mentis which, she says, is in the
last analysis the core to which all partial observations of his art
must be connected. Her attention is thus directed to both the man and
his work though her tools are not the familiar ones of biography and
literary history. Put very briefly, her conclusion is that Verga's best
work results from a dialectic tension between his actual experience of
time and what he would have liked that experience to be, between his
perception of time as fleeting (the fantasmagoria of experience) and
his aspiration to a timeless universe in which movement would be at
a standstill. With the general concept of time Dr. Böhm naturally
touches upon - though only tangentially - the basic concept of narrative as a succession of events, while with her insight into the unresolved conflict in Verga between Zeiterfahrung and Zeitgestaltung she
brings new light to bear upon the romantic as against the realistic
bent in his personality as man and writer.
    Dr. Böhm begins her investigation with a reading of Fantasticheria.
She reduces the formal structure of the story to the "opposition and
playing out of the opposition" (Gegensatz und Gegeneinanderausspielen)
of two worlds (the fishermen's and the addressee's) which lead to a
statement of Verga's message: that the restlessness of city life would
find its resolution and peace in the unchanging rhythm of life in the
Sicilian countryside. Dr. Böhm then examines this message within
the context of Verga's own feelings regarding time, expressed directly in his correspondence and indirectly in the novels of the years preceding Fantasticheria, or, it might be said, in the time span in which
he himself was living the experience of the woman to whom the story

is addressed. On the basis of this evidence Dr. Böhm is able to see
the woman as "incarnating" Verga's own experience of time and the
world, an experience from which he - though not the woman - seeks
to escape. The "sharp, polemical tone" of the piece is attributed by
Dr. Böhm to Verga's deep psychological involvement in the situation
he is portraying: "With every critical word Verga attacks himself"
(24). Read in this light Fantasticheria becomes on a deeper level than
in the interpretation of other critics (34) the link between Verga's early
works and his choice of milieu for Vita dei campi and I Malavoglia.

In her analysis of I Malavoglia Dr. Böhm adds a spatial concept,
derived from a number of critics but principally from Ernst Cassirer,
to the underlying temporal one which she uses to show how even in
this work Verga's desire to create a timeless universe revealed itself
illusory. Neither his effort to efface narrative time through the unbroken continuity of the plot line and the melting together of past and
present, nor his emphasis on the cyclical recurrence of events succeeded in obliterating the reflection in I Malavoglia of his own experience of time as passing and evanescent. Trezza did not become a
world outside time, as Dr. Böhm proves through quotations from passages in which Alfio laments the changes which have occurred in his absence. But it is Dr. Böhm's application of the spatial concept to the
novel which is particularly relevant to our discussion. The tension felt
by Verga in his dual perception of time is repeated in the polarities of
distance and nearness which are given not topographical but psychological and symbolic meaning in the experience of the characters in I
Malavoglia. Specifically with reference to the cart heard passing in the
night, Dr. Böhm points out its identification in the minds of the inhabit-
ants of Trezza with the evil characteristics of everything which is connected with distance: "restless movement, meaninglessness, homeless-
ness, boundless distance, estrangement, as for instance they can be
perceived in the motif of passing carts on a country road at night" (84).
Thus Dr. Böhm's reading of the famous Malavoglia passage coincides
essentially with mine and diverges from Cecchetti's. But while I approached the problem of assigning the correct meaning to the appearance of the cart in this passage by attempting to reconstruct the genesis
of the image in Fantasticheria and the earlier sections of the novel,
Dr. Böhm arrived at it incidentally, presenting the image as issuing
from Verga's basic forma mentis as uncovered through her analysis of
his attitude to time. We would both have to subscribe, I believe, to the
assessment of Verga's style which sees it as resulting from the novelist's persistent romanticism. (35) His identification with the world he
creates is constantly blocked at the very moment in which it occurs.
One such moment is the passing of the cart in what is ostensibly
Mena's erlebte Rede, checked immediately by the parenthetic statement così pensava Mena which has been revealed to be in essence a
subconscious protestation of perfect objectivity and as all excessive

protestations suspect.

(1972)

NOTES

1. Giovanni Cecchetti, Il Verga maggiore: Sette studi (Florence, 1968).
Page references are made parenthetically within the text.
2. On this point, see especially Cecchetti's belaboring of Lawrence's
difficulties with the word palmento (207-8). Ironically enough, the
translation into Italian of Cecchetti's essay which had originally appeared in English (Comparative Literature, IX [1957], 333-44), presented its own problems. Thus, the palmento passage which read
" . . . Verga uses the word palmento, a storehouse on Sicilian farms,
housing the mill . . ." becomes in Italian, " . . . si legge la parola
palmento, il nome dato dal Verga a una specie di capannone dei poderi
siciliani . . .", where the expression il nome dato dal Verga creates
the impression that Cecchetti thinks of palmento as a Verga coinage.
3. I shall make only one observation on the essays that I do not discuss. In speaking of the revisions made for the 1897 edition of Vita
dei campi, Cecchetti notes that the only change in the short story La
Lupa is the substitution of zitella for vitella in Nanni's words of rejection of the older woman: "Ed io invece voglio vostra figlia ch'è vitella"
(55). Cecchetti correctly observes that the change entails a loss of
"quel sapore terragno e villereccio" of the original expression. I find
it difficult, however, to accept that the change was made by Verga
himself. How likely is it for Nanni to tell la Lupa that he prefers her
daughter to herself because the daughter is unmarried (zitella) rather
than because she is fresh and young (vitella)? In the story Nanni not
only rejects the older woman but he also scorns her. Verga's substitution of zitella for vitella would imply not simply the expunction of a
"struttura espressiva locale" but a change in attitude toward the scene
he has written. I find no proof that such a change of attitude occurred.
As a matter of fact, the play which was drawn from the short story
(performed 1896) has Nanni say to la Lupa at the corresponding moment of the plot: "Datemi vostra figlia ch'è carne fresca invece . . . ."
On the basis of this evidence, I find it more likely to suppose that the
change from vitella to zitella was made by a north Italian proof reader
or even type-setter, a one letter change being the typical correction of
what is felt to be a typographical error. Thus Verga would have made
no changes at all in La Lupa.
4. Spitzer's essay, "L'originalità della narrazione nei Malavoglia",
can be read in Belfagor, XI (1956), 37-53. My remarks are based
almost exclusively on 41-44.
5. Giovanni Verga, I Malavoglia, Chapter II. The translation that

follows is the present writer's. For the balance of the essay quotations from this passage will not be accompanied by their translation.
6. Cecchetti objects to the use of the term leitmotif (96) and takes a polemical stand against Wido Hempel's Giovanni Vergas Roman I Malavoglia und die Wiederholung als erzählerisches Kunstmittel (Cologne-Graz, 1959), damning it with the usual faint praise, "È un lavoro molto diligente." Here, as in the section of the essay devoted to his three predecessors (110-13), Cecchetti is exaggeratedly concerned with vindicating the originality of his method in contrast to that of other critics. This often leads him to force his position with consequent distortions in his supporting material. Apropos of the leitmotif discussion, for instance, he speaks of recurrent images that by dint of repetition become symbols and he cites as an example "la nappa del berretto di Turiddu che finalmente si dice che ha fatto il solletico nel cuore di Santa" (95). Repetition of the image is seen by him as a means of poetic transfiguration, "anzi la trasfigurazione poetica in atto". But what we actually have in the tassel of Turiddu's cap which "tickles" the heart of Santa is a typical concretization of metaphor such as is found in popular imagination and speech. Such a concretization may of course be felt to be poetic, but I don't see how that prevents it from being used as a leitmotif.
7. In La narrativa italiana tra romanzo e racconti (first published in 1959, now 205-71 in the author's Pazienza e impazienza, Florence, 1968), Leone Piccioni proposed the distinction between narrare breve and narrare lungo to characterize what many critics have felt to be the basic contrast between the style of I Malavoglia and that of Mastro don Gesualdo. This distinction within the genre seems to me more fruitful than Cecchetti's contamination between genres.
8. By the simple expedient of reviewing the order of composition of Verga's works Leone Piccioni has shown, as far as I'm concerned, conclusively, that "questi due modi, se esistono, tuttavia non si succedono, ma si alternano durante tutta la vita e tutta l'opera del Verga" ("Per la narrativa del Verga: descrizioni e sondaggi", 107-85 in op. cit. The quoted sentence can be found on 111).
9. Cecchetti accepts Nedda (1874) as marking the beginning of Verga's mature style. For a dissenting opinion, which puts Primavera (1875) in that place, see Aurelio Navarria, Lettura di poesia nell'opera di Giovanni Verga (Messina-Florence, 1962), 46-54. Navarria's view, to which I subscribe, is that neglect of Primavera results from the dominating prejudice in Verga studies according to which only "his works dealing with the fishermen of Trezza and the peasants of Vizzini" are supposed to have achieved artistic merit.
10. Terminologically, a distinction should be made between stream of consciousness and narrated monologue (for the latter term, see Dorrit Cohn, "Narrated Monologue: Definition of a Fictional Style", Comparative Literature, XVIII [1966], 97-112). But inasmuch as Cecchetti

is not concerned with terminological distinctions, I have used the two expressions interchangeably. Verga's narrative technique is called dialogo raccontato or racconto dialogato by Luigi Russo (Giovanni Verga, Bari, 1959, 352). For a comprehensive presentation of Verga's modes of storytelling, see, in addition to the Spitzer article cited, Giacomo Devoto, "Giovanni Verga e i 'piani del racconto' ", 202-14 in his Nuovi studi di stilistica (Florence, 1962).

11. Werner Günther, Probleme der Rededarstellung, Untersuchungen zur direkten, indirekten und "erlebten" Rede im Deutschen, Französischen und Italienischen, Marburg a.d. Lahn, 1928 (Die Neuren Sprachen, Beiheft Nr. 13). The Verga passage is discussed on 133-34.

12. Here is an instance where greater attention to terminology would have resulted in greater clarity. Obviously Cecchetti is equating style indirect libre with stream of consciousness at this point, for it would be otherwise impossible to justify his contention that the content of the collective mind cannot be rendered through use of that technique. On the other hand, stream of consciousness may be said to imply a single mind.

13. Had Spitzer thought of genre as the dominating category, he would probably have ended the sentence with "battute" (speech). As we shall see below, however, his formulation here was strongly influenced not only by his stylistic orientation but also by the Günther passage he had just translated. The afterthought regarding Nature, which he placed in parentheses, comes directly from Günther.

14. Although the two occurrences of pensava have much in common (quasi identity of content, terminal position in the sentence), they also point to the basic difference between the two passages. In the one case we have straightforward storytelling by an omniscient narrator; in the other a lyrical effusion in which subject (the narrator) and object (what is narrated) merge.

15. Because of the programmatic, though not always actual, absence of an omniscient narrator in I Malavoglia, no details of Bastianazzo's death are given in the novel. As a matter of fact, the manner in which his death is referred to ("Maruzza [his wife] non diceva nulla, ma nella testa ci aveva un pensiero fisso, che la martellava, e le rosicava il cuore, di sapere cos'era successo in quella notte . . .": Chap. IV) would seem to underline Verga's intentional approach and make explicit his use of a controlled point of view.

16. The best reconstruction of the period of elaboration of I Malavoglia is still L. and V. Perroni, "Storia de I Malavoglia: Carteggio con l'editore e con Luigi Capuana", Nuova Antologia, CDVIII (1940), 105-31 and 237-51.

17. L. Russo, Giovanni Verga, 136-48.

18. In the prefatory note to Eva and in the opening paragraph of Nedda Verga also speaks directly to the reader. For Fantasticheria it is

more precise to say that Verga's persona speaks to the reader's stand-in. The opening of Nedda throws considerable light on Fantasticheria, as do also the two prefaces to I Malavoglia.

19. On this point, see my own Verga's Milanese Tales (New York, 1964), 6-14.

20. For the terminology used here, see Norman Friedman, "Point of View in Fiction: The Development of a Critical Concept", now 113-42 in Approaches to the Novel, ed. Robert Scholes (San Francisco, 1961), 124-25.

21. In his "La natura nelle opere di Giovanni Verga" (Italica, XXXVII [1960], 89-108), Giovanni Sinicropi analyzes the function of landscape in the work of Verga. Description of nature as such is shown to be almost totally absent.

22. The narrator in one case is Verga's persona who recalls to the woman what she had been doing; in the second case it is of course Verga himself, making use however of the impersonal and generalizing si udivano.

23. Spitzer did not translate the whole passage but only from "Mitten im Satze . . . " ("Nel mezzo di una frase . . .") to " . . . eine unerklärliche Schicksalsmacht" (" . . . una forza del destino inspiegabile pesa su tutti").

24. Spitzer's translation reads: " . . . il poeta sente il russare del mare e il cigolío del carretto nella notte, e ambedue sono per lui rivelazione della grande natura, del tutto e dell'uno, dello spirito eterno che abita in tutto". The missing clause would have followed notte.

25. Giulio Herczeg, Lo stile indiretto libero in italiano (Florence, 1963) 219-46, is useful for placing Günther's work on erlebte Rede in relation to that of his predecessors, among whom were Bally, Lips, Kalepky, Lerch, and Spitzer himself. The problem of characterizing Günther's position is more complex than Cecchetti's brief description would seem to indicate.

26. Cecchetti writes: "Ma bisogna essere d'accordo con lo Spitzer quando asserisce . . . che il monologo di Mena rappresenta . . ." (112). Spitzer had written: "Günther . . . il quale dedica una pagina intiera a questo passo che rappresenta forse . . ." (41). Italics mine.

27. In commenting on the passage Devoto (Nuovi studi di linguistica, 206-207) calls attention to the preceding page in the novel where the self-same sea is portrayed in the identical act of "snoring". He says that at that point the sea is no more than an insignificant part of the village scene at night. A similar observation could easily be made with respect to the different values acquired by the appearance of the cart in different contexts. This would, however, in no way change the essence of my argument.

28. The observation is acute and deserves to be quoted: "Si potrebbe dire che la stilizzazione 'omerica' ridà al narratore qualche cosa

dell'autorità che perde nell'erlebte Rede semi-oggettiva. Ma d'altra parte quella stilizzazione è anche adattata, come abbiamo detto, al ritmo interiore del pensiero collettivo. Oscilla così tra il linguaggio dell' autore e quello dei personaggi" (44).

29. To explore fully the value to be assigned to the "così pensava Mena", all similar instances of the use of such parenthetic statements in the novel should be examined. Cecchetti himself cites one, "così correvano i pensieri della sua testa", calling attention to how it parallels the "così pensava Mena" (89). Examination of this passage in the novel (Chap. V) corroborates my reading of the "così pensava Mena", for there too, the assertion follows directly on an observation which is obviously Verga's rather than Mena's and which moreover is not even rendered in style indirect libre: "Mena cogli occhi seguiva l'ombra delle nuvole che correva per i campi, come fosse l'ulivo grigio che si dileguasse; così correvano i pensieri della sua testa."

30. The reference cited by Günther in a footnote to his discussion (134) is particularly suggestive in this connection and throws some light on what must have helped form his understanding of the passage in question. He quotes a sentence from Natale Scalìa's Giovanni Verga (Ferrara, 1922, 91), which characterizes Verga's fatalism by contrast to that of the Russians as being "contenuto in linee di chiarezza veramente italiane". Scalìa had illustrated his contention by referring specifically to the vague feeling of mystery released by the "carretto solitario che cigola nella notte". Readers of Leopardi cannot fail being reminded at this point of some verses from La sera del dì di festa:

> Ahi, per la via
> odo non lunge il solitario canto
> dell'artigian, che riede a tarda notte
> dopo i sollazzi, al suo povero ostello;
> e fieramente mi si stringe il core,
> a pensar come tutto al mondo passa,
> e quasi orma non lascia.

The causal relationship between the sound heard at night and the emotion it evokes is stated explicitly by Leopardi. In the case of Verga it must be inferred. Not an unnatural inference to make, considering that the theme of the sadness of the life of the vagabond is recurrent in Verga's work.

31. G. Herczeg, Lo stile indiretto libero in italiano, 207. Within his comprehensive treatment of the problems connected with style indirect libre in Italian, Herczeg's view of the use of the technique by Verga is consonant with that of the majority of Verga critics who have consistently asked themselves, "How does Verga handle indirect discourse?" rather than, "How does he handle narrative?" Herczeg's whole argu-

mentation is dominated by the desire to unseat the author as creator. Thus, for instance, he glosses over Th. Kalepky's view that style indirect libre is an efficacious means for making it possible for the author to manifest himself behind the shoulders of his characters (222-24), and Nicola Vita's emphasis (in "Genesi del discorso rivissuto e suo uso nella narrativa italiana", Cultura neolatina, 1955) on the preponderant role of the author (233). Herczeg feels special sympathy for works of literature which deal with the life of the lower classes and would seem to look forward to the total eclipse of the author retreating before the autonomous expression of his characters.
32. In Paragraph IV of his essay Cecchetti shows strong awareness to the narrative structure of the novel, following Verga step by step as he builds up his story and prepares for and develops episodes which are tied together by the plot line and not simply by the unity of the psyche of the protagonists. But Cecchetti enunciates no cohesive narrative principle to set beside his expressive one.
33. Dorothee Böhm, Zeitlosigkeit und entgleitende Zeit als konstitutive Dialektik im Werke von Giovanni Verga (Münster/Westfalen, 1967).
34. Gorizio Viti in his school manual, Verga verista (Florence, 1961), includes a comprehensive reading of Fantasticheria, presenting the story as introductory to the world of the poor in I Malavoglia. On an esthetic level he expresses the usual reservations centered around its supposed lack of unity.
35. Sandro Briosi, "Sullo stile del Verga", Lettere italiane, XXI (1969), 200-206. Briosi lists a number of images, though not the one of the cart, whose recurrence is one indication of Verga's romanticism.

PIRANDELLO AND VERGA

. . . Pirandello and Verga - not, as chronology would dictate, Verga and Pirandello - in order to make clear at once that this does not aim to be a conventional study of the influence of an older writer upon a younger one. Pirandello would have become and would have been Pirandello even if there had been no Verga, for as a man of genius he was endowed from the start with what was essential to his art.

   Yet there are three areas at least in which a study of the relationship between the two writers might lead - and has indeed in some respects already led - to significant results. First, Verga played an important role in Pirandello's perception of his own place in the tradition of Italian literature. Second, Verga is a figure that cannot be overlooked in any examination of what is commonly referred to as Pirandello's naturalistic period. And third, in I Malavoglia - as I hope to show - Verga supplied an initial statement of the basic pattern of all Pirandello's art: his vision of the relationship of the individual to the social group, a vision which finds its ultimate formal shape in "the plot within the plot", an expression I prefer because of its greater comprehensiveness to the more usual one of "the play within the play".

In his anniversary speech on Verga Pirandello consciously and publicly expressed the meaning which he gave the older writer's work. The speech was delivered the first time in Catania in 1920 to celebrate Verga's eightieth birthday, and it was repeated eleven years later at the meeting of the Italian Royal Academy in Rome which marked the fiftieth anniversary of the publication of I Malavoglia. (1) The two versions differ in some not insignificant respects, but for the present purpose the two speeches can be considered as one. (2)

   If we were dealing not with what is essentially a literary essay but with a work of fiction, we could say that three distinct and well-rounded characters emerge in the course of the speech: Verga, Pirandello himself, and D'Annunzio. D'Annunzio is Pirandello's antagonist, the butt of his underlying polemic. (3) Verga is in many respects a shielding figure behind which Pirandello places his own personality, but there is never any real confusion between the two. It is the Catania version of the speech that contains the famous statement, "Verga is not, nor can he be, in the fundamental meaning of the word, a humorist" (419). This means that Verga did not, like Pirandello, doubt his own view of reality. In Pirandello's words, and they are tremendously precise at this point: "The world in itself is in no one reality, except if we give it that reality. Therefore, since it is we who have given it that reality, it is natural that we should think that it could not be otherwise. To do so we would have to doubt ourselves, to doubt the reality of the world as posited by us. Fortunately for him, Verga does not doubt the reality of the world as posited by him, for he feels that the world cannot be any different from what it is" (419). (4) This is no doubt one of the corner-stone statements to which we must always return when we seek to define Pirandello's divergence from verismo. The whole question of Pirandello's verismo has however been confused by the fact that Pirandello continued to be viewed as a regionalist - and in that sense a verista - long after that designation no longer suited him. (5) But it is typical for all truly original writers, for all authentic innovators - not flashy proclaimers of the new - that the magnitude of the break they represent becomes inescapably apparent only in retrospect. In the case of Pirandello it took all the years down to our own time to recognize in him not a cause célèbre but one of the prime poetic imaginations of his time, in European and not simply Italian terms. (6)

In the speech on Verga Pirandello's attitude is throughout polemical. The polemical tone is apparent not only in his condemnation of D'Annunzio but also in his praise of Verga. In praising Verga, he is not satisfied until he feels quite certain that the audience understands exactly what he is praising. This desire for clarity in communication is typically Pirandellian, (7) and is related to the driving purpose of all his work which I find to be the expression of a moral - not moralistic - message. In the Preface to Sei personaggi Pirandello calls himself a philosophical writer, in contrast to the historical writers. (8) I would propose that the designations moralists and realists would be more appropriate and more immediately understandable: realists, for writers who, as he says, are satisfied with representing figures, narrating events, or describing landscapes for the sheer pleasure of doing so; moralists, for those other writers (among whom he places himself) who have a deeper spiritual need and will consider figures, events, or landscapes only if they are imbued "with a particular sense of life", which gives them universal value.

In the Verga speech Pirandello's rhetorical strategy in the effort to state his message with perfect intelligibility is to define the character of Verga's work by appealing to the broadest field of associations available to him. The thrust of the definition is thus given by the opposition of two types of writers, two categories that between them, he says, divide the whole range of Italian literature. This part of the speech, incidentally, appears first in the second version, thus invalidating one critic's charge that Pirandello did little more in this version than adapt an old speech to a new occasion. (9) The two types of writers are those who have a style of objects (gli uni dotati d'uno stile di cose) and those who have a style of words (gli altri d'uno stile di parole). As has been pointed out, (10) Pirandello is here making use of the distinction first made by Francesco Berni when in praising the poetry of Michelangelo by contrast to that of the Petrarchists he wrote: "He speaks things, and you speak words" (Ei dice cose, e voi dite parole). The same opposition was used by Galileo to contrast Ariosto and Tasso, and was taken up much later - in a milieu to which the young Pirandello was very close - by Capuana (who was following in the footsteps of De Sanctis) in his Gli "ismi" contemporanei to define, as in Pirandello, the contrast between Verga and D'Annunzio.

In taking D'Annunzio as the object of his attack, Pirandello was of course choosing the writer best suited to represent an antithesis to both Verga and himself. D'Annunzio was Pirandello's almost precise contemporary (the four years' difference in their birth dates had dwindled to insignificance by 1920), and the youthful D'Annunzio's meteoric rise to fame occurred exactly in the same years that witnessed the niggardly recognition granted to the by then almost middle-aged Verga: Vita dei campi was published in 1880, one year after D'Annunzio's Primo vere; and at the other end of Verga's most productive period, Mastro don Gesualdo, like Il piacere, in 1889. Pirandello's anti-D'Annunzianism is even more pronounced in the second version of the speech than in the first, where he had at least recognized, however fleetingly, D'Annunzio's contribution to the enrichment of the Italian literary language through his verbal splendor.

From the center of the definition, constituted by the two figures of Verga and D'Annunzio, Pirandello moves outward to the two categories of writers mentioned - Dante as against Petrarch, Machiavelli as against Guicciardini, Ariosto as against Tasso, Manzoni as against Monti - and beyond this, stepping outside the domain of literature and art, to what he sees as the two human types that in Italy provide the socio-cultural background against which the stylistic differentiation of stile di cose and stile di parole takes place. The 1931 version of the speech starts out, after a few brief words devoted to the occasion of its delivery, with the forceful and eloquent statement:

It is probable that every nation produces two human types from its stock: the builders and the adaptors, the necessary beings and the beings of luxury; the former endowed with a "style of objects" and the latter with a "style of words". These two great families or categories of men, living contemporaneously within every nation, are quite distinct and easily recognizable in Italy, perhaps more so than anywhere else. But only for someone who knows our situation well and is able to analyze it with understanding. Because inattentive observers, be they Italian or non-Italian, are easily deceived by the noise, the pomp, the frequent self-display of those whom I have called of the "style of words", and think that this type only exists in Italy . . . So much so, that when one thinks of Italy, of its natural beauty and its traditions, it is almost

impossible, especially for a foreigner, not to picture all
Italians living the life of the senses . . . . And the men who
best represent Italy are pictured as imaginative men of letters
speaking a sonorous tongue, magnificent adorners and evokers
of the glories of the past. All in all, a people that lives . . . .
as though all were a game or a fantastic pageant where everything is dreamlike and there are no needs, and everything is
easy and already accomplished, and nothing is difficult or
still to be done.
   Of course this is not so. There are the others in Italy, too:
those who shine less and contribute more, those whom I have
called of the "style of objects". (391-392).

It goes without saying that in the oratorical sweep with which Pirandello gives voice to what I have called his moral vision it makes little
difference that he is less just and less correct in his comparative
evaluation of Verga and D'Annunzio than Federigo Tozzi had been in
an article that preceded the 1920 speech by only two years. (11) Nor
does it matter that present-day critical opinion would find it hard to
subscribe to Pirandello's denigration of Petrarch, or Guicciardini,
or Tasso. Nor again, that Pirandello's division of Italians into two
contrasting groups is highly controversial if not actually provocative
and malicious. (12) What matters in this opposition of D'Annunzio and
Verga is the meaning Pirandello gives to the former's "prestigious
literary adventure . . . which for so many years captured and held
the public's attention in a fascinated dazzle" (394), as against "the
lucid effort of the writer whose aim is to say nakedly the things he
has to say, outlining their harsh contours: objects and not words, ty-
rannical objects that demand our absolute respect for their naked inno-
cence" (393). What matters in this survey of Italian literature is the
depth which Pirandello's bird's-eye view of the great opposing forces
in its development lends to his definition of his own place, and of
course of Verga's, in the tradition. And what matters in his psychological analysis of the two types of Italians is that it leads him - probably unconsciously - to epitomize in the Sicilian the type that he opposes to the loud and voluble Italians who in their easy and superficial
sociability are the first to impress the casual visitor to Italy:

   Sicilians, almost all of them, have an instinctive fear of life;
   they shut themselves up within themselves, apart from others,
   content with the little they have, as long as it gives them security. They note with diffidence the contrast between their own
   closed personalities and the nature that surrounds them, wide-
   open and flooded by the sun. And they withdraw even further
   within themselves, distrusting the openness about them, the
   sea that isolates them, cuts them off, leaving them lonely and
   alone. Each one becomes an island to himself and enjoys his

small share of pleasures - if he has any - soberly, by himself. Alone, silent, without seeking comfort, he suffers his
often desperate unhappiness (398-99).

Most important, however, is what the opposition - be it between
Sicilians and Italians, between writers of the style of objects and
writers of the style of words, or between Verga and D'Annunzio -
means concretely in terms of the written page, which is the one, indeed the only place, where a writer finally reveals himself:

> For the first [the writers of the style of words] a thing is
> valuable not so much in itself as for how it is said; the writer,
> the seducer always shines through, the actor who wants to
> prove how good he is at saying it even if he does not actually
> show his hand. For the second [the writers of the style of
> objects] the word states the thing and has no independent value
> as a word; so that, between the thing and the person who is to
> see it, the word as word disappears and only the thing itself
> remains. There we have the showy structure of carefully
> chosen musical words that are intended to have their own value
> besides the value of the thing named; but in the long run the
> artifice is apparent and they satiate and tire. Here we have an
> inner construction; things that appear and place themselves be-
> fore you so that you walk among them, breathe among them,
> touch them: stones, flesh, those particular leaves, those eyes,
> this water (392).

I know few statements more eloquent than this one on the complete ab-
sorption of the writer's personality into the things that clamor to be
said, those things that in the phrase "things that appear and place
themselves before you" Pirandello describes not only in their concreteness but in their autonomy and self-generation. (13) Verga achieved
this ideal magnificently in some of his short stories and certainly in
I Malavoglia, so much so in fact that Flaubert's famous dictum,
"L'auteur, dans son œuvre doit être comme Dieu dans l'univers, présent partout et visible nulle part", (14) is beautifully illustrated in this
novel. Pirandello's own idea of the self-effacement of the writer, his
strong rejection of all hedonistic gratifications appears in the final
paragraphs of the speech in the phrase, "the exigent, humble and sad
task of expressing things" (405), with which he describes Verga's
commitment to his art. The urgency that Pirandello elsewhere portrays
in the characters' rush into his study during the few hours each week
which he devotes to "interviewing" the figures of his imagination, their
peremptory and insistent pleading that they be given eternal life in art,
(15) is seen here in the answering urgency felt by the writer to abandon
all else, to place his being in the service of his art, until there is

nothing left of him as a man except his function as an instrument of
expression, as a vehicle for what presses to be heard and said. As he
was to say with reference to himself in an autobiographical sketch
written around 1912 and published in Le Lettere in 1924, "There is
nothing noteworthy in my life. It is a completely inner life, concentrated in my work and in my thoughts."(16) And in the beautiful passage of Colloqui coi personaggi, the "story" that documents so touching-
ly his most intimate feelings at the time of the World War when in a
kind of magic gesture against destruction he opened wide the flood-
gates of life:

> In the darkness that gathered slow and tired at the end of those
> long sultry summer afternoons . . . I had for the past few days
> no longer felt alone. There was something teeming in that dark-
> ness, in a corner of my room. Shadows in the shadow, that
> sorrowfully shared my anxiousness, my longing, my disappoint-
> ments, and my sudden fits - all of my feelings, from which they
> had perhaps been born or were just beginning to be born. They
> looked at me, they watched me. They would look at me until
> finally, against my will, I would be forced to turn to them.
> With whom could I communicate at a moment like that, except
> with them? And I approached that corner and forced myself to
> look at them one by one, those shadows born of my passion,
> and I began to speak with them quietly.(17)

Pirandello's identification of himself with Verga has annoyed those
critics who feel little sympathy for the subjectivity and egocentricity
which marked the literature of the early twentieth century. Only outright malice, however, could lead anyone to maintain that Pirandello
set out intentionally to see himself in Verga so that his own place in
Italian literature would thereby appear magnified.(18) Rather, he read
Verga as he had read Cervantes or any other writer for that matter.
In the Knight of the Sad Countenance he saw a poetic image, one of
the many madmen and eccentrics that populate his own fictional world.
(19) In Verga he saw a fellow-writer, a Sicilian like himself, whose
actual world, whose perception of it, and whose effort to express that
perception had many traits in common with his. But outside of the
speech we have just considered, we must not expect the traces left by
his reading of Verga to be obvious and obtrusive - and surely they will
be undocumented in the conventional, academic, sense of the word.
(29)

Pirandello's naturalistic period may be said to go - but as for all
period divisions the limits are only approximate - from his earliest
known narrative work, the "Sicilian sketch" Capannetta (1884), to Il
fu Mattia Pascal (1904), the first major formulation of his mature

view of the human condition in one of the major characters of his
work. Pirandello's naturalism has been studied in quite a number of
analyses of the novel L'esclusa and of the novel (or the short story?
Pirandello himself was undecided) Il turno. (21) It has also been
studied in such short stories on Sicilian themes as Visitare gli in-
fermi, Sole e ombra, Lumíe di Sicilia, and Prima notte;(22) and in
other stories which are more specifically linked to themes treated
also by Verga, La giara and Ciáula scopre la luna. (23) Of the plays,
Il berretto a sonagli, which however falls outside the chronological
limits of Pirandello's naturalistic period, has also been directly connected to Verga. (24) It is surprising that almost no attention has been
paid to Pirandello's earliest extant play, La morsa, initially written
in 1892 with the title L'epilogo, and performed with that title in 1910.
(25) This one-acter falls squarely within Pirandello's naturalistic
period and might be expected to yield important hints of what Pirandello learned from Verga during this period, in terms of dramatic if
not of narrative technique. Surely, if we have at least two extensive
analyses of the very slight Capannetta, (26) it may be considered
proper to devote some attention to the play which, as far as I know,
takes chronological precedence over all those that have come down to
us. (27)

In his Storia di Pirandello Leone De Castris emphasizes, in contrast
to many other studies on the writer, the continuity in development between Pirandello the short story writer and Pirandello the dramatist.
How Pirandello turned to the theatre is for the critic not an external
but an internal story, part of a continuous elaboration whose most
important aspect, even in the short stories, is the thrust toward an
always stricter isolation of character from setting, of the individual
from his environment. (28) Eventually - in the years that saw Pirandello's first concentrated production for the theatre - the thrust led
to a structural change. To speak metaphorically, King Lear, whom
in his 1893 Arte e coscienza d'oggi Pirandello had seen in the guise
of modern man, the humiliated king of the universe, "armed with a
broomstick", jumping before us in all his tragic comicality, (29) is
now set raving upon the stage; to be joined later by "Enrico IV" caught
in the gesture of drawing the mantle of his equally humiliated regality
more tightly around his hunched shoulders. Given continuity, the structural change from narrative to dramatic writing must naturally be
underlain by a similarity of technique in the two genres. For Leone
De Castris both the short stories and the plays are characterized,
among other features, by the central position of the protagonist, the
almost total absence of plot in the traditional sense of a well-con-
structed concatenation of events, and by the direct entrance into
medias res, into a crystallized situation which reveals antecedent
facts but has no need to state them. (30) As Leone De Castris puts it,
"Not actual moments of experience succeed one another in the conti-

nuity of the story told, but the set, fixed situation of the present appears as on a stage. "(31)

In the light of these observations one cannot help being struck by the contents of the note which in 1912 Pirandello sent to a prospective producer together with the manuscript of his one-act play Il dovere del medico: "Here is a little drama of mine. It too is an epilogue, the epilogue of a sudden cruel drama which I thought it unnecessary to represent, but which clearly shines through the souls of the characters and in the new situation which it has determined." (32) By "it too is an epilogue", Pirandello meant to call attention to the relationship between this work and the earlier La morsa, performed, as already stated, in 1910 under the title L'epilogo.

L'epilogo deals with the typical triangle situation for which Madame Bovary provides the nineteenth-century model. Giulia betrays her husband, Andrea, with a family friend and business associate, Antonio, who turns out to be a vulgar selfish individual. When the play opens Antonio has just returned from a business trip with Andrea and tells Giulia that he suspects that her husband has discovered her infidelity. He is filled with anxiety because he fears that Andrea will kill him, and his weak attempt to make his fear pass as concern for Giulia's safety convinces no one. He leaves, and Andrea arrives shortly thereafter. The rest of the play is the confrontation of husband and wife.

If we make use of the title La morsa, then the emphasis would naturally appear to be on an element of plot, on the cruel pressure applied by Andrea in order to discover the truth and destroy his wife who has become an object of hate for him. As spectators we would be interested primarily in what happens: will Giulia confess and what will her husband do to her?

But if we use the title L'epilogo and bear in mind what Pirandello said in the note just quoted, I believe that we can arrive at a more correct individuation of Pirandello's intention. The conclusion, the epilogue which the play represents, is not the outcome of a tale of adultery, but the tragedy of a marriage. In forming the marriage, husband and wife had equal responsibility. Giulia had left her wealthy family to marry Andrea and was disowned by them. Andrea then turned all his energies to making money so that Giulia would not be deprived of the luxuries to which she was accustomed. Giulia soon tired of a husband who was always busy and exhausted. We have, in short, the familiar collapse of what psychologists call romantic love. At the end of the play, Giulia kills herself, continuing in the role of the strong, dominant marriage partner.

If we use the figure of the vise - which incidentally appears not only in the title that was eventually the preferred one but also in one of Andrea's speeches (33) - Giulia is the victim of the situation, the tragic heroine. But if we use the metaphor of the epilogue, Andrea, too, becomes a victim; he is perhaps the more tragic character of the two, for he is condemned to live, that is to relive his experience. (34) This makes me suggest tentatively that Andrea is the first shadowlike prefiguration of the Pirandellian character in a dramatic work "caught in situation" at the culminating moment of his distress. (35) Pirandello's representation of Andrea's inner torment is sympathetic; his is the most imaginative, the only "poetic" language spoken in the play. He would appear to be the character who imposed his speech upon the author, the one who - to take up the image, in Pirandello's essay L'azione parlata, of Aeschylus animating "the majestic figures of the tapestry of Homeric epic" - moved speaking. (36)

The argument in favor of Andrea's rather than Giulia's centrality - and this brings us back to Verga - is also supported by a statement attributed to Pirandello but actually Verga's, on the difference between what is referred to as the so-called naturalistic storytellers and novelists, and the psychological narrators:

> For the former, the naturalists, a thought can be written down insofar as it can be described, that is, insofar as it has turned into an action or a spoken word. For the psychologists thoughts are important even before they have a palpable life outside of the person who thinks and feels. The two methods are not therefore mutually exclusive. They could as a matter of fact be merged, and they should be fused in the perfect novel. The psychologists, after all, exhibit what for the naturalists is only preliminary. They give us the first whys. The naturalists scrutinize these same whys with equal intensity . . . but in the end they show only their results. (37)

The naturalist is, thus, as analytical as the psychologist, but he is more direct and immediate - more dramatic - in his rendition. Contrary to the general belief, it is the naturalist who requires the greater effort of active involvement from the reader, for the reader is left to reconstruct motives from actions, and is therefore asked to "collaborate" with the writer in the achievement of the total effect. Verga's famous statement in the prefatory remarks addressed to his fellow-novelist Salvatore Farina, in the story L'amante di Gramigna, cannot fail to come to mind here: "Here is not a story but a sketch for a story. The mysterious process whereby passions get entangled, are woven together, and develop . . . will for a long time to come continue to be the powerful attraction of that psychological phenomenon which is called the subject of the story . . . Of the one I'm telling you today, I'll give you only the point of departure and the point of arrival, and for you this will be sufficient, and perhaps one day it will be sufficient for everyone."(38) That Pirandello knew this passage well is proved by his using in the speech on Verga a long quotation from the original text of L'amante di Gramigna as it appeared in the 1880 edition of <u>Vita dei campi</u>. (39) This quotation underscores Verga's ambition to achieve perfect impersonality in his work as he voices his desire to write a novel which will appear "to have produced itself" in words strongly reminiscent of the Flaubert statement cited earlier. (40) Here then is further evidence for what must have been one of the sources for Pirandello's own feeling of self-effacement before the impetuous figures of his imagination.

Allusion and parataxis (i.e., the omission of connecting links) are not usually thought of in connection with naturalism. And indeed, the naturalism Pirandello has in mind is not Zola's experimental method but Verga's <u>verismo</u>, which in spite of its name is in technique closer to symbolism and impressionism than to realism. Critics have treated the relationship between Verga and Pirandello almost exclusively in terms of similarity in themes but divergence in unifying vision. As a self-conscious writer, however - and there is enough proof that for all his verve Pirandello was well aware of what he was doing (41) - Pirandello recognized that the affinity which links him to his senior is primarily one of style and technique. To understand this fully, it is perhaps necessary for a moment to forget what divides Pirandello from Verga, and concentrate instead on what brings them together.

Viewed in the context of the whole tradition of nineteenth-century realism, neither Verga nor Pirandello can be called a realist in the sense that Maupassant and Tolstoy are realists. I know no passage in the works of either capable of creating a vicarious experience comparable to Maupassant's achievement in the first chapter of <u>Une Vie</u>, or Tolstoy's in the famous episode at the races in Anna Karenina. In the first instance, the reader is <u>in</u> the travelling coach that takes Jeanne back to her home in Normandy. He sees the passing landscape; he feels the atmospheric changes. When Jeanne and her parents arrive, <u>he</u> has arrived. In the second instance, the reader is <u>on</u> the horse that Wronski rides at the races, and when Wronski to his shame and horror breaks the horse's back the reader is there, in his place, feeling the same jolt and the same collapse as they <u>both</u> fall to the ground together.

The reader is of course very much involved in Verga's <u>I Malavoglia</u>. As a matter of fact, if he is not, if he does not read attentively and closely, he will soon have to shut the book, lost amid the anonymous crowd, not one of whose members is anonymous for Verga who never for a moment forgets where each one is and what each one is doing. Yet, whatever sympathy the reader may feel for Verga's characters, he feels for characters well outside himself as he <u>watches</u> their destiny relentlessly closing in to destroy them. The same is true for Pirandello's fictional world. The spectator watches it. He may translate the single experiences portrayed into universal terms and apply these terms to himself, but he does not feel that he <u>is</u> Mattia Pascal, or that he <u>is</u> the Father in <u>Sei personaggi</u>, or even - which is more likely - that he is one of those hateful busybodies in <u>Così è (se vi pare)</u>. The situation in which the spectator finds himself before the stage repeats the situation in which Pirandello finds himself before the living character that bursts into his study to have his life made permanent in the realm of art: there is a distance which must be bridged through an act of involvement. Thus the spectator or reader has a role in Pirandello and in Verga - at least insofar as the great short stories and I Malavoglia are concerned - that he does not have in Maupassant or Tolstoy.

What is the reader's reaction to the role assigned to him? Does he enjoy the intellectual challenge of having to derive meaning for himself? I would answer that as long as he remains unsophisticated and untrained, he is <u>not</u> grateful, for in the stories he is told he seeks the reassurance that life is after all structured by some force outside himself so that experience <u>can</u> be transmitted and he <u>can</u> live it vicariously. This explains the negative reaction of the first readers of I Malavoglia. The book began to be understood only when through the successive editions of his work on Verga, Russo offered a clue as to how it could be read: the formula however enclosed the novel's vitality in a rigid scheme that inhibited further discoveries. (42) The reader's reluctance to step into an active role also explains why Pirandello's first audiences walked out on him: they did <u>not</u> accept the challenge but felt that they had been cheated out of the resolution, the pacification of reality which they expected from the artist. They began to stay only later, when they had been <u>taught</u> (by Tilgher and others) what their more enlightened reaction should be. Or, to go back to the words that Verga addressed to Salvatore Farina, the reaction of his readers, like the reaction of Pirandello's audiences, showed that telling only the point of departure and the point of arrival - that a technique of allusion and parataxis - was <u>not yet</u> sufficient for everyone.

To do full justice to the contention that in I Malavoglia we have an initial statement of the basic pattern of all Pirandello's art would require a series of analyses that the following pages can barely hint at.

Ask almost any reader who comes unprepared to I Malavoglia what the book is about, and he will mention the family of fishermen that gives it its title and the boat "Provvidenza" whose name seems to signify an ironic comment on the traditional belief in divine Providence. The two points, that is, which seem to attract the first attention are the socio-economic condition of a family of fishermen living on the eastern coast of Sicily in the years immediately following Italian unification, and the author's ideological position regarding the Catholic faith, a topical subject of great controversy in late nineteenth and early twentieth-century Italy. Critics and readers have been constantly drawn back to these points. (43) A slightly more sophisticated reader may refer to psychology, but it will be mostly a kind of social-psychology which sees the reactions and the choices of the people involved as determined by their class and their environment. Thus many readers of Verga get no further than local color in both historical and geographical terms. They feel Verga's "distance". (44) Literary critics and historians, on the other hand, have spent a great deal of time and energy on Verga's poetics, on his theoretical statements in relation to his artistic production: did he or did he not achieve objectivity and impersonality? Others have played the game of labels: how much does he owe to the French? what does he have in common with Capuana? is he too pessimistic? does he belong to Italian literature at all? what are the esthetically valid as against the unsuccessful parts of his work? The perplexities are many. (45) Sometimes one is forced to wonder whether Piero Nardi, ironically enough in a school edition of I Malavoglia, (46) is not perhaps the only one to have looked at the book closely, read it word by word, and tried to understand it word for word. For even the stylistic critics (47) who left aside extrinsic considerations - such as the work's documentary value or the credibility of its story (I am thinking here especially of Mena's renunciation which causes many present-day readers to reject her in the same way and for the same reason that they reject Lucia) - even such critics in the final analysis look at only isolated moments of the work, at samples of Verga's narrative technique which they use, brilliantly of course, as illustrations of their basic contentions.

But there is also the book as a whole, with its structure which must be examined in terms of the critical vocabulary given currency by those discussions of the theory of the novel which in Anglo-Saxon countries grew out of the attention devoted to the problems of the novel by its great fin de siècle practitioner and theorist, Henry James. James, by the way, was a precise contemporary of Verga's - his dates (1843-1916) match Verga's (1840-1922) perfectly. Of course, Verga knew nothing of James' existence, who was in Italy a late discovery. (48) The critical vocabulary referred to consists of the well-known concept of "point of view", (49) and involves such questions of narrative technique as (1) how transitions are indicated, (2) how the passage of time is treated, (3) how theme is expressed. In I Malavoglia, for instance, there is in Chapter IX, just before the report of the Battle of Lissa, a beautiful example of the naturalness - i.e., the great art - with which Verga handles transitions. A study could be made of Verga's mastery in using the contrast between showing (i.e., drama, scene) and telling (i.e., the strictly narrative passages which take the action forward). (50) Through such a study, light could be thrown on such questions as how much time actually elapses between the beginning and the end of the story told and how the reader perceives the passing of time: does he feel it as well as know it? Such analyses tell more of the writer's craft and of the work's effect on the reader than any number of moral, or ideological, or even esthetic commentaries. On the subject of theme, I Malavoglia offers almost unlimited opportunities for study. For, in it, theme is expressed through metaphors: "At one time the Malavoglias had been as numerous as the stones on the old road of Trezza"; "Now the house was as large as the sea"; " . . . the room is dark and the door shut, as though those who have gone had taken the key with them for ever". (51) Theme is expressed through repetition of episodes: in Chapter XII, for instance, when Piedipapera eggs 'Ntoni on against don Michele, he does so with the remark, "If 'Ntoni had any guts, he'd get rid of that Don Michele", thus exasperating in him that sense of inferiority which from the start has been shown to be 'Ntoni's Achilles heel. And theme is expressed also through the overt comment of the author - if nowhere else, then in the famous Preface. Questions of narrative technique, of course, involve also such matters as the relationship between major and minor characters, the presentation of setting (in Pirandello's words, " . . . the sea [but not the divine, poetic sea])", and in I Malavoglia its central contribution to Italian narrative literature, the use of style indirect libre, erlebte Rede, or to use an English term suggested later, narrated monologue. (52)

These general considerations on problems of approach to I Malavoglia suggest that both the usual historically oriented view - the study of Verga in his time - and the Crocean distinction between art and non-art have failed to do full justice to the work. Moreover, though in the speech on Verga Pirandello speaks of the discussions in Capuana's circle at which he was present - discussions which, he recalls, dealt with esthetic views, schools and methods of art, ideas on the evolution of artistic forms, and so on (53) - there is no doubt that as a practicing writer he could never nor would ever read Verga with the eyes of the literary theorist or historian. The question, therefore, of what Pirandello probably saw in I Malavoglia, which remained a permanent acquisition to his art, is an open one. Pirandello's only direct reference to the novel, as far as I know, occurs in the speech on Verga. There is a youthful article of his devoted to Mastro don Gesualdo, written while he was in Germany and published in the Florentine review Vita nuova. (54) But it is a disappointment to find that the young philologist and budding literary journalist deals not with the novel but with the perennial uneasiness of the Italian writer faced by a traditional and static literary language felt by him to inhibit spontaneity and inventiveness. This essay on Mastro don Gesualdo thus offers no clues for the matter that concerns us here.

The basic pattern of Pirandello's art, I suggested earlier, is his vision of the relationship of the individual to the social group, which vision finds its ultimate formal shape in the plot within the plot. (55) To fit I Malavoglia into this pattern a radical - but not too radical - operation is necessary. Radical, because we shall have to discount the lyrical element in the novel, which has caused many readers to

concentrate almost exclusively on the unfortunate members of the
Malavoglia family and to read the book as though it were an elegy of
their fate, and by extension an outpouring of Verga's own emotional
attachment to Sicily and the family hearth.(56) Not too radical, because the work is after all a novel, and the downfall of the Malavoglias is not only the outcome of Verga's disconsolate, subjective
vision of reality, but also the outcome of a plot (57) - plot both in the
novelistic sense and in the sense of scheming: the plot, that is,
created by the self-interest, the meanness, the lack of charity and
compassion of the antagonists, those despicable individuals who contribute to and indeed machinate the family's collapse. For in the destruction of the Malavoglias nature may deliver the first blow - with
the sinking of the ''Provvidenza'' and the death of Bastianazzo - but
man, cruel, grasping man delivers almost every subsequent one.
There are, of course, the Horsemen of the Apocalypse: war, pesti-
lence and famine. They appear in I Malavoglia as they do in I promessi sposi, but how muted is their appearance in the later book!
Verga expends all his energies on the construction of the plot, on the
interactions of that famous crowd, that famous chorus which critics
reduced to anonymity but which Verga created as distinct individuals
each with his own unmistakable role. There are first of all the ''big''
villains - zio Crocifisso and Piedipapera. There is don Michele, the
customs agent who should enforce the law and instead helps to break
it. There is the group of smugglers - their operations are like an in-
curable disease which drains the whole village while it appears to give
it life. And then there are the less sinister but equally ruthless antagonists (or are they even more ruthless?): all those girls looking for
husbands. Their aspiration is legitimate enough, but it is they, no
less than the smugglers and the usurer, who precipitate the catas-
trophe. Chapter VIII is the magnificent center of a plot worked out
with mathematical precision. And where is the family meanwhile? It
stands at the center, as Christ surrounded by his deniers. Only
Cousin Anna, the widowed mother of a brood of children, and the little
girl Nunziata who, abandoned by her father, is raising her even younger brothers and sisters - and Compare Alfio of course - do not join in
the throwing of stones.

But is this not the precise situation of Così è (se vi pare)? In this
case it is not material gain that drives the small-town gossips desirous
of discovering the ''truth'', that is, the facts of the private lives of a
family of newcomers in their midst, but it is an equally heartless and
selfish goal. The play, described by Pirandello himself as a parable,
is usually interpreted as demonstrating the truth and teaching the
lesson of the relativity of reality. But before the veiled woman appears
at the end to give this message, a great deal of suffering has occurred.
Spectators and readers are wont to laugh about the reciprocal accusations of insanity made by mother and son-in-law, but surely insanity,

even imputed insanity, was no laughing matter for Pirandello. Moreover, why are these accusations made? Surely not to provide comic
relief. They are made to protect - to protect, as Laudisi puts it generalizing, each man's right to his "phantom". (58) They are made to
shield the small inner group - Ponza, Signora Frola, and the veiled
woman - from the destructiveness of the outer group, those who have
understood nothing, the respectable society of the well-adjusted.

Inner as against outer group: the center, the dot, the microscopic
individual lashing out against others, in defense of his inner freedom
Padre 'Ntoni, pleading with his creditors that he may be given the
chance to pay off his debt. "Henry IV", reduced to an act of murder to
defend his right to the tragic insight that made him one day take on
willingly and consciously the cloak of madness. Ersilia Drei (in
Vestire gli ignudi), probably the most tragic character of all, who
must really die - not just die to ordinary life as "Henry" does - in
order to be permitted to have her form, to have not the mantle of an
emperor but her "decent little dress".

We look at the great central figures, we follow Pirandello's cer-
ebrations, and often we forget the other figures, the "chorus", not
one of whom is simply a walk-on for Pirandello. Belcredi, a repulsive
villain if there ever was one: it was he who through one of the idiotic
jokes that society condones (he had pricked "Henry"'s horse during
the cavalcade and thus caused him to fall) precipitated the tragedy,
that is, destroyed a man's life. Pirandello does not need to dwell on
this point any more than Verga needs to dwell on the implied zio
Crocifisso-Judas parallel (Chapter VI), in order to take sides, to express his horror and revulsion for evil, for men in their evil. Ersilia's
four antagonists: the journalist (Pirandello's familiar meddler now
justified by his profession), the novelist (ready to help, but only at the
cost of imposing his reality on hers), her ex-fiancé (opportunistic and
sentimental), and the Consul of Smyrna, the man from whose house
she was dismissed (a weakling torn between respectability and passion).
And in a lighter vein, a much lighter vein, Mattia Pascal's antagonists;
the grotesque mother-in-law, the swindler Papiano.

Leone De Castris would subsume these and other instances of the re-
curring pattern under the category of the centrality of the protagonist
and see the pattern as a pattern in Pirandello's technique. But the
pattern involves not only technique but content, that is, subject matter
or element of plot.

The formal aspect of the pattern is, as has already been suggested,
the plot within the plot. A rapid reference to Sei personaggi will, I
hope, explain what this means. Everyone knows about the inner and
the outer story. The outer story, the play as we see it in performance,
consists of the six characters appearing on the stage, of their efforts
to remain on that stage, and of their eventual dismissal from it. The
inner story concerns the actual content of these characters' lives,

what happened to them. The two stories are played out not only one within the other, but one in opposition to the other (in the play, the opposition produces the typical Pirandellian meditations on the problem of artistic creation) - in opposition, that is, exactly with the same tension with which in the story (in the inner plot) the individual fights against the group.

Is the identity too tenuous? The purpose of this essay, however, was not to try to prove or analyze the influence of Verga on Pirandello, but to speak more generally of affinities, or of meanings that Pirandello gave to Verga's art. For some of these meanings there are actual documents; others must be reconstructed or deduced. It is, after all, both a very modest and an immodest proposal to suggest that Pirandello saw in the village square of I Malavoglia a stage upon which the basic conflict between individual and society was being fought, and that he then saw himself watching that stage (sentimento del contrario), so that the ultimate statement of his art - which many critics see in the trilogy of the theatre - dramatizes both the struggle and his perception of the struggle.

" . . . always the same square . . ." Pirandello had said in his speech on Verga. And Fergusson in his "Action as Theatrical"(59) speaks of "two boards and a passion" - the passion, perhaps, which Mommina lives in the final scene of Questa sera si recita a soggetto, when she shows the children what the theatre is ("The theatre, the theatre, now I'll tell you what it's like") without even needing the two traditional boards. I see an identity between these two places, the square and the stage, because if you pull away all the superfluous - Verga's and Pirandello's kinship as Sicilian authors, as fin de siècle authors, as narrators of deeds of violence and injustice - you come to the bare minimum, the essential, that ascetic stylistic ideal which Pirandello never tired of praising in Verga.

(1968)

NOTES

1. "Giovanni Verga" in L. Pirandello, Saggi, poesie e scritti vari, a.c. di Manlio Lo Vecchio Musti (Milan, 1960), 391-430. All references are to this edition and are cited in the text. Translations are the present writer's.
2. Specifically on the speech see Adriano Seroni, Verga, (Palermo, 1960), 36-7; Gaspare Giudice, "Pirandello e Verga", Galleria, XV no. 1-2 (1965), 27-32; and Gaetano Ragonese, "Verga visto da Pirandello", in Interpretazione del Verga, (Palermo, 1965), 288-306; now also in Atti del Congresso internazionale di studi pirandelliani, (Florence, 1967), 611-12. Only Ragonese has noted the difference in basic themes

in the two versions of the speech. Giudice is throughout critical of
Pirandello: he calls the speech "parzialmente insincero" (20), and
goes so far as to imply that Pirandello lost the letter Verga wrote
him about Il fu Mattia Pascal because he held Verga in low esteem
(21). In the comparative evaluation of Verga and Pirandello, critics
of Marxist inclination have gravitated towards Verga as the more
compassionate of the two: cf. Giudice's comparison of Rosso Malpelo
and Ciáula scopre la luna (22-25) and Ragonese's comment on it (303).
3. Ragonese (296) speaks of "la polemica spiegata e sottintesa contro
il Croce" which he sees as going hand in hand with Pirandello's anti-
D'Annunzianism. I have not investigated the interlocking of the two
polemics.
4. In "Symbol and Metaphor in the Transformation of Reality into Art",
Comparative Literature, XX (1968), 45-54, John V. Hagopian offers
this classification of definitions of reality: "Reality is that which exists
independent of man and remains largely even beyond man's potential
perception of it; the object exists irrespective of the subject. Reality
is that which exists independent of man, but is meaningful only if perceived or is potentially perceivable; the object and subject are engaged in a transactional or dialectical relationship. Reality is man's
internal construct; the subject exists irrespective of the object." If
we were to apply these categories to the case of Verga as against
Pirandello, we might say that Verga stands between the first and the
second of the definitions, Pirandello between the second and the third.
The massive use of style indirect libre in I Malavoglia points to
Verga's moving in the direction of the transactional position; but the
total effect of the novel, with its sense of inevitability and its deter-
ministic "closure", points to the survival of the metaphysical position. This conflict could be illustrated by an analysis of Verga's
attitude to religion as against his attitude toward God, bearing in
mind that anti-clericalism in literature declined as the metaphysical
position was abandoned in favor of the solipsistic - not the transactional - one.
5. Thus, for instance, among the Marxist critics who habitually emphasize Pirandello's veristic period and whose parallels between him
and Verga consistently favor the latter, Giuseppe Petronio (Pirandello novelliere e la crisi del realismo, Lucca, 1950) arrives at some
amazing conclusions: "La novella di Pirandello, e così il suo teatro,
raramente giunge alla tragedia . . . Dove ci è solo un mondo in dissoluzione, la tragedia non può essere pura . . . Mena e Diodata
(taken to exemplify 'vite mancate') sono personaggi di tragedia in
quel loro dolore senza parole. Anche quella del prof. Terremoto è
una vita mancata, ma il prof. Terremoto non è una pescatrice o una
contadina (!), né Pirandello ha la capacità di accostarsi ai vinti con
simpatia così pura da intenderne il chiuso dolore" (45). Or again:
"La larga comprensione umana che è ancora in Verga non può essere

più in Pirandello, che appartiene ad una generazione nuova, più corrosa, più egoisticamente attenta ai propri individuali problemi, meno aperta ad una solidarietà generosa con tutti gli altri uomini" (29). In both these observations a value judgment on matters extrinsic to art has conditioned the critic's comparative evaluation: peasants and fisherwomen are in themselves more tragic than professors; an individual's ability to feel human sympathy for others is conditioned by his generation. That the implicit awareness to "un mondo in dissoluzione" may in itself be tragic - and that this awareness lies at the very core of Pirandello's vision, as is proved by the theory of umorismo - seems never to have occurred to Petronio.

When Verga and Pirandello are brought together as Sicilians, that is, as regional writers of the late nineteenth century, the resulting critical insight is almost always unsatisfactory. Let one example among many suffice: I fail to see, for instance, what the critic has told us when he has written: "Pirandello scrisse la seconda parte dell'opera cui aspirava Verga, il dramma della piccola borghesia venuta fuori dal Risorgimento" (G. Giudice, Pirandello, Torino, 1963, 18). Gramsci, too, although on a more sophisticated level, is led to oversimplify for the sake of effect when he considers Pirandello in his Sicilian dimension: "Pirandello è criticamente un 'paesano' siciliano, che ha acquisito certi caratteri nazionali e certi caratteri europei, ma che sente in se stesso questi tre elementi di civiltà come giustapposti e contraddittori. Da questa esperienza gli è venuto l'atteggiamento di osservare le contraddizioni nella personalità degli altri; e poi addirittura di vedere il dramma della vita come il dramma di queste contraddizioni" (Antonio Gramsci, Letteratura e vita nazionale, Torino, 1954[4], 52). Here the characterization of Pirandello's vision is not incorrect, but the mechanistic description of its genesis is: Pirandello did not develop his vision after he had passed from Sicily to Italy to Europe. A quite different aspect of Pirandello's "regional" background, his bilingualism (dialect and language), must have played a more important role in sharpening - perhaps even in forming - his vision of the contradictory aspects of human life. This aspect has, as far as I know, never received adequate attention and I would like to take this occasion to make the following remarks.

Bilingualism means not only the availability of two words, two expressions, but of two structures of thought - dialect being in this respect comparable to language, and language being structured thought. An interesting light is thrown on this point by the use in the story Lontano of the word impuparsi, a so far unnoted clue, I believe, to the origin of the concept of the man-puppet in Pirandello: "E veramente quella mattina don Paranza non poteva andare alla pesca, come da tanti anni era solito. Gli toccava invece (porco diavolo!) vestirsi di gala, o impuparsi secondo il suo modo di dire. Già! perché era viceconsole, lui, di Svezia e di Norvegia" (L. Pirandello, Novelle per un

anno, Milan, 1956, I, 800). There seems to be no reason why Pirandello should have found it necessary to insert the dialect expression
at this point, except for its connotative value to him. What needed to
be said for the sake of the story had already been said, and Pirandello
is not given to indulging in local color as such. Moreover, the passage
is not in dialogue (though there are traces of style indirect libre) so
that it is not here technically a case of the character imposing his own
speech. Pirandello quite simply wrote the word because he could not
pass up an opportunity to use it, it being one of the key words of his
private vocabulary, from which derives one of the central metaphors
of his intuition of the human condition. When he will get to Ciampa's
great speech in Il berretto a sonagli, "Pupi siamo, caro signor Fifi!
Lo spirito divino entra in noi e si fa pupo . . .", the word will have
gained a quite different resonance and will express the deepest existential anguish. But at the very root lies the notion of a fisherman
getting dressed to play another role: "Kleider machen Leute" - only
one more indication of the absolute concreteness of Pirandello's meta-
phoric vocabulary and the continuous evolution of his art. The concept
of the man-puppet in Pirandello has normally been studied in relation
to the marionette theatre and the Theatre of the Grotesque (see D.
Radcliff-Umstead, "Pirandello and the Puppet World", Italica, XLIV
[1967], 13-27), rather than following the more fruitful line of the intrinsic genetic approach to the development of Pirandello's thought.
6. That Pirandello won the Nobel Prize should not obscure the fact
that his work was long misunderstood and diminished. This does not
mean, of course, that there were no good critics: among others,
L. Bàccolo, Pirandello, Milan 1949[2] (1938); A. Di Pietro, Saggio su
Luigi Pirandello, Milan, 1941, and Pirandello, Milan, 2nd ed. 1951;
and A. Janner, Luigi Pirandello, Florence, 1948, can continue to be
read with great profit.
7. Giudice, Pirandello, 21, cites Pirandello as recalling, "Ricordo
che da bambino avevo piena fiducia che avrei potuto farmi intendere
da chiunque. Un'ingenuità, che naturalmente mi costò amarissime
delusioni. Ma di qui trassi lo stimolo ad affinare le mie facoltà es-
pressive, e anche il bisogno di studiare gli altri per rendermi conto
di coloro con cui avrei avuto da fare; fermo sempre nella fede in-
crollabile di poter comunicare quando che sia tutto a tutti."
8. " . . . a me non è mai bastato rappresentare una figura d'uomo o
di donna, per quanto speciale o caratteristica, per il solo gusto di
rappresentarla; narrare una speciale vicenda, gaja o triste, per il
solo gusto di narrarla; descrivere un paesaggio per il solo gusto di
descriverlo. Ci sono certi scrittori (e non pochi) che hanno questo
gusto, e, paghi, non cercano altro. Sono scrittori di natura più propriamente storica. Ma ve ne sono altri che, oltre questo gusto, sentono
un più profondo bisogno spirituale, per cui non ammettono figure,
vicende, paesaggi che non s'imbevano, per così dire, d'un particolare

senso della vita, e non acquistino con esso un valore universale. Sono
scrittori di natura più propriamente filosofica. Io ho la disgrazia d'ap-
partenere a questi ultimi.'' L. Pirandello, Maschere nude, Milan,
1958, I, 58.

9. Giudice, "Pirandello e Verga", 30-1: "In quest'occasione [For the
Accademia d'Italia meeting], sempre lontano dal desiderio di ri-
leggersi l'opera verghiana, egli non fece che riprendere dal cassetto
in cui l'aveva deposto nel 1920 il suo discorso per rimaneggiarlo un
po' nella disposizione delle parti . . .''. It is surprising to find such
deep misunderstanding of Pirandello as reader of great works of
literature. Over and over again Giudice appears to expect to find a
literary historian or a critic, not a poet, in Pirandello reader of
Verga. One of the reasons for the bias may be that Giudice was
writing for an homage number dedicated to Verga. A more revealing
reason no doubt is that the periodical for which he was writing is politically committed and that he took the occasion to speak at length of
Pirandello's "Fascism". He misconstrues, in my opinion, the conventional expressions of approval for governmental initiatives which
we find - and would expect to find - in an official speech such as this,
reading them as indications of Pirandello's political allegiance or at
least of his political dishonesty. This is of course not the place to
enter into a discussion of Pirandello's political involvements nor of
the influence they have had on the story of his "fortune" and reputation. But how can anyone reading the final paragraph of the 1931
version of the speech fail to remain deeply amazed? One wonders
whether Pirandello is fully aware of what he is doing. For what he
does is first to separate the content of Verga's view of life, its deter-
ministic pessimism, which he allows may well appear depressing to
his audience or at least opposed to its present state of mind ("conce-
zione . . . contraria all'animo nostro mutato e non più da vinti"),
from Verga's commitment as a writer, from his style which he had
described earlier as "asciutta magrezza e povertà nuda di parole e
di cose, la piazza sempre quella e le vecchie case d'un umile villaggio,
il mare (ma non il poetico divino mare), il mare avaro e crudele dei
pescatori, e deserte campagne infestate dalla malaria, e gli stenti,
i bisogni, le passioni chiuse, originali e sospettose di un'infima gente
che vuol salire, o che è già salita e ne ha l'affanno che le vieta non
solo il riposo, ma ogni consolazione" (394-95). And he sets this commitment, this ideal of style, as the moral imperative that should
guide not only individuals but also nations, or more precisely his
nation, the Italy of Fascism, in the conquest of its style. This exhor-
tation with which the speech ends in a moving crescendo far outweighs,
as far as I am concerned, that peculiar intrusion of the Duce among
the writers of "the style of objects" which occurs in a variant of the
speech later rejected by Lo Vecchio Musti (L. Pirandello, Saggi,
a c. di M. Lo Vecchio-Musti, Milan, 1952, 429), and which a close

examination reveals as an obvious afterthought, a last minute addition before the delivery of the speech. For there can be no doubt, at least for me, that Pirandello was fully aware of the incongruity of the situation (avvertimento del contrario, as he calls the concept of the comic in L'umorismo): he in the role of speaker, himself beribboned and beplumed, exhorting his beribboned and beplumed audience to lay aside the superfluous, the style of words, in order to conquer that other style, the essential style of objects. "Spogliarsi d'ogni superfluo" are the words he uses: the contrary of impuparsi (see note 5, above), to divest oneself, to undress, to lay aside one's clothing, man in his nakedness as against man in his finery. On the political implications of the speech, see also Giudice, Pirandello, 453-54, and C. Alvaro in Novelle per un anno, I, 34ff.

10. F. Rauhut, Der junge Pirandello, oder das Werden eines existentiellen Geistes, (Munich, 1964), 86.

11. F. Tozzi, "Verga e noi", Messaggero della domenica, 17 nov. 1918 (reproduced in Seroni, 93-6).

12. Giudice, Pirandello, 343-46, has a good analysis of Pirandello's "volontà di provocazione".

13. This expression is to be related to a similar one in a passage of the 1899 essay L'azione parlata, where Pirandello maintains that the secret of success in writing dramatic dialogue lies not in observation and objective representation but in the author's ability to identify himself completely with the figure he creates, "fino a sentirla com'essa si sente, a volerla com'essa si vuole" (Saggi, poesie e scritti vari, 982, italics mine). The theological vocabulary is unintentional, but seeing the union of author and character in terms reminiscent of the union of God and man in salvation is typically Pirandellian, one of the compensatory strategies in a godless universe. Cf. Seroni, 49, on Momigliano's interpretation of "immedesimazione" (identification) and "impersonalità".

14. Letter of December 9, 1852 (Correspondance, Paris, Librarie de France, 1922, vol. I, 486).

15. See especially La tragedia di un personaggio and the repetition verbatim in Sei personaggi of Dr. Fileno's eloquent description of the condition of the character without author.

16. Saggi, poesie e scritti vari, 1246.

17. Novelle per un anno, II, 1131.

18. Giudice, "Pirandello e Verga", 28-9.

19. Pirandello's analysis of Don Quixote appears at the end of Chapter V of L'umorismo, Part I.

20. Giudice, "Pirandello e Verga", 28, speaks of the "idiosincratica maniera pirandelliana di trattare l'opera altrui" as though this were a fault rather than a mark of his originality.

21. Among good critical discussions of L'esclusa and Il turno are A. Di Pietro, "Luigi Pirandello", in I contemporanei, Milan, 1963,

I, 52-57; Leone De Castris, 45-9 and Bàccolo, 31-3, 35-6.
22. See Petronio on the "novelle paesane", passim; Leone De Castris,
60-6; in Atti del Congresso internazionale di studi pirandelliani, 553-
58.
23. On La giara and La roba, G. Poggioli, "Pirandello in Retrospect",
Italian Quarterly I, 4 (1958), 19-47; now in The Spirit of the Letter,
Harvard University Press, 1965, 146-70. On Ciáula scopre la luna
and Malpelo, Giudice, "Pirandello e Verga", 21-5, and Ragonese,
290, 303 n.
24. On Il berretto a sonagli and Cavalleria rusticana, Poggioli, cit.
25. L. Ferrante, Pirandello, 1958, 80-1, analyzes the play in his
chronological discussion of all Pirandello's plays. His reading is
diametrically opposed to mine. G. Andersson, Arte e teoria. Studi
sulla poetica del giovane Luigi Pirandello, Stockholm, 1966, 129,
does not discuss the play in the section devoted to Pirandello's
writings in the periodical Ariel because he had been unable to locate
a copy of the number in which it appeared.
26. Rauhut, 157-62; Andersson, 19-39.
27. Giudice, Pirandello, 99-100, speaks of a number of plays written
by Pirandello between 1886 and 1888, but these plays do not survive
and we have only indirect references to them. On Pirandello's efforts
to have L'epilogo performed in 1892, also see Giudice, 153-54.
28. Leone De Castris, 111-15.
29. "Che è divenuto l'uomo? Che è divenuto questo microcosmo,
questo re dell'universo? Ahi povero re! Non vi vedete saltar dinanzi
Re Lear armato d'una scopa in tutta la sua tragica comicità? Di che
farnetica egli?" Saggi, poesie e scritti vari, 870.
30. Andersson, 124, brings an interesting corroboration to this point.
He quotes from a short article "Romanzo, racconto, novella" which
has not been included in the edizione definitiva of Pirandello's works,
and shows the similarity between Pirandello's and Tommaseo's definitions of the short story. In his Dizionario estetico Tommaseo had
drawn a parallel between the short story and classical tragedy because they both concentrate on the final climax of the action, "gli
ultimi passi, l'eccesso insomma".
31. Leone De Castris, 112.
32. Quoted by Silvio D'Amico in the Preface to Maschere nude, I,
12-3.
33. Andrea quotes an old man he had met on the train, who described
his method for discovering his wife's infidelity thus: "Venuto questo
momento mi rivolgerei a mia moglie . . . e poi, come se nulla fosse
. . . le racconterei una storiella di questi amori . . . che s'aggi-
rasse intorno alla colpa di lei, stringendola in cerchi più sottili, sempre più sottili . . ." Maschere nude, II, 176 (italics mine).
34. An episode related by Giudice, Pirandello, 307-08, corroborates
my reasoning on this point. Se non così, originally written in 1896

with the title Il nibbio and published in 1917 as La ragione degli altri, was Pirandello's first three-act play to be performed in 1915 in a regular commercial theatre. During rehearsals a clash occurred between the leading lady, Irma Gramatica, and the author because they could not agree on the play's central character. Gramatica insisted that it was Elena, the mistress who is forced to give up her child; Pirandello that it was Livia, the sterile wife who cruelly - but with stringent logic - claims the child for herself. This disagreement, which led Pirandello to preface the printed version of the play with a letter addressed to the protagonist Livia, is an indication of the unconventionality of Pirandello's conception: just as the tragic character is not necessarily the one who dies at the end of the play (Giulia in La morsa), so the greatest suffering does not necessarily take place outside the pales of respectability - the tragedy of a wife can be more moving than the tragedy of a rejected mistress. But, as Pirandello points out in the Preface, it was a view for which the audience, and not only Irma Gramatica, was not ready.

35. Leone De Castris, 158, specifically excludes La morsa and La ragione degli altri from the history of Pirandello's theatre which he sees as "momenti successivi in cui la bipolarità della rappresentazione (realistico-simbolica) si attua in misure sempre piú delicate e risolte" (157).

36. "E le figure s'eran mosse parlando" (Saggi, poesie e scritti vari, 981).

37. The passage, published by Pirandello together with other fragments from his notebooks in Nuova Antologia, January 1, 1936, under the general title "Taccuino", appears in L. Pirandello, Saggi (1960) 1210. It is actually part of Ugo Ojetti's 1894 interview with Verga included in the young journalist's Alla scoperta dei letterati (Milan, 1895). As Mario Pomilio has shown (La formazione critico-estetica di Pirandello, Naples, 1966, 71), Pirandello was well acquainted with this work; as a matter of fact, he quoted part of the same passage in his review of Capuana's Il marchese di Roccaverdina, which appeared in Natura ed arte, July 1, 1901, and is included in the 1965 edition of Saggi (959). The passage, however, is apparently still attributed to Pirandello in this later edition where it continues to appear as part of the section, "Appunti" editi dall'autore (1250).

38. G. Verga, Tutte le novelle, Milan, 1959, I, 167-68 (italics mine).

39. This text was reproduced in reissues of Vita dei campi published by Treves and Bemporad. On the textual problem, see G. Cecchetti, Leopardi e Verga, Florence, 1962, 145-52.

40. The passage as quoted by Pirandello (404-05) reads: . . . il trionfo del romanzo si sarebbe raggiunto "allorché l'affinità e la coesione di ogni sua parte sarà cosí completa che il processo della creazione rimarrà un mistero, come lo svolgersi delle passioni umane; e che l'armonia delle sue forme sarà cosí perfetta, la sin-

cerità della sua realtà cosí evidente, il suo modo e la sua ragione di essere cosí necessarie, che la mano dell'artista rimarrà assolutamente invisibile, e il romanzo avrà l'impronta dell'avvenimento reale, e l'opera d'arte sembrerà essersi fatta da sè, aver maturato ed esser sorta spontanea come un fatto naturale, senza serbare alcun punto di contatto col suo autore . . . ch'essa stia per ragion propria, pel solo fatto che è come deve essere ed è necessario che sia, palpitante di vita ed immutabile al pari d'una statua di bronzo di cui l'autore abbia avuto il coraggio divino di eclissarsi e sparire nella sua opera immortale."

41. Immediately preceding the passage quoted above, Pirandello had described Verga's artistic achievement in I Malavoglia and had added: "E non è a dire che tutto questo non sia voluto, perché era nell' aspirazione e dunque nell'intenzione dello scrittore, se, dedicando a Salvatore Farina la novella L'amante di Gramigna nella Vita dei campi, scriveva che . . ." etc. This statement shows Pirandello's full awareness of the connection between intention and execution in artistic creativity.

42. L. Russo, Giovanni Verga (Naples, 1919) and subsequent editions for which see the 6th ed. (Bari, 1959).

43. It is a well-known fact that Verga's literary beginnings occurred in an environment of social awareness and that the first reviews of his works emphasized his humanitarian ideals. Cf. Seroni, 5-12.

44. "Qualcuno è lontano, in luogo glorioso da cui non lo vorremmo disturbare: Verga . . .": R. Serra, Le Lettere, Rome, 1914 (now in Scritti di Renato Serra, a c. di G. De Robertis e A. Grilli (Florence, 1938, I, 321). "Oggi un poco guardiamo Verga. Ma è certo che Verga abbia potuto influire con la sua riservata arte narrativa, sulla formazione del nostro temperamento? Meglio i verghiani considerassero la distanza incalcolabile a cui è rimasto il grande siciliano e a cui lo teniamo, malgrado ogni cura, ogni amoroso trasporto, fatalmente, noi stessi, con la certezza di essere diversi da lui. Di D'Annunzio non possiamo non sentirci migliori; ma da Verga lontani, diversi": E. Vittorini, Diario in pubblico, Milan, 1957, 9-10 (the passage is dated ottobre '29).

45. For a rapid survey, see the whole of Seroni's introductory essay, esp. 44-64.

46. G. Verga,. I Malavoglia, a c. di Piero Nardi, Milan, 1964[28].

47. G. Devoto, "I 'piani del racconto' in due capitoli dei Malavoglia", Bollettino di studi filologici e linguistici siciliani, n. 2, 1954; now in Nuovi studi di stilistica, Florence 1962; L. Spitzer, "L'originalità della narrazione nei Malavoglia", Belfagor, XI (1956), 37-53.

48. For an aperçu on Henry James's reputation in Italy, see n. 27 of "Stendhal, Lampedusa, and the Novel", included in this volume.

49. G. A. Cesareo's "estetica dell'arte creatrice" (cf. Seroni, 45), especially in the statement" . . . 'la rappresentazione della realtà',

che qui vuol dire la creazione della realtà", would seem to have some connection with James' concept of "point of view" and with the more general notion of "organic form". Pirandello repeatedly speaks of Verga's visione but he does not approach the subject of how the "vision" is translated into form. On p. 404, for instance (see n. 57 below), he is content with the generic adjectives mirabile and prodigiosa to describe Verga's creative achievement, thus eschewing any consideration of "craft".

50. On "showing", "telling", and related techniques, see N. Friedman, "Point of View in Fiction: The Development of a Critical Concept", PMLA, LXX (1955), 1160-84.

51. Emphasizing the structural importance of such passages (i.e., their importance in the plot) will result in a more correct definition of Verga's use of dialect, which is by no means determined by its documentary value.

52. D. Cohn, "Narrated Monologue: Definition of a Fictional Style", Comparative Literature, XVIII (1966), 97-112.

53. M. Pomilio, La fortuna del Verga. Parte II, Naples, 1963, 160-64, very correctly relates this reference to Capuana to Pirandello's own essay, Soggettivismo e oggettivismo nell'arte narrativa.

54. Saggi, poesie e scritti vari, 852-855.

55. Si gira (1916) uses the device of the plot within the plot in a manner as effective as the later trilogy of the theatre.

56. This approach is most clearly apparent in the first edition of Russo's study on Verga.

57. In comparing Mastro don Gesualdo and I Malavoglia in the speech on Verga (404), Pirandello raises the latter above the former because of its "compatta e schietta naturalezza . . . tanto più mirabile e quasi prodigiosa, in quanto non si sa come risulti così fusa attorno quella casa del Nespolo tutta la vita di quel borgo di mare e come venga fuori senza intreccio e pieno di tanta passione il romanzo in cui le vicende sembrano a caso". This impression of a novel without a plot in which the events appear to be controlled by chance and not by the author is what many critics have experienced. My contention, instead, is that the plot controls the action with tremendous force and that it is this that gives the work its structure.

58. "Fantasma" is the word used by Pirandello; the same word, for instance, used by De Sanctis when he speaks of Ariosto's imagination in the Orlando furioso: "Niuna opera fu concepita né lavorata con maggior serietà. E ciò che la rendeva seria non era alcun sentimento religioso o morale o patriottico, di cui non era più alcun vestigio nell'arte, ma il puro sentimento dell'arte, il bisogno di realizzare i suoi fantasmi" (Storia della letteratura italiana, a c. di Luigi Russo, Milan, 1960, II, 55-56).

59. Francis Fergusson, The Idea of a Theatre, Doubleday Anchor Books, 1953, 198.

PIRANDELLO'S LA PATENTE: PLAY AND STORY (1)

Pirandello's one-act play La patente has enjoyed a theatrical history
of uncommon success, not matched however by an equally rich, varied,
and perceptive history in Pirandello criticism. It was first performed
at the Teatro Alfieri in Turin, on 23 March 1918, but this performance
has gone almost completely unnoted. (2) It is more usual instead to hear
of the Rome performance of 19 February 1919, in a Sicilian version,
'A patenti, (3) prepared by Pirandello himself and with the famous
character actor Giovanni Grasso junior as Chiàrchiaro, or of the
Milan performance of the following year with the even more famous
Angelo Musco in the same role. The two interpretations represented,
in Leonardo Bragaglia's broad synthesis, the two faces of Sicily and
the two faces of the Sicilian theatre - the Sicily of knives and duels
against the Sicily of broad humour and folklore, and the Sicily of Greek
tragedy against that of the puppet stage. (4) La patente was later performed in a Roman dialect version (with Ettore Petrolini as Chiàrchiaro),
a Genoese one, a Venetian one, and a Neapolitan one (with Peppino De
Filippo always in the same role). The 1953 film adaptation, one of four
Pirandellian episodes constituting Questa è la vita, is remembered for
the tense and lugubrious interpretation of the great dead-pan comedian
Totò, (5) while the 1959 television play was distinguished by the
"brilliant, grotesquely modern" interpretation of Mario Scaccia. (6)
   In criticism, on the other hand, the work has been pushed to the
side, caught among a crowd of more significant three-act plays that
preceded and followed it chronologically, and subordinated in the one-
act category to the variously more striking Lumíe di Sicilia, La giara,
All'uscita, and L'uomo dal fiore in bocca. Thomas Bishop, for instance,
calls it "a short, inconsequential play" of some interest only because
of its treatment of illusion, and invokes the name of Kafka to characterize its kind of absurdity. (7) Ferrante groups it with Il berretto a
sonagli and Bellavita as a folk comedy on the theme of the revolt of the
underdog offended in his sense of honour. (8) J.-Th. Paolantonacci,
J. Chaix-Ruy, Aldo Borlenghi, Sandro D'Amico, and Benvenuto
Terracini fail to mention it or the short story on which it is based entirely, while Giuseppe Giacalone speaks only of the short story. (9)
Leone De Castris does no more than name Chiàrchiaro in passing as
one of the lesser brothers of Ciampa, Baldovino, Leone Gala, Martino
Lori, and Fulvia, all of them troubled and disturbed persons in search
of something, in whom Pirandello discovered the underlying human
condition and the grotesque conventions by which they live. (10) Tilgher,
with considerable felicity but understandable brevity, inserts La
patente in his schematization of the whole of Pirandello's work, by

seeing it as a central link in the thematic development of the clash between Life and Form. (11) Pasini discusses it together with La giara, L'altro figlio, and Lumíe di Sicilia under the heading of "Cose minori. Alla maniera antica" and summarizes it following the schemes of L'umorismo, Pirandello's essay on humour, as a drama of "illusion creating reality". (12) Although Janner finds that, together with Il berretto a sonagli, La patente is one of the two most original of Pirandello's early plays, he also feels that it does not go much beyond the story from which it is drawn, a judgment he then seems to contradict with his rapid enumeration of the characters and scenes that have been added to heighten the "widespread atmosphere of grotesque terror" so necessary to the situation. (13) Starkie uses the play to illustrate the Sicilian character of Pirandello, especially insofar as his style, "full of jerks and jolts", is concerned. (14) More recently a critic who describes his approach as a combination of literary criticism and stage directing has pointed out that Chiàrchiaro with his sunken cheeks, his dark-rimmed glasses, and his gravedigger's garment was visualized in terms of the contemporaneous expressionist theatre. (15) A students' guide to the work of Pirandello includes the short story though not the play in its analysis of the major works, but its discussion is marred by an overemphasis on the moral and psychological at the expense of the formal. (16) More perceptive and incisive are the observations on the relationship between the play and the story in Giuseppe Morpurgo's annotations to his school edition of the Novelle. (17) But the two best readings that have come to my attention are Franz Rauhut's in his "Pirandello als Sizilianischer Mundartdramatiker" and Domenico Vittorini's in The Drama of Luigi Pirandello. (18) Rauhut's insight into the character of Judge D'Andrea is truly exceptional, for in the literature on La patente this second protagonist (or antagonist) almost never comes in for mention. (19) For Rauhut, instead, he is like Professor Toti in Pensaci, Giacomino! one of the Pirandellian philosophers of "love of neighbour", opposed to Chiàrchiaro who is seen by Rauhut as a Pirandellian philosopher of "hatred of neighbour". Vittorini, who calls the play "a little jewel of its kind", does not overlook D'Andrea either, but places him next to Chiàrchiaro as one of the two protagonists that carry the meaning. Yet both Rauhut implicitly, by discussing the play in the context of Pirandello's dialect theatre, and Vittorini explicitly, by classifying it with the naturalistic drama which is seen as treating "humble themes of Sicilian life", end up by limiting its wider implications. In conclusion, however, we must add to Vittorini's special credit that, no more than Leone De Castris, did he miss the resemblance of Chiàrchiaro to other Pirandello characters: "Chiàrchiaro is the first character that gives evidence of traits which, enriched and deepened, will blossom into more complex personalities in later plays. "

Of course the proverb says "Del senno di poi son piene le fosse" (It

is easy to be wise after the event) - and to no one does hindsight offer
greater satisfaction than to the critic who turns back from his vantage
point to consider earlier appraisals of an artist's work. Yet a measure
of surprise at finding La patente so generally slighted may be permitted. Not that its first reviewers, working under the peculiarly
awkward conditions of journalism, could have been expected to tran-
scend the dialectal dress in which it first appeared (20) in order to
relate it to its author's broader message in Così è (se vi pare), by
common agreement the work that marks the turning-point in Pirandello's development and which was already well-known. But surely
in retrospect the play should more readily have been seen to fall within that period of extraordinary activity which witnessed the composition
of more than twenty plays in six years, some of them written with
amazing speed in a matter of weeks, if not days. The rapidity with
which Pirandello was able to write at that time is naturally not significant in itself but because it offers concrete proof of his intensified
creativity, of that fire which in a short span of time refined his ideas
to their essence and concentrated them in ever more readily perceivable and recognizable concepts and images. Composed between
Pensaci, Giacomino!, Liolà, Così è, Il berretto a sonagli, and Il
piacere dell'onestà on the one hand, and Il giuoco delle parti, Tutto
per bene, Sei personaggi, Enrico IV, and Vestire gli ignudi on the
other, La patente belongs by chronology and conception to that central-
ly important group of plays analysed by Leone De Castris as embodying the progressive unfolding of the character without an author. In
this connection, one of the purposes of the present essay is to show
how at the confluence of Pirandello's Sicilian and Italian experiences,
and under the compelling impact of his sudden discovery of the dramatic conventions as they operate on the stage, (21) Chiàrchiaro, the
character who was to become the protagonist of the play, burst into
full theatrical life. Moreover, since La patente, like many others of
Pirandello's plays, is derived from an earlier short story, the essay
also aims at being a contribution to the so far all too brief tradition
of the close study of the transformation of narrative into drama within the Pirandello corpus. (22)

Inasmuch as the play is available in English translation whereas the
story is not, it seems advisable to begin the discussion with an analysis of the play. What first strikes the reader is that the work is a
well-made problem play, both terms being understood here in the technical meaning they have for late nineteenth-century realistic drama.
The author's mastery of his craft is evident in the ease with which one
scene leads into the next, climaxing in an effective and striking dénouement, which is followed, somewhat exceptionally, by a second and
lesser falling action, the clinching demonstration in this cold blooded
dialectical encounter that, regardless of the facts of the case,

Chiàrchiaro and not Judge D'Andrea was correct in his interpretation of the practical aspect of the existential situation presented. Though both characters are non-conventional in their attitudes and are thereby antagonists of society, faced by a common social problem to be solved, their distance from their fellow-men creates no solidarity between them but opposes them in a duel in which the realist defeats the idealist and the irrational forces win out over the rational. The two-step dénouement is thus the logically necessary conclusion to the full unravelling of the action - but Pirandello did not hit upon it at once.

Greater clarity can be achieved, I believe, by breaking up the single and compact act into its component scenes, a division which does not, of course, occur in the printed version where no separations are indicated when there is a change of characters on stage. Yet it is obvious that, in distributing the action, Pirandello was thinking in terms of scenes, just as though he had been working in the more usual three-act format. (23) Thus Judge D'Andrea's initial solo appearance with the business of the two bird cages and the papers on his desk (SC. 1) is followed by a short scene with the usher, Marranca, whom he sends to get Chiàrchiaro (SC. 2), and Marranca's exit coincides with the entrance of the Three Judges for a choral scene, in which talk of D'Andrea's goldfinch, of Chiàrchiaro, and of the administration of justice in general serves to reveal preceding circumstances important for understanding the Judge's forma mentis and the paradoxes of the case to be tried (SC. 3). Marranca's return from his errand, accompanied not by Chiàrchiaro but by the latter's daughter Rosinella, is the cue for the departure of the Three Judges and for a change of focus from the case as a legal and social problem to the case as a human one (SC. 4). Rosinella's pleading with D'Andrea to try to convince Chiàrchiaro to withdraw his accusation provides information about the family background and foreshadows in the most explicit manner so far the grand entrance that Chiàrchiaro will eventually make (SC. 5). The entrance is delayed by a short scene in which Marranca announces Chiàrchiaro's arrival and D'Andrea helps Rosinella escape by a back exit (SC. 6). The rest of the play is given over to the confrontation between Chiàrchiaro and the Judge and this ends with the coup de scène of the goldfinch's death: "as though pushed by a gust of wind", Pirandello writes ambiguously in the stage directions, a window opens and knocks the cage from its stand (SC. 7). At D'Andrea's outcry, the Three Judges and Marranca run in again, thus bringing all characters except Rosinella on stage for the finale (SC. 8).

But though the play falls easily into its component scenes and divides further into two balanced parts, of which the first finds D'Andrea on stage without Chiàrchiaro while the second unites the two protagonists, there is no break in the action rising to its climax and resolution, and each scene contributes to the continuity of the whole, not only in terms of plot and characterization but specifically in the observance of the basic dramatic rule of showing rather than telling. Thus, up to Chiàrchiaro's entrance we have a series of reiterations and variations through which he and the other characters in relation to him are defined; after his entrance we have on stage, _coram populo_, the two opposing and contradictory views of the man, so similar to the unsettling effect created in _Cosí è (se vi pare)_ by the successive "explanations" of signor Ponza and signora Frola.

In first introducing Chiàrchiaro Pirandello has recourse to descriptive epithets in the mouths of those who speak of him and to gestures of reaction to the mention of his name. "Benedett'uomo!" (That tiresome man!)(24) D'Andrea exclaims impatiently at sight of the documents on his desk (SC. 1). And Marranca, when he hears the Judge pronounce Chiàrchiaro's name, makes a sign of exorcism of the evil eye (SC. 2). The Judge comes to Chiàrchiaro's defence, calls him "un pover'uomo" (a poor devil of a man), but Marranca is unconvinced of his innocuousness: three times he avoids saying his name. In scene 2 he hesitates a moment before coming upon the expression "questo galantuomo" (this gentleman) with which to refer to him; in scene 4 he reports on his errand by using the emphatic "Lui" (He - Pirandello's italics); and in scene 6 he ushers in Chiàrchiaro with "Eccolo!" (Here he is!). Each one of these moments, beyond being the faithful rendition of carefully observed superstitious behavior, increases the sense of Chiàrchiaro's exclusion, of his absolute difference from others which robs him even - as it will later rob "Enrico IV" - of the right to his name. And it is a measure of Pirandello's deftness at rapid characterization and of his unerring attention to telling detail that he has not overlooked these almost imperceptible opportunities for creating suspense but has known how to exploit fully the possibilities offered by an essentially functional character like Marranca. Later, when D'Andrea speaks to the Three Judges of the unjust trial which as public prosecutor he must institute, he again refers, generically this time, to "un pover'uomo" who is also "una vittima" (a victim). But when the Three Judges learn that the "pover'uomo" is none other than Chiàrchiaro, they too jump back in alarm and, like Marranca, make signs against the evil eye (SC. 3). D'Andrea's next use of "pover'uomo" refers directly to Chiàrchiaro, "questo pover' uomo" (this poor devil of a man - italics mine) who is also "un disgraziato" (an unfortunate wretch of a man). And though the Second Judge concedes that "disgraziato" is descriptive of Chiàrchiaro's plight, he repeats at the same time what the First Judge has already said, "È un pazzo!" (He's a madman!). The connotation of "disgraziato" used in conjunction with "pover'uomo" is, of course, different from that of "disgraziato" used with "pazzo", insanity being by itself the ultimate social exclusion. Two additional attributes are assigned to Chiàrchiaro in this important scene (still SC. 3): violence and a kind of awesome frightfulness - the violence of his protests against those who have given him the reputation of having the evil eye, and the terribleness of his supposed power and perhaps even of his physical appearance.

So much for the effectiveness on stage of words and gestures. Rosinella's scene (SC. 5) brings about a change in perspective. While characterization through epithets continues ("fustigato da tutti, sfuggito da tutto il paese come un appestato" [scourged by everyone, avoided as though he had the plague], "È come impazzito mio padre" [He's like a man gone mad, my father], Rosinella says of him), the audience now moves closer to Chiàrchiaro. There is no need, of course, for the Judge to do so, for he has stood by Chiàrchiaro all along, although, as the action will show, he has been mistaken in his estimate of how to help him. And indeed it is not D'Andrea who summons Rosinella, but it is she who comes running to him in apprehension for her father. Is Rosinella's scene expendable? In a certain sense it is, and the fact that there is no place for her in the final choral grouping is a hint that her presence continues in some ways to be felt as an intrusion. Moreover, all the information that she gives - and it is considerable - will be repeated in a more direct form by Chiàrchiaro himself. We learn, it is true, that there are four persons involved in the family tragedy, that Chiàrchiaro has been unemployed for a year, that he is the object of a heartless persecution. And we learn most importantly that there is nowhere for his family to go, for his reputation would follow them like a second skin: "Ce la portiamo appresso la fama", Rosinella says, "dovunque andiamo. Non si leva più neppure col coltello" (We'd carry this reputation with us wherever we'd go. We couldn't get rid of it even by cutting it off with a knife), and in her expression the coalescing of mask and being is forcibly implied. The audience learns all this and, what is especially useful in terms of drama, learns it in a manner particularly favourable to Chiàrchiaro. Rosinella is an appealing intercessor for her father. Her youth, her evident poverty, her decency elicit sympathy on basic human grounds, something, it will be seen, that Chiàrchiaro has little use for, but which is a sine qua non in the direct encounter between fictionalized world and spectator in realistic drama. Thus Rosinella's scene is a bridge in more ways than one, but principally in containing a description of the change that has come over Chiàrchiaro and a recital of some of the reasons for it: the most important reason will be told later by Chiàrchiaro himself. Yet the scene is also a postponement, part of a fundamental strategy in drama, where time no less than space must be treated differently than in narrative. So that it is this aspect rather than its content, which, together with its function in generating audience sympathy for Chiàrchiaro, stands out when one considers Pirandello's theatrical know-how.

All is ready now for Chiàrchiaro's entrance, prepared for, as we have seen, in dramatic terms by showing the reaction both of those who feel pity for him and of those who fear him, and by having a person close to him, especially invented for the purpose, tell facts about his background which only she can know. But Chiàrchiaro has not yet spoken for himself; he has not yet presented his own case. There is one passage in scene 5 in which something of his inner torment, of that life of feeling which appears to the outside world only in the actions and attitudes to which it gives rise, appears to shine through. It is the important exchange between the Judge and Rosinella:

ROSINELLA. . . . Per carità, signor giudice: gliela faccia ritirare codesta querela! Gliela faccia ritirare!
D'ANDREA. Ma sì, carina! Voglio proprio questo. E l'ho fatto chiamare per questo. Spero che ci riuscirò. Ma voi sapete: è molto più facile fare il male che il bene.
ROSINELLA. Come, Eccellenza! Per Vossignoria?
D'ANDREA. Anche per me. Perché il male, carina, si può fare a tutti e da tutti; il bene, solo a coloro che ne hanno bisogno.
ROSINELLA. E lei crede che mio padre non ne abbia bisogno?
D'ANDREA. Lo credo, lo credo. Ma è che questo bisogno d'aver fatto il bene, figliuola, rende spesso così nemici gli animi di coloro che si vorrebbero beneficare, che il beneficio diventa impossibile. Capite?
ROSINELLA. Nossignore, non capisco. Ma faccia di tutto Vossignoria!
ROSINELLA. . . . Please, Your Honor, have him drop this case! Have him drop it!
D'ANDREA. But, of course, my child. That's exactly what I want. And that's why I've had him come. I hope I'll be able to convince him. But, you know, it's much easier to do harm than to do good.
ROSINELLA. No, Your Honor! For you too?
D'ANDREA. Yes, for me too. Because harm can be done by anyone and to anyone, but good can be done only to those who need it.
ROSINELLA. And do you think that my father doesn't need it?
D'ANDREA. I know he needs it. But it is this need, my child, that so often embitters the hearts of those we would like to help so that we can do nothing for them. Do you understand?
ROSINELLA. No, sir, I don't understand. But please do everything you can, Your Honor.

But it is obvious that in its statement of a fundamental paradox the passage is essentially generic: that it refers more to the difficulties of helping any poor devil of a man rather than this particular one; that the insight that those most in need of help are often the least willing to accept it, that their would-be benefactor is more often proudly rejected than gratefully acknowledged, is the consequence of

D'Andrea's tendency to ruminate, to "philosophize", a tendency only briefly referred to in scene 3 when the First Judge says to him: "Sèguita, sèguita, mio caro, con codesta filosofia, e vedrai come finirai contento!" (Just keep on with that kind of reasoning of yours and you'll see how happy it'll make you!), but more fully developed in the story. The insight is of course applicable to Chiàrchiaro's case, but it is not yet Chiàrchiaro's case itself. The Judge for all his understanding of Chiàrchiaro cannot tell us his <u>ragione</u> (reason). It is Chiàrchiaro himself who must do so, and he <u>must do so</u> with the intense and desperate anguish to which there is no answer, not with the calm reasonableness of conviction that can issue into the optimistic rhetorical question, "Capite?" (You do understand, don't you?).

I have spoken so far only of the first part of the play, pointing out elements of continuity, contrast, and suspense in its inner dynamics and devoting some attention to the two functional characters, Marranca and Rosinella, for one of whom there is no counterpart in the story and for the other only a very shadowy one. There is in other words an usher in the story whom D'Andrea sends out to get Chiàrchiaro, but he is nameless, featureless, and lacks speech. As far as Rosinella is concerned, one may wonder whether to the reasons for her invention already discussed there should not also be added a possible practical one - in terms of production of the play - the need for a role for a female character to accommodate the leading lady of a troupe of actors. (25) Obviously, without Rosinella, the play would have an all male cast, something which would not at all be unsuited to the nature of its story, but which would be contrary to normal theatrical practice. There are three other characters who have roles in the play while their counterparts were only briefly mentioned in the story. The transformation of what were originally some vague colleagues of D'Andrea into the Three Judges offers a fascinating insight into Pirandello's workshop. In the story D'Andrea seeks advice on how to handle Chiàrchiaro's case from his colleagues: "ma questi, appena egli faceva il nome del Chiàrchiaro . . . si alteravano in viso e si ficcavano subito una mano in tasca a stringere una chiave, o sotto sotto allungavano l'indice e il mignolo a far le corna, o s'afferravano sul panciotto i gobbetti d'argento, i chiodi, i corni di corallo pendenti dalla catena dell'orologio" (But they, as soon as he would mention the name of Chiàrchiaro . . . blanched and either stuck a hand in their pockets to touch a key, or with their index and little finger made a sign against the evil eye, or grasped the silver hunchbacks, the nails, the coral horns hanging from their watchchains on their waistcoats). In this passage the number of colleagues involved is unspecified but their reactions upon hearing Chiàrchiaro's name are three-fold: they either slip their hands into their pockets to touch "iron", or they make signs of exorcism with their fingers, or they grasp the talismans hanging from their watchchains. In the play, the stage directions - "i tre Giudici . . . danno un balzo indietro, facendo scongiuri, atti di spavento e gridando . . ." (the Three Judges . . . leap backward, making signs against the evil eye, making gestures of fright, and shouting . . .) - are much less explicit, eschewing all reporting of the specific signs against the evil eye, but the judges are three. For each type of gesture a character has emerged!

Aside from the intrinsic interest of these observations regarding the minor characters of La patente, there is also the fact that they all belong to the first part of the play. For one of the striking aspects of the transformation of story into play in this case is that the work of re-elaboration required for the first part was quite different from that required for the second. Though the story is divided asymmetrically into three sections, the balancing of its action is very similar to that of the play, Parts I and II corresponding to scenes 1 through 6 and being dominated by the presence of D'Andrea; Part III corresponding to scene 7 and consisting exclusively of the meeting and clash of D'Andrea and Chiàrchiaro. There is nothing in the story to balance scene 8 and we shall return to this point later. It is a fact of considerable interest and well worth noting that the meeting of D'Andrea and Chiàrchiaro presented itself to Pirandello from the beginning in dramatic form. From the moment that D'Andrea catches sight of him in his office to the end of the story practically everything is in dialogue. In reworking this section Pirandello therefore had little to do except transfer the dialogue almost verbatim to the play and permit the connecting narrative material to be absorbed into stage directions. The procedure is a common and familiar one in Pirandello's adaptations of his stories for the stage and need not be further illustrated here: a rapid glance at the two texts side by side will show what has happened. (26) The problem was different for the first part. In that instance a play had to be fashioned out of descriptive, narrative and style indirect libre passages. It was in fashioning this play that, as we shall see, Pirandello took a radical step in displacing D'Andrea and in shifting the determining weight of protagonist to the shoulders of Chiàrchiaro.

In turning from Pirandello's dexterity in the medium of drama to the emergence of Chiàrchiaro as the play's protagonist, we move from an area in which Pirandello has much in common with other playwrights to one in which he is quite unique. For the Pirandellian character is different from other characters not only because his perception of reality is a distinct and recognizable one, but also because he imposes himself upon author, fellow characters, and spectators in a characteristic and unusual manner. This is already true of the Chiàrchiaro of the short story whom Judge D'Andrea finds standing in front of him when he raises his eyes from his desk: " . . . Chiàrchiaro che

gli era entrato nella stanza, mentr'egli era intento a scrivere"
(. . . Chiàrchiaro who had come into his room while he was busy
writing), Pirandello writes. The important words here are "che gli
era entrato nella stanza", for the expression unmistakably echoes
the "mi trovai davanti" (I found in front of me) repeated twice of the
Six Characters in the Preface to that play, the "me lo vidi entrare in
camera" (I saw him coming into my room) which announces the arrival of Icilio Saporini in La tragedia di un personaggio, and the "vi
trovai un insolito scompiglio" (I found an unusual fuss there), which
signals the presence of dottor Fileno among Pirandello's Sunday
morning habitués in the same story. In each case the character imposes his presence decisively and palpably upon a passive (at least
at that moment) and helpless receiver. The reaction of the latter is
not always the same. Pirandello accepts Saporini and finds a place
for him in a story (although, as he adds wryly, he is to die there).
He refuses to satisfy Fileno and drives him into non-being. What he
does with the Six Characters is too well-known to warrant repeating
here. Judge D'Andrea also reacts to Chiàrchiaro's appearance:

> Ebbe uno scatto violentissimo e buttò all'aria le carte, bal-
> zando in piedi e gridandogli:
> - Ma fatemi il piacere! Che storie son queste? Vergognatevi!
> He was violently startled and throwing the papers off his desk
> leaped to his feet, shouting:
> - What do you think you're doing? What nonsense is this? You
> should be ashamed of yourself!

The violence of his reaction and his indignation are not dissimilar
from the impatience expressed by other Pirandello characters in
comparable situations. As a matter of fact, a case might be made
for seeing in Judge D'Andrea's reaction an abbreviated model for the
long and varied tug of war between characters (specifically the Father
and the Step-Daughter) and Capocomico (director) in Sei personaggi.
The licence which Chiàrchiaro demands would thus become the material and therefore ludicrous equivalent of the artistic form which
other of Pirandello's characters plead for, the stamp of reality and
identity - someone else's or, more broadly speaking, society's -
conferred on an individual who has lost his own sense of it because
his personality has in some way been mutilated. (27)
But while it is true that a close reading already shows traces of
the character without an author in the story, it is only in the play
that Chiàrchiaro makes the fully prepared grand entrance of which
we spoke earlier. To appreciate what has happened to Pirandello's
conception of him, three texts must be placed next to one another at
this point: the story, the play, and the play as it reveals itself in
performance. In the story the famous description of Chiàrchiaro's

transformation from "povero disgraziato" (a poor devil of a man) to "jettatore" (man who has the evil eye) follows immediately upon the passage quoted above in the preceding paragraph:

Il Chiàrchiaro s'era combinata una faccia da jettatore, ch'era una meraviglia a vedere. S'era lasciata crescere su le cave gote gialle una barbaccia ispida e cespugliuta, s'era insellato sul naso un pajo di grossi occhiali cerchiati d'osso, che gli davano l'aspetto d'un barbagianni; aveva poi indossato un abito lustro, sorcigno, che gli sgonfiava da tutte le parti. Chiàrchiaro had fixed himself up to look like a "jettatore" and he was a wonder to behold. He had let a rough, bushy beard grow on his sunken yellow cheeks, had put a pair of thick, horn-rimmed glasses on his nose, which made him look like an owl; then he had put on a shiny mouse-coloured suit which hung around him on all sides.

In the text of the play the sequence in which D'Andrea's reaction and Chiàrchiaro's appearance are recorded is reversed. According to the usage which places the description of a new character immediately after his first entrance on stage, the equivalent of the passage just quoted precedes D'Andrea's reaction and his exclamations of annoyance and disgust. In performance, of course, this temporal dimension is lost, for the spectator perceives visually what in narrative or stage directions can be told him only by the author. The visual perception makes present what in the story was past. "Chiàrchiaro gli era entrato nella stanza" (Chiàrchiaro had come into his room), says the story. "Tiene una canna d'India in mano col manico di corno. Entra a passo di marcia funebre, battendo a terra la canna a ogni passo, e si para davanti al giudice" (He carries a bamboo cane with a handle made of horn. He walks in funereally, tapping the cane on the ground at every step, and takes a stand in front of the Judge's desk), say the stage directions. As can be seen, there is in the play, in addition to the change in tense, the introduction of a detail of Chiàrchiaro's "masquerade", which in the story had been postponed to a later moment. (28) The cane beating rhythmically on the ground accompanies the impression of black magic made by Chiàrchiaro's costume with an ominous aural undertone. The Chiàrchiaro, who in the story had come into D'Andrea's study almost surreptitiously, in the play strides across the stage attracting a strange hypnotic attention to himself.

I should now like to examine some of the reasons which may account for the greater forcefulness of Chiàrchiaro's entrance in the play, and turn then to Pirandello's final rounding out of his figure in the course of the rest of his encounter with D'Andrea.

But there are two anecdotal explanations of the origin of the play

which must first be dealt with. One occurs in Musco's memoirs <u>Cerca</u>
<u>che trovi</u> . . .; the other is reported as having been given by Piran-
dello himself. (29) In recalling moments of his long and fruitful association with Pirandello, Musco speaks of an encounter which he says
occurred on the day after the Rome première of <u>Liolà</u>. He was walking
with Pirandello and Rosso di San Secondo, the other important dramatist of those days of Sicilian origin, in Piazza Poli, the little square
behind the Galleria Colonna in the heart of Rome, when they witnessed
an attack by two brutes upon a poor ragged wretch of a man. Upon
asking what had happened, they were told that the man who was being
mistreated had the reputation of being a fearsome bearer of bad luck,
a "jettatore". Thereupon talk turned to this superstitious belief and,
Musco concludes, the first idea for <u>La patente</u> came to Pirandello. The
story attributed to Pirandello, though not identical, bears a strong
resemblance to Musco's. According to it, Pirandello, who did not himself believe in the evil eye, had met a man in Rome who was reputed
to have that magic power and was as a result so thoroughly shunned by
others that he was forced to live alone, a social outcast. Overcome by
pity for him Pirandello wanted to befriend him, but he was warned
against doing so by his acquaintances. It then happened that in a minor
street accident Pirandello was hit by a car and thrown into the arms of
this very man who saved him from harm. "And that was the first germ
of <u>La patente</u>", he is quoted as having said, "which I then forthwith
wrote". In spite of the slight variations, the two stories may very well
refer to the same incident. We can be sure, however, that the first
idea for <u>La patente</u> did not come to Pirandello after the 4 November
1916 performance of <u>Liolà</u>, for the story by that name on the same
subject had been in print since 1911. Yet something may very well
have happened on the day remembered by Musco to revive the original
idea in Pirandello and to suggest how this story too could be changed
into a play for the Sicilian comedian. (30) At any rate, the version of
the play which was published in <u>Rivista d'Italia</u> in January 1918 is described in the subtitle as a <u>novella sceneggiata</u> (dramatized short story)
and it can be presumed that it was this text which served as the basis
for the 23 March 1918 Turin première. The fact that the anonymous
<u>La Stampa</u> reviewer referred to earlier makes no mention of the play
being in dialect may point to one of two alternatives: either the performance was in Italian or the principal actor or actors improvised a
dialect translation as he or they went along. This latter possibility
may account for the fact that in the extant dialect text only the part of
Chiàrchiaro (but I am almost positive - as positive as one can be without having actually seen the evidence - also the part of Rosinella) is in
dialect. (31) But it is not so much this matter which is of significance
here as the light the two anecdotes shed on the primacy of the theatre
for the growth of Pirandello's reputation. It is fully understandable
that, when Musco first played the role of Chiàrchiaro, he was not

acquainted with the details of the play's history and pre-history, and that as a result the encounter on Piazza Poli and the emergence short-ly thereafter of the character of Chiàrchiaro seemed to him incontro-vertible proof of the inevitability with which the raw materials of life are turned into art. As for Pirandello, there is in point of fact nothing in the anecdote as he told it to suggest, as critics have implied, that it was the play he was thinking of as the work directly inspired by his meeting with a real life and blood "jettatore". It might just as well have been the story. In any case, it is in the two texts, play and story, more than in any possible effects of contingent circumstances, that we must seek evidence for Pirandello's artistic creativity. And yet the fact that the anecdote exists, that it was transmitted, and that it is mysteriously suggestive, by itself tells something about the strong-ly haunting quality of the figure of Chiàrchiaro.

In looking now for the internal reasons that determined the evolution of Chiàrchiaro, we must consider first of all the different development given D'Andrea in the play and in the story. Put very briefly, in the story D'Andrea is presented more fully than in the play. His role in terms of plot is the same, but Pirandello tells more about him, de-tails of his appearance, of his life, of his feelings, which in the play are omitted altogether. While in the play we learn that D'Andrea has the reputation of being an eccentric, nicknamed Giudice Cardello (Judge Goldfinch) because of his habit of taking his goldfinch with him to the office every day, in the story we are told of the sleepless nights he spends gazing at the stars, establishing geometric relationships between them, and sending his soul wandering among them "like a little lost spider". (32) While in the play we hear him discussing the case with the Three Judges on the day that he has called Chiàrchiaro to his office, in the story we learn of the long period of indecision that has preceded his calling Chiàrchiaro, of his frequent attempts to draw advice from his fellow judges, of his particular dislike of the two op-position lawyers, Grigli who has the profile of an aged bird of prey, and Manin Baracca who bought an enormous talisman against the evil eye for the occasion and wears it on his fat belly, "ridendo con tutta la pallida carnaccia di biondo majale eloquente" (laughing with all his overflowing pale flesh which made him look like an eloquent blond pig). (33) Finally, while in the play we are given no physical descrip-tion (the spectator, it is true, sees D'Andrea step on stage and there-by receives an immediate physical impression of him, but that is the doing of actor and director and not of Pirandello), in the story there is an elaborate one which tells of his age, his thick woolly hair, his broad bulging forehead, his wrinkles, his small leaden eyes, his crooked stooped shoulders on which he seemed to carry an unbearable weight. In the story, in other words, we get one of "those minute pe-dantic portraits" which are so common in Pirandello's stage directions and which he was in the habit of simply lifting from his stories: "fine

psychological indications", as one critic has said, "most precious
for his future interpreters, but extending to physical particularities
with which no make-up man would ever be able to endow an actor". (34)
But in the case of D'Andrea, Pirandello did not follow the usual procedure and by the time he came to the play he let this part of the
characterization drop completely.

What induced Pirandello to suppress other aspects of D'Andrea as
well? As we have already seen, scenes 1 through 6 were fashioned
with material from Parts I and II of the story, reorganized in such a
way as to fit the new medium. Characters were created and scenes
devised so that what was important to the plot and to characterization
could now take place on stage. The many paragraphs devoted in the
story to D'Andrea's attitude to his work and to his struggle with the
case of Chiàrchiaro are reduced to a few quick notations (some of
them invented for the play): his walking on carrying a tiny bird cage
in his hand, his words to the bird, his exclamation of impatience at
sight of the papers of the case on his desk, and later, in conversation
with the Three Judges, his recollection of the "court" game of his
childhood and its relation to the "game" he is forced to play now. The
narrator's voice, which in the story had expressed that deep identification between author and character which lies at the root of Pirandello's penetrating attention to D'Andrea, is now silent. The action on
stage, with its quick give and take, its entrances and exits, its mounting expectation of the direct confrontation with Chiàrchiaro, leaves
little room for a more leisurely and thorough presentation of D'Andrea.

But it is not only the play in contrast to the story that minimizes the
role of D'Andrea. In the course of the story itself a shift of emphasis
from D'Andrea to Chiàrchiaro was already apparent. For while it is
the Judge who there, as later in the play, takes the initiative of calling
Chiàrchiaro to his office to discuss the merits of his case, it is
Chiàrchiaro who once in the office does most of the talking. It is as
though, in the very act of writing, Pirandello, beset by the urgency
and oddity of Chiàrchiaro's plea, found it more and more difficult to
permit D'Andrea to dispute his views. The tables are subtly turned.
No longer is it the Judge who tries to convince the plaintiff to withdraw his case because it is contrary to his interests, but the plaintiff
pressing the Judge to institute the case so that he can the more rapidly lose it, and thereby win it! For the paradox of the situation is that
Chiàrchiaro has understood something which D'Andrea, in spite of his
inclination to reflection, his indignation at the injustice done Chiàrchiaro, and the long hours spent pondering a course of action, has not.
What Chiàrchiaro has understood is that there is no way back to a
status quo ante. (35) Nothing will ever convince, not just the two men
against whom he has brought proceedings, but the whole town including
lawyers and judges (with the exception of D'Andrea) that he is not a
"jettatore". Therefore, D'Andrea's sympathy is of little use to him.

D'Andrea's rationalistic impatience with the ignorance which lies at the basis of superstition can find no answering chord in Chiàrchiaro. Chiàrchiaro lives under pressure: he must find a solution to his plight immediately and cannot wait for the rosy morrow which the dream of progress through education and enlightenment promises. He must transform ignorance not into knowledge, as D'Andrea would like to do, but into salvation for himself. Thus, instead of fighting against the reputation that has blighted his life, he will now strengthen his claim to it. If he has been unjustly accused of being a "jettatore", he will show his accusers that he is indeed the bearer of bad luck and that his power is more deadly than they had supposed. To achieve this, he has already clothed himself in a new uniform and he comes now to demand a certificate. He argues his case lucidly, with a disconcerting logic which rests on an absurd notion of the social meaning of a legally conferred privilege, in which a high level of abstraction and a shrewd understanding of the world of practice mingle. Just as the Judge had to earn his degree to exercise his profession, so he too, the outcast, is applying for the right to collect a fee for a service rendered. In his case the service will be withholding his supposed but firmly be-lieved-in influence of evil. In the story Chiàrchiaro foreshadows what he will do: "Mi metterò a ronzare attorno a tutte le fabbriche; mi pianterò innanzi a tutte le botteghe; e tutti mi pagheranno la tassa, lei dice dell'ignoranza? io dico della salute!" (I'll start hanging around all the workshops. I'll take up a stand in front of all the stores. And everyone will pay my tax. You call it the tax of ignorance? I call it the tax of my salvation!). In the play he goes further and mimics the scenes that will ensue:

CHIARCHIARO. Mi metterò a ronzare come un moscone attorno a tutte le fabbriche; andrò a impostarmi ora davanti a una bot-tega, ora davanti a un'altra. Là c'è un giojelliere? - Davanti alla vetrina di quel giojelliere: mi pianto lì,
eseguisce
mi metto a squadrare la gente così,
eseguisce
e chi vuole che entri più a comprare in quella bottega una gioja, o a guardare a quella vetrina? Verrà fuori il padrone, e mi metterà in mano tre, cinque lire per farmi scostare e impostare da sentinella davanti alla bottega del suo rivale. Capisce? Sarà una specie di tassa che io d'ora in poi mi metterò a esigere!
D'ANDREA. La tassa dell'ignoranza!
CHIARCHIARO. Dell'ignoranza? Ma no, caro lei! La tassa della salute!
CHIARCHIARO. I'll start buzzing around all the workshops like a blue bottle fly. I'll take up a stand in front of this store

and that store in turn. Is there a jeweller's there? - I'll
take a stand in front of his shop window (he does so). I'll
look people straight in the face (he does so). Who do you
think will still want to go in there to buy a jewel in that
shop, or to look at the window? The owner will come out
and will place three, five coins in my hand to have me move
on and to take up a stand in front of his competitor's window.
Do you get it? It'll be a kind of tax that from now on I'll start
collecting!
D'ANDREA. Sure, the tax of ignorance!
CHIARCHIARO. Of ignorance? No, sir! The tax of my salvation!

This is the argument which in the story, as in the play, bit by bit reduces D'Andrea to silence. It is driven home by Chiàrchiaro's insistent tapping of his cane on the ground, by his repeated threats, and by
his calling D'Andrea more than once his bitterest enemy. It is an argument, however, which leaves the Judge intellectually unconvinced.
Even the great self-revelatory statement which occurs in both story
and play: "Perché ho accumulato tanta bile e tanto odio, io, contro
tutta questa schifosa umanità, che veramente credo, signor giudice,
d'aver qua, in questi occhi, la potenza di far crollare dalle fonda-
menta una intera città!" (Because I have heaped up so much bitterness
and so much hatred against this loathsome human race that I really
think, Your Honor, that here in my eyes I have the power of shaking
a whole city to its foundations!)(36) is powerless to move D'Andrea
from his position. Chiàrchiaro's lines parallel "Enrico IV"'s "capii
. . . che sarei arrivato con una fame da lupo a un banchetto già bell'e
sparecchiato" (I understood that I would be arriving with ravenous
hunger at a banquet which had already been cleared off the table), and
permit a glance at the inner abyss that the cruelty of man to man has
created. They are the sudden illumination which makes an apparently
insane decision appear to be the most rational, the only rational, in
the world. In the story D'Andrea is overwhelmed by pity at this point
and embraces Chiàrchiaro. In the play he is similarly touched but his
reaction is more restrained: he gazes at Chiàrchiaro stunned. The
hesitant and perplexed question, "La patente?" with which in both instances he answers what is no longer Chiàrchiaro's request but his
command to get on with the trial - "Istruisca subito il processo" (Get
on with the case at once) are Chiàrchiaro's words in the story, and
"Si metta a istruire questo processo" (Get down to this case) in the
play - is an indication not of his having been won over, but of his
having been hammered into psychological exhaustion. And if there
should be any doubt about this reading of D'Andrea's reaction, Chiàrchiaro's line in the play, "Lei è rimasto come una statua di sale!"
(You're struck dumb like a pillar of salt!), to which there is no equi-

valent in the story, is enough to dissipate it. The direct encounter with Chiàrchiaro has shown D'Andrea that it is not only difficult to help this man in distress but that it is downright impossible.

But for the situation to be pushed to its logical conclusion it is not enough for D'Andrea to have been reduced to silence. He must also be destroyed. For to Chiàrchiaro's singlemindedness, even if only one individual survives who does not believe in his power, there is danger that in the end no one will. It is here that the play goes further than the story and by doing so brings to full light the second cause of antagonism between the two. Beyond their disagreement about the expediency of the trial lies Chiàrchiaro's determination to persuade D'Andrea of the actual existence of his supernatural powers. We pass from the social and existential dimension of the situation to an aspect of that vast area of the occult to which Pirandello returned again and again throughout his career.(37) Superstition in this context is no longer a cultural blindness which enlightenment can cure, but a key to a suprarational understanding of reality. Indeed Chiàrchiaro had from the very beginning of his appearance insisted on the authenticity of his magic powers: "Lei dunque non ci crede?" (So, you don't believe in it?) are his first words in both the story and the play, and later when D'Andrea thinks of humouring him by feigning belief, he cuts him short sharply, "Nossignore! Lei deve crederci sul serio, e deve anche dimostrarlo istruendo il processo!" (No, sir! You must believe in it seriously, and you must also show that you do by instituting the trial!). But D'Andrea had taken these repeated admonitions no more seriously than Chiàrchiaro's dress or, to be more precise, he had taken them seriously only inasmuch as they were the clue to Chiàrchiaro's deep and intolerable anguish. Now, however, after Chiàrchiaro's emphatic, "La patente, sissignore!" (The license, yes sir!) with which in both story and play he counters D'Andrea's benumbed stammer, the window opens unexpectedly and a gust of wind upsets the bird cage on its stand. From this point to the end of the play the only words that D'Andrea speaks refer to the death of the goldfinch. And the very last ones he utters, the disconnected "Il vento . . . la vetrata . . . il cardellino" (The wind . . . the window . . . the goldfinch) - his answer to the excited questions of the Three Judges and Marranca - are the rational interpretation of the accident, in which there is absolutely no room for the action of the supernatural even reduced to its most abstract formulation, fate. Chiàrchiaro disputes this interpretation at once and brings his clinching argument to bear on D'Andrea:

CHIÀRCHIARO (con un grido di trionfo). Ma che vento! Che vetrata! Sono stato io! Non voleva crederci e glien'ho dato la prova! Io! Io! E come è morto quel cardellino, subito, gli atti di terrore degli astanti, che si scostano da lui,

così, a uno a uno, morirete tutti!
CHIÀRCHIARO (with a cry of triumph). What wind? What
window? It was I! He didn't want to believe in my power
and I've given him proof! I! I! And just as that goldfinch
died (<u>at once all those present draw back from him with
gestures of fright</u>) so one by one you too shall die!

The three <u>io</u>'s (I's) mark the high point of Chiàrchiaro's transformation. The threat, implicit in the grotesque dress with which he
underscored his exclusion from the fellowship of men, tapped out by
the rhythmic beating of the cane, at various times openly made to
D'Andrea, has become a reality. What D'Andrea had interpreted as
play-acting on the part of Chiàrchiaro was deadly earnest. But the
argument - the bird's death turned by Chiàrchiaro with lightning
rapidity to his interest - convinces only those who have been convinced all along. The TUTTI (All) who answer Chiàrchiaro's intimi-
dation with the usual invocations and entreaties, "Per l'anima vostra!
Ti caschi la lingua! Dio, ajutaci! Sono un padre di famiglia!" (Think
of your soul! May you be struck dumb! God, help us all! I have a
family to support!), obviously do not include D'Andrea. If D'Andrea
has been defeated by Chiàrchiaro, he has been so only in the sense
that his superior learning and his training in dialectic have been unsuccessful in impressing upon the latter the absurdity of demanding
official recognition for his fearsome status. As far as the results of
a lifetime of scepticism are concerned - "la certezza di non poter
nulla sapere e nulla credere non sapendo" (the certainty of not being
able to know anything and of not being able to believe in anything,
not knowing), as the story states - these have not been overturned.
    What then is the irreparable something that, in contrast to the
story, the final action of the play brings about? While with his
specious arguments and the various demonstrations of the harm that
had been done to him Chiàrchiaro has all along rejected the helping
hand proferred him by D'Andrea, it is only through the death of the
bird and through his assuming responsibility for it that he definitely
shuts the door in his face. Hate has triumphed over love. The meanness and stupidity of men have been answered by a cunning and an
ill-will strong enough to destroy. The sympathy felt for Chiàrchiaro
earlier is now suddenly turned to frozen horror. For while Chiàrchiaro's self-congratulation might have been understandable and
even justified as a response to anyone else on stage, it is not so in
the case of D'Andrea. The effect is disproportionate to the cause.
Chiàrchiaro has killed - or assumed responsibility for killing, the
two things being equivalent here - what D'Andrea held dearest. In
D'Andrea's life the goldfinch, the gift of his deceased mother, had
taken the place of all human affections and stood for his sense of
continuity and identity.(38) It is this that at the existential level

Chiàrchiaro has taken from him. The action, begun when Chiàrchiaro appeared before D'Andrea, dressed not in his own clothing but in a masquerade costume which revealed his inner being, is concluded. Events will now follow their course. The trial will take place, Chiàrchiaro will lose it, and by losing it he will have found his way back into society, a scarecrow from which men will flee but which they cannot ignore. Unable to earn his living by contributing to the material well-being of men (his job as a bank clerk thus has a symbolic and not merely a naturalistic meaning), Chiàrchiaro will still have a function in catering to the dark, mysterious underside of their nature. (39) In the final reversal it is not Chiàrchiaro, the apparent victim, who is excluded, but D'Andrea, the man who was isolated all along. Through his progressive swelling, first in the short story and than in the play, Chiàrchiaro has robbed him of his Lebensraum.

To find out who and what D'Andrea really is one must, of course, turn back from the play to the story which is its indispensable subtext. D'Andrea, I hope I have made clear, is neither one of Pirandello's chorus figures nor is he comparable to a spokesman such as Laudisi. While Chiàrchiaro stands between Ciampa(40) and "Enrico IV" on the trajectory of the emergence of the character without an author, D'Andrea is rather much like Serafino Gubbio, the cameraman whose voice has been silenced by the horror of a scene he involuntarily filmed. In Pirandello's version of the anecdote relating to the conception of La patente, he himself has a role or a possible role in the life of the unfortunate man reputed to bring bad luck. In Musco's version there are no second roles: there is only the actor, the "jettatore". The stage history of the play reflects this latter vision of it. The internal history of its genesis and growth, instead, reflects – and how could it not? – Pirandello's vision of it. In this vision, the complete meaning of the story of Chiàrchiaro is understandable only in terms of what happens to D'Andrea. For Pirandello never intended the "triumph" of the former to be a cause for rejoicing (as it would have been had only the Manin Baraccas been his adversaries), but only for reflective sadness at the condition of "questi poveri piccoli uomini feroci" (these poor little cruel men). So that without aiming at a comparative aesthetic judgment of the respective merits of play and story – something which in the final analysis would only reflect subjective preferences – the greatest pleasure to be derived from letting play light up story, and story play, is that of once again watching creativity at work in that great poet of the creative act who was Luigi Pirandello.

(1973)

NOTES

(1) The play La patente was first published in Rivista d'Italia, 31
January 1918. Shortly thereafter it was issued together with Lumíe di
Sicilia and Il berretto a sonagli as Volume III of the first collection
of Maschere nude (Milan, 1920). Together with L'imbecille, Lumíe
di Sicilia, and Cecè, it later formed Volume XX of the second collection of Maschere nude (Florence, 1926; Milan, 1933). It is now
in Opere di Luigi Pirandello (Milan), Maschere nude (1962), II, 601-
18. All quotations in the present essay are from this edition. The
first English translation, by Elizabeth Abbot, appeared with the title
By Judgement of the Court, in Luigi Pirandello, One-Act Plays (New
York, 1928). It has more recently been translated by William Murray
with the title The License, in Pirandello's One-Act Plays (Garden
City, NY, 1964; New York, 1970).
    The short story by the same title, first published in Corriere della
sera, 9 August 1911, was included in the collection La trappola
(Milan, 1915) and later in Volume III, La rallegrata, of Novelle
per un anno (Florence, 1922; Milan, 1934). It is in Volume I of
the "Omnibus" collection of Novelle per un anno (Milan, 1937),
with minimal notes giving the variants. Like the play, it is now in
Opere di Luigi Pirandello, Novelle per un anno (1966), I, 512-19.
According to Frederick May (Luigi Pirandello, Short Stories, selected,
translated and introduced by Frederick May [London, 1965]), there is
no English translation of the story.
(2) Leonardo Bragaglia lists it in the chronology of the play in his
Interpreti pirandelliani (Rome, 1969), 96, with the erroneous information that it was given at the Teatro Carignano. However, in the
body of his discussion he fails to mention it and gives the 19 February
1919 performance as the prèmiere. Luigi Ferrante, both in his Pirandello (Florence, 1958), 96, and in Pirandello e la riforma teatrale
(Parma, 1969), 109, cites only the 19 February 1919 Rome performance, as does M. Lo Vecchio-Musti under the heading "Prime
rappresentazioni", in his Bibliography in L. Pirandello, Saggi, poesie,
scritti vari (Milan, 1960), 1276. The anonymous review which appeared in Turin's La Stampa, 24 March 1918, reports that the performance
was given in honour of the actress Jole Campagna and that Angelo
Musco took the role of Chiàrchiaro. (Jole Campagna belonged to a
well-known family of Sicilian actors and in September 1917 she had
played in 'A vilanza [La bilancia], the dialect comedy written in collaboration by Pirandello and Martoglio.) In summarizing the plot, the
La Stampa reviewer mentions that the job Chiàrchiaro lost was that
of teacher. This detail, reminiscent of the figure of Toti in Pensaci,
Giacomino!, differs from what we have in the printed text, but it need
not surprise us, for dialect comedies followed many of the traditions

of commedia dell'arte, including improvisation. In commemorating Musco's death, for instance, Silvio D'Amico spoke of "the eternal phenomenon of the popular comic and dialect theatre where in the beginning is the actor and not the author", and of Musco's "fatal lack of discipline, his congenital faithlessness as far as the texts were concerned, his physical need to betray and remake them", so that he never rose to the level of "interpreter" but always remained an actor and a clown (Nuova antologia, CCCXCIV [1937], 111-13). But the nature of Musco's art must not be misunderstood: perhaps a traitor to the author, but for E. Gordon Craig he was the greatest actor in the world and for Antoine "an overflowing comic energy" such as had never been seen on the stage before. Both these opinions were recorded by Silvio D'Amico in Tramonto del grande attore (Milan, 1929) and are now quoted in D'Amico's Cronache del Teatro, E. Ferdinando Palmieri and Sandro D'Amico, eds. (2 vols., Bari, 1963-4), II, 457, n. 16.

(3) The manuscript of the translation is extant and is scheduled for publication in the new edition of Pirandello's opera omnia under the editorship of Giovanni Macchia.

(4) L. Bragaglia, Interpreti, 69. On Pirandello's own feelings regarding the contrast between Grasso and Musco, see his 4 February 1917 letter to Martoglio, published by Sandro D'Amico in "Itinerario di Pirandello al teatro", Il Veltro, 8 (1968), 93.

(5) Vito Pandolfi, "Quattro atti di Pirandello", Il dramma, no. 94 (May 1956), 18.

(6) L. Bragaglia, Interpreti, 70.

(7) Thomas Bishop, Pirandello and the French Theater (New York, 1960), 19.

(8) L. Ferrante, Pirandello, 97. See also Ferrante, Pirandello e la riforma, 109, where the scalognati, "the unlucky ones", of I giganti della montagna are added to the category of social victims.

(9) J.-Th. Paolantonacci, Le Théâtre de Luigi Pirandello (Paris, n.d.); J. Chaix-Ruy, Pirandello: Humour et poésie (Paris, 1967); Aldo Borlenghi, Pirandello o dell'ambiguità (Padua, 1968); Sandro D'Amico, "Itinerario"; Benvenuto Terracini, "Le Novelle per un anno di Luigi Pirandello", 283-398 in Analisi stilistica (Milan, 1966); Giuseppe Giacalone, Luigi Pirandello (2nd ed., Brescia, 1969). Of the commonly used reference works there is no entry for La patente in Dizionario Letterario Bompiani (Milan, 1947-68) which otherwise covers the works of Pirandello rather thoroughly, nor is the play discussed by Giovanni Macchia in his chapter on Pirandello in Vol. IX of the Cecchi-Sapegno Storia della letteratura italiana (Milan, 1969). In Enciclopedia dello spettacolo (Rome, 1961) Alberto Spaini groups La patente with L'altro figlio and Bellavita as works which consist of a series of monologues, with the "chorus" represented in turn by

a judge, a doctor, and a lawyer: "The antagonist has not yet been born. " My view of La patente in part challenges this judgment.

(10) Arcangelo Leone De Castris, Storia di Pirandello (Bari, 1962), 170.

(11) Adriano Tilgher, Studi sul teatro contemporaneo (Rome, 1923), 192.

(12) Ferdinando Pasini, Luigi Pirandello (Come mi pare) (Trieste, 1927), 293-4.

(13) Arminio Janner, Luigi Pirandello (Florence, 1948), 291-2.

(14) Walter Starkie, Luigi Pirandello (3rd ed., Berkeley and Los Angeles, 1965), 88.

(15) Maurizio Del Ministro, "Lettura di testi pirandelliani", Letteratura, no. 94-6 (1968), 135.

(16) Gaetano Munafò, Conoscere Pirandello (Florence, 1968), 147-8.

(17) L. Pirandello, Novelle, a cura di Giuseppe Morpurgo (20th ed., Milan, 1946), 106-17.

(18) Franz Rauhut, "Pirandello als Sizilianischer Mundartdramatiker", 148-172 in Der Dramatiker Pirandello. Zweiundzwanzig Beiträge herausgegeben von Franz Norbert Mennemeier (Cologne, 1965); Domenico Vittorini, The Drama of Luigi Pirandello (Philadelphia, 1935; New York, 1957), 54-7.

(19) Only one of the drama reviews I have seen even mentions the role of D'Andrea: Vito Pandolfi in Il dramma, May 1956, speaks of the actor Mario Siletti who played the Judge with "pathetic resignation", giving him an air of "disconsolate and good-natured" gentleness.

(20) Some of the early reviewers, such as Eugenio Cecchi who wrote for Il giornale d'Italia under the pseudonym Tom, were unable to understand Sicilian and objected vigorously to plays in dialect (see L. Bragaglia, Interpreti, 27 and 41-2). Moreover, there was considerable antagonism elicited by the provincial Musco among sophisticated intellectuals, as can be seen, for instance, in Piero Gobetti's "Pirandello e il buffone Angelo Musco", Energie nuove (Turin), 1-15 December 1918 (now in Le riviste di Piero Gobetti [Milan, 1961], 90-1). Pirandello's own feelings regarding the dialect theatre were ambiguous, as is apparent from his 1909 essay "Teatro dialettale?"

(21) Leone De Castris (Storia, 111-15) has spoken of the dramatic dimension of certain stylistic procedures in Pirandello's short stories. But there is a difference between drama in narrative and drama on stage, something Giovanni Macchia saw clearly when he gave the title "Teatro e palcoscenico" (Theatre and Stage) to one of the subdivisions of his chapter on Pirandello (Cecchi-Sapegno, IX, 467-70). What I have in mind here, however, is specifically related to the context of Pirandello's working with dramatic techniques in the first part of La patente.

(22) Occasional references to this whole area of Pirandello studies abound, but only two thorough explorations of particular relationships between stories and plays have come to my attention: Ulrich Leo's seminal "Luigi Pirandello zwischen zwei literarischen Gattugen" (Luigi Pirandello between two Literary Genres), Romanistisches Jahrbuch, XIV (1963), 133-69, which deals with L'uomo, la bestia e la virtù, O di uno o di nessuno, and especially Così è; and J.H. Whitfield's elegantly executed analysis of Tutto per bene, "La metamorfosi della novella", in Atti del Congresso internazionale di studi pirandelliani (Florence, 1967), 735-42. The discussion of La patente, play and story, contained in Nino De Bella, Narrativa e teatro nell'arte di Luigi Pirandello (Messina, 1962), 57-9, leads to the conclusion that the narrative version is superior to the dramatic because it is a better expression of Pirandello's "humourism".

(23) The fact that Pirandello thinks in terms of scenes does not preclude the experimentation with respect to this very point which takes place in the trilogy of the theatre within the theatre: the ingenious way, for instance, in which Sei personaggi, although only "a play in the making", is divided into acts through the accidental lowering of the curtain at the end of what thereby becomes a de facto Act I.

(24) All translations throughout the essay are mine.

(25) The fact that this play in which the woman's role is so very minor should have been chosen for a performance in honour of a leading actress is not irrelevant in this connection.

(26) Useful observations on the relationship between stage directions and parallel passages in the stories are found in Aldo Vallone, "Le didascalie nel teatro", 501-7 in Atti . . . studi pirandelliani.

(27) In her "Pirandello and the Theatre of the Absurd" (Cesare Barbieri Courier, VIII, Spring 1966, 6), Beatrice Corrigan says on this point: "Pirandello holds that the individual cannot feel secure in his illusion unless he can persuade others to share it." Pushed to an extreme this is the strategy and the anguish of the schizophrenic; Pirandello's characters stop short of complete disintegration, but they express their desire for consistency with the intense and desperate desolation which appears on Fileno's face when Pirandello rejects him: "una così intensa e disperata angoscia si dipinse sul volto del dottor Fileno, che subito tutti quegli altri [i miei personaggi che ancora stavano a trattenerlo] impallidirono e si ritrassero" (an anguish so intense and desperate appeared on Dr. Fileno's face that immediately all those others [my characters who were still trying to hold him back] grew pale and retreated).

(28) In the story the cane appears only when Chiàrchiaro is already seated and is rolling it back and forth along his thighs as though, Pirandello writes in one of his arresting comparisons, it were a rolling-pin. The episode is transferred without change to the play

where, however, coming after the initial visual and aural impressions of Chiàrchiaro's entrance it acquires a more threatening resonance than it had originally: the domestic object, one suddenly remembers, has often figured prominently in acts of violence. But the pleasure of this discovery is reserved for the reader of the play only, for when stage directions are translated into actions they lose the specific values and connotations of the words in which they are couched. Another instance of the loss of a strong, commonplace comparison in the transformation of narrative into drama is the "sfagliò come un mulo" (he started back like a mule) said of Chiàrchiaro in the same scene and which is replaced in the stage directions by the colourless "tirandosi indietro" (stepping back).

(29) Angelo Musco, Cerca che trovi . . . (Bologna, 1929), 169. Pirandello's own story is told by Ottavio Profeta in De Roberto e Pirandello: Note (Catania, 1939); I have not been able to see this work and derive my information from Rauhut, "Pirandello als . . . Mundartdramatiker", 165.

(30) Pirandello had already written in Sicilian or translated the following plays for Musco: Lumìe di Sicilia, Pensaci, Giacomino!, Il berretto a sonagli, Liolà, and La giara.

(31) Rauhut, 166, reports that Sandro D'Amico showed him the manuscript of the Sicilian version and pointed out "that only Chiàrchiaro as a man of the people uses dialect; the others speak Italian because they belong to a higher class". I am quite sure that a closer examination of the manuscript would show that Rosinella too speaks dialect. Rauhut also mentions (361, n. 31) Pirandello's interview in Corriere della sera, 10 October 1923, where he spoke of two of his regional plays translated into Sicilian by Musco. Rauhut supposes that if Musco actually translated any Pirandello works into Sicilian, these have not yet come to light. On the basis of the evidence presented in this essay, however, I would propose that 'A patenti may very well be one of the two plays Pirandello had in mind: the circumstances reviewed here suggest that a translation of La patente was extant prior to the official one performed in February 1919.

(32) The image of the spider as an emblem for man already occurs in a letter of Pirandello to his sister, 31 October 1886. "Luigi Pirandello, Lettere ai familiari", presentazione di Sandro D'Amico, Terzo Programma, no. 3 (1961), 273-80.

(33) In contrast to what happens to the anonymous judges in being transferred from story to play, these two very "real" lawyers are reduced simply to a name (Lorecchio).

(34) Alberto Spaini, "Pirandello autore drammatico", in Enciclopedia dello spettacolo, VIII, 156.

(35) The theme is a familiar one in Pirandello from Il fu Mattia Pascal to La nuova colonia, but as far as I know it has never been studied as such.

(36) Chiàrchiaro's lines as they appear in the play (the version quoted here) are only slightly different in the story. I have not examined the two texts for stylistic divergences of this kind, nor indeed have I stopped to consider the evidence which the available intermediate text of the Rivista d'Italia brings to this point. Yet one example among many might be cited. In the passage in which Chiàrchiaro describes how he will go about collecting the tax, the Rivista d'Italia text reads: "Mi metterò a ronzare come un calabrone attorno a tutte le fabbriche; mi stabilirò ora davanti a una bottega, ora davanti a un'altra: mi pianto cosí (eseguisce), e mi metto a guatare la gente cosí (eseguisce); e chi vuole che entri piú in quella bottega? Vien fuori il padrone, e mi mette . . ." (I'll start buzzing around all the workshops like a wasp; I'll establish myself first in front of one store and then in front of another; this is how I'll do it [he does so]. I'll stare at people this way [he does so]. And who do you think will still want to go into that store? The owner will come out and put . . .). I have italicized only those words of Chiàrchiaro that are different in the two versions, but a comparison between the passage as quoted here and as quoted earlier will show in the later version the insertion of whole new phrases as well. Some of the changes between the Rivista d'Italia text and the definitive one were no doubt the results of experiences during rehearsals and performance. The difficulties encountered by Pirandello with the actors who interpreted his works are well known, but it might not be inappropriate to refer here to a letter he wrote Martoglio (12 February 1917) apropos differences that arose during Musco's rehearsing of Il berretto a sonagli. Musco had complained about lines he considered difficult and contorted. Pirandello wrote: "Words must be given a soul if they are to live. It is the soul that was lacking during the rehearsal of Musco and the others. Lacking the soul, the actors found themselves embroiled in long sentences full of parenthetical expressions which they didn't know how to recite to the end! Why is it that all those long sentences, those parenthetical expressions were not noticeable when I said the lines? Because I gave a soul to the characters; in reading, I communicated to them their spoken action. Because this is the characteristic of my dialogues: they are made not of words but of psychological feelings" (S. D'Amico, "Itinerario", 94). A stylistic study of the transformation of the story into the play, especially insofar as the dialogue passages (second part of La patente) are concerned, would involve a careful examination of at least four texts, the three already available and the text of the Sicilian version soon to come.

(37) In Cecchi-Sapegno, IX, 453-7, Macchia has some extremely illuminating observations to make on this point.

(38) The meaning of the goldfinch for D'Andrea is in some respects identical with that of the canary for Adriano Meis (Il fu Mattia Pascal, end of chap. IX). While D'Andrea's lines in La patente, "Gli parlo

. . . che noi esistiamo" (I speak to him . . . that we exist), can in no way be called a direct borrowing from the novel, "Non potendo con gli altri . . . della nostra vana illusione" (Not being able to do so with others . . . of our vain illusion), the two passages follow exactly the same line of development. Morpurgo in his edition of the Novelle, 107 n. 34, instead of Il fu Mattia Pascal refers to the story Un gatto, il cardellino e le stelle (first published in Penombra in 1917) as embodying the bird theme. In this story a neighbour's cat finds its way into the house of a carefully guarded and deeply cherished goldfinch and devours it. There are some obvious parallels to the situation of La patente: the goldfinch in the story belongs to a couple whose granddaughter had trained it before dying; their loss is thus comparable to D'Andrea's loss. Less obvious is the fact that the ruthlessness of the cat, a being inferior to man, is very similar to the ruthlessness of Chiàrchiaro. In both stories, as in Cinci (1932), nature is a spectator without feeling. The crossing of influences, always significant in Pirandello, is especially interesting in La patente because it is an additional indication of the bipartite division of the play: in fact, as far as the bird episode is concerned, it is the mood of the passage from Il fu Mattia Pascal that is echoed in the first part of the play; the mood of Un gatto, il cardellino e le stelle that is recaptured in the second part.

(39) What I earlier referred to as the second dénouement, Chiàrchiaro's collecting money from the Three Judges and Marranca in scene 8, is a projection of what is expected to happen later on a larger scale. This scene is incomplete in the Rivista d'Italia version, which ends with Chiàrchiaro's defiant "Io! Io!" The difference between the two versions is further proof of the progressive development of the character of Chiàrchiaro.

(40) It is instructive to compare the description of Ciampa and that of Chiàrchiaro at their respective entrances. Ciampa is himself, even though his eyes "flash like a madman's". However, he wears thick metal-rimmed glasses, comparable to Chiàrchiaro's horn-rimmed ones. All the details of Ciampa's appearance are naturalistic; none of Chiàrchiaro's is. And yet there can be no doubt that Ciampa's tension is in every way comparable to Chiàrchiaro's, and I would say that the eyeglasses are the outward sign of their kinship.

"THE LIGHT IS SPLIT IN THE PRISM . . .":
SVEVO'S UNFINISHED PLAY, CON LA PENNA D'ORO

Among Svevo's papers there is the draft of a curious letter which to
all appearances was never sent to its addressee. In it Svevo asks an
unidentified but obviously successful playwright for assistance in
completing one of his own plays. "You know only too well", he writes,
"that however complex the thought in a play, the actual writing must
be clear and lucid. I know it too, only the trouble is, when I try to
achieve this lucidity (what a painful business) everything falls to
pieces in my hands. I hack and patch and mangle, but can let no light
in; the light is split in the prism and is lost. Is it my ear or my hand
that is at fault? I don't know and perhaps I will never know unless
you help me. "(1)
  Of the Svevo scholars who have made mention of this letter, none
has seen it as the excellent piece of self-criticism that it is. The
failure to do so is no doubt due to the gingerliness with which critics
in general have approached the subject of Svevo's plays. They have
been content mostly with examining them for the additional light they
throw on the author's favorite themes: his concern with illness, with
old age, with middle-class attitudes, with gay paradoxical situations,
with ineptitude. Almost all have shied away from the central and crucial problem: the dramatic effectiveness of the plays. (2) It is thus
refreshing to find that Svevo himself was well aware of his limitations
as a playwright and that he was not embarrassed to recognize them.
  These limitations are abundantly illustrated in a play which for a
number of more positive reasons can attract and fix our attention.
Con la penna d'oro is an unfinished work dated 1926, available only
in a version which is in part a reconstruction by Umbro Apollonio. (3)
The fact that the play is incomplete and the sequence of scenes often
uncertain is ample proof of the special difficulties Svevo encountered
in its composition. Its thematic richness, however, undoubtedly the
principal reason for its failure as a play, invites that closer look
which some of the other finished works do only to a lesser degree. (4)
  Con la penna d'oro is built around four female characters who are
bound to one another by a succession of indissoluble relationships.
There is first of all the blood relationship of the two cousins, Alberta
and Alice, and of their aunt, Teresina. The three have always known
one another, have studied and criticized one another in the manner
typical of members of close-knit Victorian families, have dutifully
declared their affection for one another, but have at the same time
been unable to control the resentments that periodically flare up to
change that affection into something very much resembling hatred.
The family relationship is complicated by the fact that the now old and

invalid zia Teresina is dependent on her nieces for both physical care and financial assistance. The physical care is entrusted to a nurse, Clelia, who had originally hoped to be trained for office work and thus avoid the demeaning position of household servant. Though Clelia is "hired help", she has aspirations which make her a person to be reckoned with and not merely a convenient foil for constructing dialogue. The financial responsibility for zia Teresina rests on the shoulders of Alberta alone, for Alice is a widow with two small children to raise. Alberta's husband, on the other hand, is a wealthy businessman with enough money to support the needy members of his family by marriage (Teresina and Alice), indulge his passion for collecting, and finance his wife's charities.

The economic theme, a de rigueur theme in bourgeois social comedy, is thus an inseparable part of the family relationship, though it is treated by Svevo in a manner which at least partially removes it from the sphere of strictly family emotional involvements. The second unavoidable theme, love, is likewise complicated by the basic family tensions, though again it is in Svevo's treatment not simply a secondary, dependent element. Moreover, in Con la penna d'oro, love - in the sense of romantic love - is the province of the male characters: Carlo Bezzi, Alberta's husband; and the two friends of Carlo who are frequent visitors at his house: the painter Donato Sereni, and the businessman Roberto Telvi, whose wife has recently left him. Doctor Paoli and the moneylender Chermis complete the cast of characters, standing for the two forces - health and wealth - which in a deterministically conceived society are either the sources of well-being or, through their absence, of irreparable damage.

When the play opens, Alberta is interviewing Clelia for the position of nurse and companion to zia Teresina. The money theme is thus introduced quite naturally and in the context that it will maintain for most of the play: money serves to do good. But with an ironic twist, doing good is revealed to be regulated in the case of Alberta by the same caution and parsimony that make possible the accumulation of capital in the business world.

Alberta is a professional do-gooder who goes so far as to argue with her husband on the comparative difficulties each encounters in handling his or her money affairs. Though her generosity is not self-interested in the sense that she does not act primarily in the hope of being paid back in some form or other, she does tend to moral blackmail, to an instinctive summing up of debits and credits, of which she is unaware but which constantly comes to the fore in her sugary as well as in her impatient remarks.

Thus we discover in the first few scenes that, while she is willing to pay for zia Teresina's support, she is not willing to lavish time and love on her, and that she is therefore planning to have her stay at Alice's house. Since Alice too is financially dependent on her, this arrangement seems perfectly logical to her; it will moreover make it possible to keep a closer control over Alice's household, something which Alberta desires to do for a number of reasons. Again, though Alberta provides for Alice, she does not do so in a compassionate spirit. She reserves the right to be critical of how her money is spent, an attitude which runs to unbelievable pettiness when, for instance, she objects to Alice dressing the children in white because other colours would require less frequent laundering.

Alberta suffers from that common managerial illness which finds respite only in organizing the lives of others. In contrast to her husband who thinks of Alice as a beautiful young woman with two children to look after and who should therefore be helped as much as possible, Alberta is never for a moment able to forget the social and economic distance that lies between her condition and her cousin's. "If we give her everything she asks for", Alberta tells her husband in reporting Alice's increased needs because of the rising cost of living, "she will end up by demanding too much; she will soon be spending as much as we do. I'm thinking of giving her half of what she asks" (385).

The dramatic conflict which the exposition of this background situation leads one to expect occurs at the end of the first act, when Alice discovers Alberta's plans for zia Teresina. Her indignation at seeing herself treated like an object, like a slave ("The help you give me doesn't give you the right of thinking you own me", 413), bursts forth in full fury, and she rushes away from the dinner party which is about to begin, flinging the money Alberta had given her to the floor, tearing off the scarf Alberta had lent her to cover her décolleté, and promising to send back the dress she is wearing - another of Alberta's gifts - the next day. It is a good scene, in which the hatred that had lain dormant for years rises to the surface. In formal terms it is the climax not only of the intrigue that Alberta had plotted - the surface action of the play to this point - but also of the rivalry of the two girls since childhood.

Alberta and Alice had earlier (Act I, scene 4) recalled an episode which had for each fixed the image of the other by placing the latter in a position of weakness and thus neutralizing the danger she represented. Alberta, who is a year younger than Alice, remembers that when she was eight, a little boy had run after her to beat her up, that Alice had intervened, and that the boy had then turned on Alice. Since Alice had not been able to defend herself, Alberta had in her turn come to the rescue: "I remember that while I was hitting him, I was not blinded by rage, that every one of my blows was well aimed and strong, and that it was meant to teach you the use one is supposed to make of one's hands" (391, italics mine). Alice's recollection dates from a slightly later period: Alberta had just lost her mother and for a time she sat day after day with her head on Alice's lap, trying to forget - she had said at the time - that the lap was Alice's and not her mother's.

Alice's comment to Alberta's recollection is that people always remember what suits them, and that she herself had completely forgotten
the little skirmish in which she had played such a generous part. (Obviously she emphasizes the first part of the episode, which Alberta
had chosen to gloss over.) Alberta's comment to Alice's recollection
is that while she may have said that she was trying to forget that
Alice's lap was not her mother's, she had actually thought that Alice
was "good and sweet and weak" like her mother had been, and that
"if a bad boy were to attack her", she would rush to Alice's rescue.
In this exchange, a significant aspect of the plot is handled with effectiveness and economy. Sympathy is evoked for Alice who is shown to
be not merely worse off than Alberta in the external conditions of life
but also a victim of long standing of Alberta's unconscious distortions
of reality.

The conflict scene at the end of Act I is a direct outcome of this
swapping of memories. When Alice objects to having zia Teresina
forced upon her, Alberta replies that she will write Teresina to tell
her that since Alice doesn't want her, she will pay for her stay at a
nursing home:

> ALICE. How nasty of you! Now you're going to tell zia Teresina
> that I don't want her. You're not going to! Now that you've in-
> vited her to come, let her come. I want her to come. I want her
> to stay with me so that my every minute will be poisoned and so
> that every minute I shall remember what you've done to me.

> ALBERTA (frightened as by a sudden revelation). I see your hatred,
> Alice, your deep hatred of me.

> ALICE. My hatred? You're frightened at your own hatred, the
> hatred you've always felt for me. I don't ever want anything
> more from you. You've been good to me, but now I've had
> enough. Here is your money. Here is your shawl. (She tears it
> off.) Tomorrow I'll send you this dress. The one I took off just
> now in the other room is also yours. I don't ever want anything
> else from you. (413-14)

As this stands, it could be the perfect ending to a one-act play. Of the
four female characters, Teresina and Clelia would have served as
dramatic props; the male characters would have been a kind of partially
amused, partially disconcerted chorus of by-standers. Attention would
have been focussed exclusively on the two cousins. The action itself
would have been the conclusive and revealing clash that lays bare long-
smouldering passion. As a special condiment we would even have had
a dash of amateur depth analysis with consequent insight - enough to
suggest a resolution, even if only a temporary one, of the conflict, and

enough to send the audience home with the satisfaction of having seen a whole, even if only a slight, play.

The second act opens with a scene in which Teresina and Clelia discuss their life in the household of Alice. It is almost as though Svevo, having attended to Alice and Alberta, were now turning to his other female protagonists. Indeed sympathy is now marshalled for zia Teresina, though it is a qualified sympathy, for the old lady is rather insufferable with her endless self-justifications, her dwelling on the past, her fear of offending any of the three women around her. Zia Teresina is tied to her wheel-chair, at the mercies of whoever pushes it around; she compares her present situation with the freedom and consideration she enjoyed when she ruled first her father's and then her uncle's households – a time when everyone ran to do her bidding: "The more I shouted, the better things prospered. The cattle multiplied, the wine grew by the gallons, the potatoes reached sizes never seen before" (435). Teresina's old imperiousness, her desire to run things is still there, but constantly checked by the realization that her erstwhile power is gone. She has thus entered into a not too savoury association with Clelia, whom she encourages in her natural tendency to pry into the affairs of the people she works for.

Clelia could have represented a disintegrating element in the society Svevo portrays had he chosen to use her in that way, a kind of revolt of the lower, serving classes on the way up the social ladder. Instead Svevo dwells on her as a comic character, almost a survival of commedia dell'arte, as is hinted at in one of Alberta's remarks to her: "How dare you play such practical jokes (lazzi) on your employers!" (441), or in Clelia's rather idiotic excuse (one of Svevo's famous Witze ?) for pushing out zia Teresina's chair when Alice wants to speak to her on stage: "I'm so sorry. I forgot to take this other hand off the chair too" (420). Clelia's prying and the impudence which, egged on by Teresina's vacillations, she displays serve the purpose of relating on stage the developments in Alice's private life. They also provide the dramatic device that triggers the main action of Act II.

In broad terms, if Act I deals with money, Act II deals with love. The theme had already been adumbrated in the first act through Carlo's tolerant affection for his wife (an echo of Svevo's own feeling for Livia? a hypothesis strengthened by Carlo's use of the same term of endearment, capra capretta - 386?), through Telvi's half pathetic, half ridiculous retelling of his marital misadventures and the concomitant advances he hesitantly makes to Alice, and finally through the hinted rivalry of the two cousins for Sereni.

It is the latter fact that, we eventually realize, determines the dramatic action of Act II. When Clelia impishly tampers with the window curtains and thus sets the signal with which Alice is in the habit of informing Sereni that the coast is clear, she is acting on a discovery she has made through eavesdropping and keyhole gazing. She had observed and reported to zia Teresina the progressive rapprochement of Alice and Sereni who, under pretext of painting Alice's portrait, is a daily visitor at the house. The significance of a passage in the mutual confessions scene (Act I, scene 4) now becomes clear. There Alice had jumped directly from the recollection of the aggressive littl boy to the thought of Sereni:

ALBERTA. . . . . I used to think: Good and sweet and weak like my mother. If a bad boy attacks her, I would step between them and protect her.

ALICE (hesitating). But by now bad little boys leave me alone.

ALBERTA. Is Sereni painting your portrait?

This exchange shows how well the two cousins are able to "read" one another's subconscious: Alice knowing that Alberta has grown little boys in mind, and Alberta stepping into the trap by apparently changing the subject but actually continuing the dialogue on the unstated level that had run through it from the beginning. But the skill with which Svevo handles this transition - as a matter of fact the tremendous understatement with which he has introduced the brute fact of the girls' rivalry now for one of the men in this little social comedy - is revealed only in retrospect, upon a rereading of the passage in the light of knowledge acquired later in the play. For the dialogue itself continues thus:

ALBERTA. Is Sereni painting your portrait?

ALICE (flushing). What harm is there in that? He comes to my house.

ALBERTA. There can be no harm in it except the portrait itself.

ALICE. I think it's coming quite nicely. He's giving it to me as a present. He's doing me dressed in that peasant's costume from the Friuli we used to wear when we were girls at Tricesimo.

ALBERTA. A wonderful idea. Urge him not to put your mouth in place of your ear. You don't have to be a painter to know where ears belong. It's more difficult to paint a nude woman because of the colour of the skin. But that, too, would be easy for Sereni. He'd just make her all green or all blue . . . (392)

The shifting of attention to sly little digs at modern art (see also 389 for an earlier remark on the same subject by Alberta) has weakened the main dramatic thrust, the revelation of the extent of the two girls' hatred for one another.

Act II is a full statement of what this hatred has led to. Only a month has elapsed since Alice refused to accept any further charity from Alberta. She and Sereni have become lovers, and she has asked the children's guardian for a considerable amount of the money left them in trust. She has thus mismanaged the two important forces which the bourgeois ethic takes pride in controlling and rendering useful and productive - love and money. This would be bad enough in itself, but the situation is shown to be even worse when we discover that Alice has acted not out of love for Sereni and desire for financial independence, but out of spite for Alberta.

In her confrontation with Sereni (Act II, scene 15) she claims to have always loved him but she reveals at the same time that it was anger that precipitated the affair: "I loved you and I love you! It is difficult to know why a woman gives herself. I only remember that my heart was filled with jealousy. How dreadful! She seemed so strong! And you didn't even deny that you were paying court to both of us!" (447-48). As the scene progresses, Alice has other surprises in store. The presence of Alberta looms larger and larger. Sereni obviously finds himself with more on his hands than he bargained for. First of all, Alice tells him that though he is not married to her, she is married to him, for on her way to meet him the first time she had stopped in a church and gone through a sort of symbolic ceremony of self-dedication. Then she draws out a phial of poison she carries around her neck and which she threatens to use should Sereni resume his visits to Alberta's house. The visits had been interrupted after the night of the quarrel, but Alberta now suggests that they be continued for the sake of her husband as though nothing had happened. Alice also tells Sereni that she feels that she has been a bad mother since her affair - another way in which she tries to unload her guilt feelings on him. And finally, or perhaps we should say from the beginning of these recriminations, she declares that she would like to make their affair public, flaunt it before the eyes of others, which means essentially before the eyes of Alberta. At the end of the act, after Clelia has been discovered hovering behind the door, Alice sends her out, slams the door behind her, and turns to Sereni: "Her (i.e., Alberta's) spy is here! Oh how glad I am! How much I love you! I feel as though I were kissing you in front of her!" (453).

Act III shifts to Alberta's house where zia Teresina and Clelia are now staying. As invalid and nurse are commenting on their treatment at the hands of Alberta, this scene parallels the initial scene of the preceding act exactly. Alberta's beneficence, as we expect, lies heavy.

116

Zia Teresina already regrets having left Alice's disorderly and in-
formal household: there she had at least been accepted as a member
of the family and Alice had confided in her. At Alberta's, talk revolves mostly about money, a subject of little interest to zia Teresina
because, as she says, she has none.

Alice arrives in great excitement to see Alberta, and we have in
scene 5 the only instance in the play of two people speaking and really
reaching one another instead of pursuing their inner phantoms side by
side. Zia Teresina and Alice have the classic heart to heart talk. For
a moment zia Teresina seems to forget her own predicament to look
objectively at the life of another human being. She affirms her love
for Alice whom she claims to have always preferred to Alberta, and
this time her words have the ring of truth for they show that she has
observed Alice's self-destructive behaviour and is concerned for her
future:

> TERESINA. . . . How is it possible that you, little mother, love
> your children so much and yet are unable to guide and control
> them? You only weep for them. How can that be? The last thing
> you think of is your home. You are bent on ruining yourself.
> Aren't you aware of this, Alice?

And then again:

> TERESINA (timidly). Couldn't you leave that man who is ruining
> you?

And finally:

> TERESINA. Well, then, why doesn't he marry you? (458-59)

The novelty in Act III is Alberta's intervention to force Sereni to
marry Alice. No doubt her motives are mixed. In the preceding act,
when she had gone to Alice's house to effect a reconciliation, she had
said to zia Teresina:

> ALBERTA. Well, I'll wait for Alice. You see, we are both stub-
> born and this silly quarrel threatens to last forever. It is up
> to me to take the first step. There is no doubt of that. By
> making peace I stand to profit nothing - on the contrary! But
> if this quarrel continues, Alice will be ruined. So it is up to
> me to give in. (432-33)

Now she fears that she may have contributed to Alice's "perdition":

> ALBERTA (to Alice). Was it I who pushed you to scorn what you

used to respect? Did I make you abandon the road where you
would have found happiness for yourself and your family? I
don't know, but my conscience cries out when I think that one
day you turned your back on me and that from that day you
began to act as though life meant nothing to you! Am I to blame
for all this? (464)

And later she seems to indicate that her negotiations in favor of
Alice's marriage were determined by her desire to see the family
reputation restored.
    Alice naturally rebels at the idea of a marriage arranged by
Alberta:

ALICE (to Alberta). I refuse! . . . This is all very strange!
Why does he (Sereni) have to ask you if he can marry me?
He sees me every day and he has to seek out you to ask
me . . .

ALICE (to Teresina). Even if I were convinced that Sereni is
marrying me to please her, I would refuse that pleasure (sic).
I don't want to owe her anything! I've known for a long time
that he meant to marry me. Why did she have to interfere and
ruin my happiness? Oh, her conscience obliged her to help me?!
What nonsense! Her conscience! All she wants is to enslave me
once more! That's what she wants. (465)

Alice is so suspicious of Alberta's motives and so unsure of herself
that she even comes to Alberta's house to accuse her of planning an
affair with Sereni. Carlo himself is alerted and for the first time
manifests symptoms of jealousy. In spite of all these currents and
cross currents, the marriage seems to be decided upon: Alberta
pays the debts Alice had made through Chermis, agrees to pay for
the education of Alice's children, and exacts a promise from Sereni
and Alice that their clandestine meetings will be suspended until their
marriage. The golden pen, as can be seen, continues to write as
busily as ever, with heavier and heavier strokes.
    It is at this point that Svevo interrupted the composition of the play.
And, we may say, with good reason. For it is difficult to envisage
where the action could have led to. It would hardly seem possible to
give the play a happy ending, to imply, that is, that Sereni and Alice
"lived happily ever after". Alice's resentments are far from resolved:
obviously she does not love Sereni enough to accept him on any terms
whatsoever. Sereni, on the other hand, shows no signs of becoming
the tolerant, understanding, conciliatory, not to say blind, husband
that Carlo is. Moreover, Alberta would have to be reckoned with as
the third member of the family-to-be: in the final scene written by

118

Svevo she had succeeded in imposing that the "reconciliation" of
Alice and Sereni, after Alice's fainting fit brought on by sight of
Chermis, take place at her house and not at Alice's.

To envisage a tragic ending – Alice's suicide – is easier. It would
be in one sense the only logical conclusion, the only imaginable release to the dramatic tension generated by Alberta's unrelenting
pressure. Alice is fully aware of the implications of this pressure
for her:

> ALICE. You find yourself every day in the company of a person
> who does you no harm, indeed who thinks she is doing you
> good! And she humiliates you and takes your freedom from you,
> and you humble yourself before her. You smile when you would
> like to weep, you say words of thanks when your heart feels no
> gratitude, you go when you would want to stay, and stay when
> you would want to go. These are all small things and yet to-
> gether they add up and become so big that they fill your life.
> And you don't even realize that the efforts you are making are
> being forced on you by that person. Then, one fine day, that
> person weighs down upon you more than usual and finally
> pushes you to rebel. And then you know why for years and
> years your life was not worth living. (450)

But in spite of the mounting despair so well analyzed in this passage,
the question still remains whether Alice will ever turn her rebellion
against herself more than she has already done by starting an illicit
love affair, and whether Svevo will ever seriously permit himself to
write the tragic ending. The episode of the phial of poison supports
the notion that he at least gave that possibility a thought. And there
is of course the precedent of the suicide that ends Una vita. But between a suicide laconically reported in a business communication and
a dramatic gesture on stage (or off stage?) there is a world of difference.

The deeper reason why I feel that Svevo would not have chosen the
tragic ending is that the point of view throughout the play as it stands
vacillates. My analysis, made selectively, may have given the completely erroneous impression that Svevo built conflict scenes into the
action in order to underline the structure of the play. While a close
reading reveals the presence of such scenes and their progressively
mounting tension, a less alert approach – an approach comparable to
the experience of an average theatre audience on opening night – results in no such insight.

The focus of attention is by no means constantly on Alberta and
Alice. We have mentioned zia Teresina and Clelia: the play could
easily have become zia Teresina's, as Furbank in his reading of it
suggests it is, (5) or it could have been Clelia's, as I myself have in-

dicated. We have mentioned Telvi, whose figure is developed at considerable length in the first two acts. There is Doctor Paoli, who at
one point seems destined for a fuller role. And there is the moneylender Chermis who arrives at the end with a wonderfully ironic comment on the relative percentage of interest charged by himself and by
Alberta: "And what if there were people who prefer to borrow money
at my interest rate (30%) rather than pay what you ask?" (471).

In short, there are too many characters viewed as fully rounded
figures to permit the perspective necessary to dramatic representation. The inability to focus, acceptable in first-person narrative,
is an almost insurmountable handicap in drama. There is moreover
lacking a central conviction on the part of Svevo - some overriding
view of the world - which could shine through the variety of scenes
and characters to give unity even to what is simply recorded. It is
sufficient to think what Pirandello could have done with some of the
material of Con la penna d'oro: how Alice would have turned into a
tragic character in spite of the bourgeois setting, how her "grand"
exit scene at the end of Act I would have acquired metaphorical and
universal meaning.

"The theatre is the form of forms", Svevo is reported to have said
at one time, "the only one in which life can be transmitted directly
through precise channels".(6) But if drama can be thought to have
"realness" through its brute statement of facts on stage, realness
alone - as a long tradition tells us - does not constitute a work of art.
Svevo was of course well aware of this. Hence his 1895 letter to the
novelist and critic, Silvio Benco:

> My most heartfelt thanks for your letter which tells me in so
> many words what I myself think of the work I sent you, and -
> what is worse - of every one of my works. Fog reigns supreme
> in them, so that at a short distance the majority of readers is
> unable to see anything. Therefore rather than pardon your sin-
> cerity in telling me what is true, I am flattered that you think
> the work deserving of the trouble of trying to disentangle from
> its confusion the kernel which perhaps is there. I doubt, how-
> ever, that I shall be able to find in me - as you say - the neces-
> sary energy for rethinking my psychological insights. I suffer
> from two illnesses that prevent me from achieving anything.
> The first, which I think innate, is the inability to arrive at
> that immediate representation of reality which other men seem
> to feel in things themselves. I am resigned to this because I
> think it is an innate shortcoming . . . The second illness makes
> the first one worse. I attribute it to my fate: I have a kind of
> terror of my own ideas so that I find it almost impossible to
> stay close to them for any length of time. I write, I revise,
> but actually I do nothing but repeat myself in the development

and even in the words, because I am unable to rethink with
any intensity. (7)

It is an eloquent document, an honest laying bare of the shortcomings
of Con la penna d'oro as of all of Svevo's plays, (8) a recognition of
that lack of intellectual vigor which characterizes Svevo's work so
strongly. Should Svevo have had an assistant for the composition of
his plays? A critical alter ego who could have laid out the lines of
dramatic tension for him and used the blue pencil on the lines the
golden pen wrote with such super-abundance? Or will the generation
of the antiplay find in him the great neglected precursor?

(1969)

NOTES

(1) Livia Veneziani Svevo, Vita di mio marito con altri inediti di
Italo Svevo (Trieste, 1958), 152-53. The translation I have used is in
P. N. Furbank, Italo Svevo. The Man and the Writer (London, 1966),
143-44. Both sources comment on the letter only in an effort to identify the addressee. Mrs. Svevo believes the letter was written to
Pirandello, and Furbank follows her in this hypothesis. For a different view, see Bruno Maier, La personalità e l'opera di Italo Svevo
(Milan, 1961), 169-71. Maier argues against the Pirandello attribution and makes a strong case for Marco Praga; he dates the letter
for the early part of the century, possibly 1903, the year of Svevo's
one-act play Un marito. In Italo Svevo, Epistolario (Milan, 1966),
56-7, Maier pushes the date even further back to 1896, pointing to
the similarity in content between this letter and an 1895 letter to
Silvio Benco. The matter of attribution is only of peripheral interest
for the present essay. Regardless of the period to which the letter
belongs, it is interesting to note the degree of Svevo's literary
naiveté and his apparent inability to grasp the concept of the cohesion
of content and form in a work of art.
(2) The occasional references to Svevo's plays in A. Leone De Castris,
Italo Svevo (Pisa, 1959), in the works of Bruno Maier and P. N.
Furbank cited above, and in a few scattered articles - including
Umbro Apollonio's introductory pages to the Commedie volume -
are informative but remain essentially provisional. Among other
things there is considerable disagreement about the comparative
merits of the different plays. For instance, De Castris singles out
Le teorie del Conte Alberto, Terzetto spezzato, and especially
Inferiorità and Un marito as the most successful; Furbank follows
him in Terzetto spezzato and Inferiorità and adds La rigenerazione
to complete the group of good plays, but he finds L'avventura di Maria

"a decided failure" and Un marito "preposterous"; for Apollonio Inferiorità is unsatisfactory, while Un marito is the "most complex and rich in situations"; and finally, Maier casts his vote for Un marito and Inferiorità. In reading their several comments one sometimes wonders whether they are all writing about the same works! More inclusively, Maier, De Castris, and Apollonio are of the opinion that Svevo's talent did not find its best expression in works for the stage; Furbank notes a development in Svevo's control of the genre and claims that in La rigenerazione at least he had succeeded in finding an original formula that allowed him to reach an achievement comparable to that of the novels. At the heart of these opinions - consciously or unconsciously determining them - lie the basic facts that Svevo's plays never passed beyond the stage of literary experimentation, that he never had and perhaps never sought the advantages of seeing their effectiveness tested in performance (only Terzetto spezzato was produced - in Rome in 1927), and that as works they do not have a place in the history of the theatre. Readers of Svevo's drama are thus almost completely unaided because of the lack of any critical tradition on the subject.

(3) Italo Svevo, Commedie (A cura e con prefazione di Umbro Apollonio, Milan, 1960), 379-478, 713-29. See especially 440 n. and 756. All references in this essay are to this edition; all translations are mine.
(4) Svevo wrote a number of plays, mostly one-acters, between 1880 and 1890; Un marito in 1903; and another group in the twenties. There is a list in Livia Veneziani Svevo, 256, which includes titles not in the Commedie volume. The Commedie volume which is part of Italo Svevo's Opera omnia (Milan, 1969) reproduces the earlier edition verbatim.
(5) P. N. Furbank, 212-13.
(6) Quoted in De Castris, 48 n., from S. Benco, "Italo Svevo", Pegaso, January 1929.
(7) Epistolario, 34.
(8) I am using Bruno Maier's observation that Svevo's plays do not reveal a chronological development (La personalità e l'opera, 151) as justification for using works of different periods to throw light upon one another.

ALBERTO MORAVIA: VOYEURISM AND STORYTELLING (1)

> Interviewers: And in your own work do you see a new
> direction?
> Moravia: I'll go on writing novels and short stories.
> Interviewers: You do not foresee a time, then, when
> you will occupy your mornings otherwise?
> Moravia: I do not foresee a time when I shall have
> nothing to say.
>
> The Paris Review Interviews, 1957.

The steady rhythm of Moravia's production since the statements just
quoted proves that he was correct in his prediction, while the growing
list of translations of his works into a good many of the world's
languages attests to an international success of no mean proportions.
Periodically, Moravia's name is put forward as that of a likely, if not
actually neglected, candidate for the Nobel Prize.

But if many readers would seem to agree with him that he indeed
continues to have something to say, critics are by no means unanimous
in sharing that view. A kind of tiredness has crept into their words, as
though at least some of them were beginning to feel that there was little
that they could add to what has already been said. New novels, new
short stories, essays, and lately also new plays propose Moravia's
new comments on man and society, man and his myths, the artist and
his time, the artist and his subject matter, communism and art, eroticism and literature, but there is something familiar about much of it
that tends to inhibit the enthusiastic reception accorded to real discoveries or deeply felt rediscoveries. Moravia continues to be emphatic. He continues to repeat his key words with greater and greater
insistence. He is as persuaded as ever that to state and restate a conviction or opinion is equivalent to gaining consensus for it. He approaches the reader with a sledge-hammer, tells him what to think,
and then tries to drive the truth home with a blow. Meanwhile his
characters continue to be strangely puppet-like, moved by visible
strings, distant alike from the reader's sympathy and antipathy, sil-
houettes against a gray background, reminiscent of the geometrical
forms of metaphysical painting but without the bright colours that liven
many a De Chirico.

One clue to understanding Moravia can perhaps be found by remem-
bering that he started writing when Pirandello dominated the stage.
Take away the anguish and rage with which Pirandello's characters
tear at themselves and others and leave only the intellectual will that
drives them and you have something of the icy atmosphere of The Time

of Indifference. Or, think of Moravia the novelist as a Peeping Tom.
An eye is fixed on the scene taking place in the bright light at the end
of a dark passageway. The concentration is intense, but there is an
absolute suspension of emotion. Sensations, yes, and the intellectual
tension which comes from the need of interpreting the meaning of what
is seen without hearing the words that accompany the actions. The
dark passageway creates distance, is distance. The novelist is the eye
that sees (and not the heart that feels). What he will put on the page is
the tracework of lines and not the tonalities of music. He will try to
blot out the distance by being categorical, but the distance remains.
It is the reason for his sense of alienation and the concomitant strain-
ing toward reality. It was no accident that Moravia gave an oblique
answer to the Paris Review interviewers. His intention was indeed to
continue writing novels and short stories, and that is all. The new
directions, he was saying, are at most something critics can try their
hand at discovering.

Moravia's latest novel, The Lie, has, to my mind, come a long way
toward making explicit the Peeping Tom implicit in many of his earlier
works. I would hazard the guess that the title for the translation derives from a statement made by Moravia in the same interview already
referred to, where he is quoted as saying: "I'm a liar, in fact. That
means I'm a novelist, after all." The English title is not inappropriate,
for the novel does in part deal with the problem of sincerity, of truth-
fulness, in the writer.(2) Nor, in view of Moravia's lifelong love-hate
relationship with his great predecessor, Manzoni, would it be far-
fetched to suppose that by calling the novelist a liar Moravia intended
a kind of bravado rejoinder to Manzoni's moral scruples with regard
to the fictional (i.e., fabricated, untrue) elements in novels. But there
must have been good reasons why in his own title Moravia preferred to
emphasize a quite different aspect of the book. The Italian title is
L'attenzione, and Moravia is at pains to define what the word means to
him by opposing it to its contrary, disattenzione. He does this over
and over again, so that the two words strike a kind of thematic note
for the book. The effect is of course lost in the translation, where the
word and the concept behind it disappear not only from the title but
from the text as well. Angus Davidson translates attenzione by "attention", "attentiveness", or "involvement", as the context seems to demand; and disattenzione by "non-involvement", "detachment", or
"aloofness". These extended meanings are present in the attenzione-
disattenzione polarity, but the point is that Moravia subsumed their
abstractness into something strongly concrete.
    Briefly stated, The Lie is the story of a Roman journalist whose am-
bition is to write a novel. As a young man belonging to the upper middle
class, in search for a stimulating situation, for something that might
put him in touch with the authenticity of experience, he had fallen in

love with and married a dressmaker of humble origins. The novel was to have been a record of that story. And indeed he had finished a first draft when something unexpected happened. He ceased being in love with his wife, and his former feelings for her now filled him with shame. Here begins the process of his estrangement, estrangement from everything but especially from his writing and from his wife and her daughter. He rejects his writing by tearing up the novel, his step-daughter by forbidding her to call him Father, and his wife by ceasing to look at her and later even removing himself from her gaze:

> My uncommunicativeness finally reached a point when I avoided turning my eyes toward her, so as to allow her not even the thing that one refuses to nobody - a glance. I made some excuse for changing my seat at the table, placing myself so that I would not have her opposite me. Another mean trick was that, if she came into the room, I would contrive to slip out as quickly as possible; not merely did I not want to see her but I did not even want to be seen by her. (11)

When the low point is reached, when, that is, he has been attracted by Nothingness(3) and has encountered Death in the shape of a skeletal prostitute, the tension is relieved by his finding a job that takes him away from Rome and his family for long periods at a time. For ten years (1953-1962) he travels to different parts of the world and supplies his newspaper with reports on the countries he visits. But though he travels to observe, he "observes" very much as he had "seen".

It is another case of disattenzione rather than attenzione: the eyes are open and they perceive, but they are not concentrated upon looking. Here again the translation blurs the issue, for it substitutes feelings of aloofness and non-involvement for the physical sense of sight. Moravia, instead, is quite specific. It is true that he speaks of the state of dépaysement in which his journalist travels, but he gives as the content of that state the long succession of hotel rooms in which he sleeps, the airport busses that take him to the cities whose streets he sees only through the fog of tiredness, the landscapes that succeed one another like identical photographs of identical places. Typical symbols of alienation, one might be tempted to say, except that for Moravia they are first and foremost moments of experience that could have become "real" had the traveler been able to focus on them. No doubt in Moravia's text focusing the eyes also means focusing the feelings, but it is important to note that over and over again he expresses the idea of involvement through the image of eyes looking. This becomes particularly obvious in the diary part of the novel, in a passage which reports an exchange of views between the protagonist and his editor-in-chief. The former is by now at work on a second

novel, entitled L'attenzione, and dealing with his return to a more
normal participation in the life about him:

"A novel? And what sort of novel is it?"
"It is the story of a man who suddenly decides to pay
attention."
"Attention to what?"
"Attention to the things that are happening under his nose."
. . . .
"And what does he do?"
"He doesn't do anything. He is satisfied with looking."
"Looking at what?"
"Looking at the things he sees."
"But looking isn't enough."
"Why isn't it enough?"
"Because a character (in a book) is supposed to act."
"My character doesn't feel like acting."
"Why doesn't he feel like acting?"
"Because he has no reason to act, while he has many
reasons for looking."(4)

The protagonist is looking, but what is he looking at? After ten years
of journalism, he is still obsessed by the failure of his first effort to
write a novel. He decides to try again, but this time the subject will
not be the drama of his encounter with Cora but rather the insignificant,
everyday occurrences of his daily life. Yet the specific event which
once more sets the mechanism of his attention in motion is his receipt
of an anonymous letter which accuses his wife of running a house of
prostitution. This is the starting point of the "story" told in his diary.
It is in his effort to discover the truth that he meets his grown step-
daughter again and that he starts out, sometimes with her and sometimes without her, on what is in some respects a tour of organized
vice in Rome. We thus have the traditional fictional elements, a story,
a plot and suspense, which will engage and sustain the ordinary reader's
attention. This may come as somewhat of a surprise, for Moravia has
of late been busy celebrating the demise of just this kind of novel and
has proposed new formulas to help novelists out of the supposed cul de
sac into which the loss of philosophical certainties has forced them.
But once Moravia comes out from behind the psychological, sociological,
and literary comments which form the "essay" part of The Lie, he
finds himself face to face with the most basic of narrative forms. The
form is indeed basic: we may call The Lie a "love story", a classification justified by the fact that it is, after all, the double story of the
protagonist's love first for Cora and then for his stepdaughter. The
tension in a love story derives from the uncertainty of its outcome:
will the lovers marry and "live happily ever after"? Will something

intervene to separate them? Or, in the context of the "incestuous" attraction felt by Francesco for Baba, will they become lovers at all? Now, Francesco, once he has recuperated the ability to pay attention, lives with his eyes riveted on the story that unfolds before him. As a writer he is involved with the fictional elements of the novel; as a lover with the possibility of possessing Baba; as an ex-lover and husband with his curiosity about his wife's second profession. In all three cases, it is in the end the sex act itself that is the object of his looking.

Moravia's fiction abounds in voyeuristic scenes. The most successful are, I believe, those that involve adolescent boys: for instance, Agostino in the story that bears his name (in Two Adolescents), and Tancredi in "The Fall" (Bitter Honeymoon and Other Stories). Not only is curiosity about sex natural in adolescents, but the special aura of constraint and complicity that surrounds it in Moravia, and thereby heightens its emotional tension, is the direct result of the socio-psychological situation of his protagonists. A summer such as mother and thirteen-year-old son spend at the seashore in Agostino is not out of the ordinary for the Italian middle-class; nor is a home like the villa in "The Fall", complete with maid, the customary sexual initiator for the boys of the well-to-do. Of course, the two stories are quite different. Agostino is the case-study of an Oedipal conflict which manifests itself rather late by classical Freudian standards, but offers Moravia, in line with the whole tradition of the novel of adolescence in Europe, a richer, more complex subject matter to make use of than would otherwise be the case. With "The Fall", instead, we are frankly in the realm of the pathological. Tancredi's uneasiness, his "chronic apprehension or feeling of foreboding, as if everything concealed a trap", has a less well-defined origin than Agostino's unhappiness, and thus lends itself to the surrealistic juxtapositions Moravia favors in this story and which would be out of place in the more rationally analytic Agostino. In each of the stories there is a carefully worked out, and in its way unforgettable, voyeuristic scene: in Agostino, the final page where the boy, barred from entering the brothel because of his youth, looks in through a window; in "The Fall", the more mysteriously suggestive sight of a pair of legs which Tancredi watches through a crack in a door.

In the context of adolescence, voyeurism can thus be said to have its place. Also because, in addition to the justification already adduced, the discovery of sex can, with the familiar and basic extension of meaning, be made to stand for the acquisition of knowledge and the commencement of adult life. But what are we to make of the voyeurism of adults? What about Cora in The Lie, spying on her husband while he makes love to a prostitute she has herself supplied? How about the window scene in A Ghost at Noon, where the husband watches his rival embrace his wife and remains there motionless even when his wife has

caught sight of him? What about the famous "moonlight dance" in
Conjugal Love? What about Lisa in The Time of Indifference, spying
upon Carla and Leo in that voyeur's paradise, the dark hallway with
its five velvet-hung doors? Or again, what about the protagonist of
The Lie, whose age and experience would seem to preclude prurient
curiosity and who yet engages in regular detective work to find ocu-
lar proof of his wife's activities? Examples could be multiplied, and
each scene should of course be studied by itself so as to determine its
specific function. For it would seem legitimate to ask whether this
repetition of similar scenes is accidental, a writer's tic? Are these
scenes merely devices necessary to the development of the plot? Are
they used by Moravia to point up something in the personality formation of his characters? Or are they a kind of inevitable occurrence at
certain definite moments of tension in the narrative? In "Eroticism
in Literature" (Man As an End), Moravia himself has answered critics
who find his insistence on sex excessive, by tainting the writer who
avoids the mention of sex "when the subject matter of the book requires
it", with hypocrisy and dishonesty. While there is no reason to dis-
agree with him on this judgment, it is still possible to ask who is to
determine the "when" and the "requires". For Moravia's off-handed
"but it is necessary to talk about it when – to make a play on words –
it is necessary" will convince only those who were already convinced
to begin with or who mistake tautological emphasis for logical proof.
Moreover, it is not merely the presence of sex in Moravia's work
that is significant, but the manner in which it is present. I feel that
The Lie throws important light on that manner, emphasizing the fact
that the role played by sex in Moravia's representation of reality is
not only quantitatively but also qualitatively different from the role
assigned to other basic factors in modern society.

Moravia has been writing short stories for as long as he has been
writing novels. Only very few of the earlier ones are available in
translation, mostly in the collection Bitter Honeymoon, which first
appeared in 1956. Of the recent ones a much more generous sampling
has found its way into English. This is to be explained not by the superiority of the second group over the first, but by the circumstances
of Moravia's introduction to the English-speaking world. His success
in England and America dates from the appearance of The Woman of
Rome, which was read at the time (1949-1950) in the context of remembered or vicarious war experiences in Italy and of the vogue of neorealism. From that point, interest in Moravia was quite naturally sustained by every successive publication of a new work. What he had
written earlier (and there had been at least twenty years of literary
activity prior to The Woman of Rome) did not have the same topical
urgency, nor did it always reflect the same concerns. The surrealistic
and satiric Moravia, for instance, seemed at odds with the social critic

and the psychological analyzer. Thus, though many of the earlier
works were eventually translated and published, (5) there are gaps in
what is available to readers of English. As a short story writer,
Moravia is unequally represented in English, and it is to be doubted
that the two volumes of Roman tales and the latest collection, The
Fetish, will do much to establish or maintain his reputation in the
genre.

One trouble is that the short stories in these three volumes are not
typical of the genre, either as cultivated by Moravia himself at other
times, or as it developed in the nineteenth century. They are journalistic pieces, originally written for the literary pages of a large Italian
daily. As such, their length and to a certain extent their subject matter
and narrative development are pre-set. It is difficult for writers who
over long periods of time write on assignment for a specific type of
consumption to avoid adopting formulas. That is why these particular
stories reinforce the impression of excessive repetition and monotony
in Moravia's work. Many of them, taken singly, convince and amuse;
read in succession, they tire and exasperate.

This is especially true of the stories in The Fetish. Through a long
succession of episodes and scenes, Moravia tells of the boredom of
modern life. Many of the stories deal with the typical contemporary
couple who hope to escape from their sense of indifference and isolation through one another, but only find themselves more deeply en-
trapped than ever in the anonymous apartments and mass-produced
cars which contain their lives. In "The Bill" a young man has just arrived at a vacation paradise, Capri perhaps, and is struck by the
crowd of people around him: "They were almost always couples, some
of them young, some middle-aged, some elderly . . . It seemed to him
that all of these couples, as they passed close to him, were saying:
we're two and you're only one; we know where we're going and you don't;
we have a purpose in life and you haven't." Indeed, the couple - rather
than the family - is a characteristic of modern life, and Moravia's
portrayal of it in the different stages of its cohabitation could well be
categorized into an "anatomy". In "The Honeymoon", for instance, we
have the bride and groom who have just set off on their wedding trip.
A chance remark of his wife startles Giovanni into the discovery that
there is no true relationship between them. The rest of the train ride
is taken up by his efforts to bridge the gap of incommunicability and by
his wish at the same time that the gap might become even wider through
his wife's disappearance. An amusing twist at the end shows that the
wife had experienced exactly the same feeling, but this cannot undo the
thought the husband had had earlier: " . . . as soon as his wife came
back he would feel unhappy again. And so it would be as long as they
lived, since they were married and there was nothing to be done." In
"The Fetish" the newly married husband is annoyed by a modernistic
sculpture bought by his wife and cannot refrain from joking about it.

A quarrel ensues; misunderstandings come to the surface and are discussed; resolutions are made to be more conciliatory in the future. At the end, however, when peace is restored and his wife sits opposite him at the table again, the husband notices that "in perspective, his wife's face appeared to be closely coupled with the stupid, ferocious face of the fetish". Numerous are the stories which deal with the triangle situation, from the obsessive jealousy of the fiancé in "The Man Who Watched", to the lazy toying with the idea of unfaithfulness by the wife in "The Escape", the search for "thrills" on the part of an "enormously" bored wife in "Too Rich", and the wife's discovery in "Scatter-Brains" that her husband has a mistress. Finally, there are the stories that mark the dissolution of the love or marriage tie: for instance, "Repetition", in which two estranged lovers try to re-enact their first meeting, or "Measurements", in which a man separated from his wife looks over the rooftops he sees from his window.

I would like to comment on only two of these stories. "Scatter-Brains" introduces a wonderfully vapid society woman, "absolutely incapable of concentration" as she herself puts it, who in her conversation flits from topic to topic so that in the end everything is reduced to the same uniform level. She invites a friend, Sofia, to come to see her because she has something important to tell her. But in the conversational stream of consciousness with which she greets Sofia, she forgets the important thing she wanted to tell. Only when Sofia is already at the door, ready to leave, does she suddenly remember and she hurriedly blurts out that her (Sofia's) husband is unfaithful. Later that evening, Sofia tells her husband that she has learned something important, but . . . "It's no use. I've forgotten it, and it's useless for you, with your usual morbid curiosity, to try and find out what it was . . . I've forgotten it and there's nothing to be done about it." The story is amusing: the description of the scatterbrain quite brilliant, the final note ironic. The reader is left wondering why the wife forgot: was it a ruse to avoid telling her husband something unpleasant, or has she really forgotten, numbed by the silly patter of her friend? Obviously Moravia's treatment of the theme is radically different from what it would have been in nineteenth-century fiction, where a discovery of this kind would have led to dramatic action or tearful resignation – at any rate, to the test and revelation of character. Moravia is saying, in substance, and all the stories in The Fetish bear this out, that modern life has dulled the sense of personal identity to the point that a woman in Sofia's predicament is more likely to mimic unconsciously the reactions of a friend who is personally uninvolved, than to take a stand on her own.

The story "Measurements" is one of Moravia's contributions to chosisme, Robbe-Grillet's poetics of objects. The man looking at the rooftop opposite his window is an engineer and there is thus some slight justification for his abnormal tendency to want to measure mentally all

the different structures which have with time been built on the roof.
One day, leafing through Casanova's Memoirs, he comes upon a passage in which the Venetian adventurer makes a similar mathematical
description of the objects he sees from his prison cell at the Piombi.
Moravia's protagonist remarks, however, that Casanova, who was
planning his escape, had good reason to be interested in these details,
while his own observations are "purposeless, inexplicable, absurd".
Earlier he had also noted that the objects about which he was so
passionately curious are the very things that form "the fixed, incom-
prehensible background of every life", that as long as life goes on they
go unnoticed, but that as soon as life stops they reveal themselves.
Awareness of their presence, then, is a symptom of stasis, death, of
the imprisonment to which modern man is condemned. If with "Scatter-
Brains" Moravia commented on the disappearance of emotions, with
"Measurements" he shows that even the ability to perceive has been
attenuated, for his protagonist sees not the distinguishing features of
the scene opposite him – the turrets and stairs and balconies, man-
made objects with their historically conditioned styles – but abstract
compositional lines, distances, and relationships.

Narrative formulas predominate in the Roman tales as they do in
The Fetish, but local colour somewhat redeems them. It is a special
kind of local colour, emphasizing not the quaint and the original, but
the usual and the typical. But where the emblematic couples of The
Fetish merge into one joyless, gray mass, the garage mechanics and
cab drivers, the movie house cashiers and country bumpkins, the
chambermaids and waiters of the Roman tales have greater élan, are
quick to recover from setbacks, and live carefree lives, knowing that
tomorrow will bring its own golden opportunities. Though Moravia, in
theorizing about these stories, lumped their characters together under
the common denominator of economic man, the Marxian archetype
driven by necessity, the reader cannot help recognizing in them the
classic comic types: pranksters and tricksters with their foolish victims, bumblers and small-time crooks, gullible girls and neighbourhood gallants. Moreover, they are descendants of the skeptical and
colourful Roman populace of the past which had already left its mark
in literature through the bright dialect poetry of Belli and Trilussa.
As stories, the Roman tales are often simple faits divers, human
interest news items raised to the level of "art" through the addition of
a punch line which serves to make the ironies of life explicit. They
resemble nothing so much as the earliest examples of contes and dits,
where we find the same strong grounding of the story in a definite
social reality, the same concise delineation and revelation of character, the same quick smile which attests to the success of the final
effect. Read one by one, as a kind of daily ration of literature for
readers of the Corriere della sera, the Roman tales have their own
slight charm. But it would be difficult to claim for them any more

serious significance.

Claiming serious significance for his work is what Moravia has of late
been busying himself with more and more frequently. In the same interview to which we referred at the beginning, he was quoted as saying that today two groups, the crowd and the intellectuals, divide all
modern life between them: "The day of the crowd is all accident; the
day of the intellectual is all philosophy." Accident is of course also
what feeds fiction, and as the interest-sustaining plots of his novels
and short stories prove, Moravia has a fine eye for accident. Philosophy, on the other hand, or the will to philosophy (a more appropriate
formulation in the case of Moravia), has at most a tangential relation
to fiction. Of course, stories signify; they have meaning; often they
have several possible meanings from which the reader can select the
one that suits him best. But the narrator implants the meaning as he
is telling the story, and does not normally need to add a running commentary as well. Moravia, instead, is suffering from a kind of nervous
insecurity which compels him to compete with the critics of his works.
This, too, is not an uncommon phenomenon, especially in the careers
of writers whose work spans long periods of time and whose success
insures wide attention. Pirandello discovered a new dimension to his
writing after Tilgher had pointed it out to him, and from that moment
Pirandellism was born. I do not know who played the same role for
Moravia, but I would not be surprised if some future thorough study
of his work should reveal a similar moment for the birth of Moravia-
nism. It is not without significance, for instance, that Moravia should
have said over and over again that The Time of Indifference "was not
a reaction against anything", that it did not represent an ideological
position, that it was simply a novel and that is all. Yet, at some point
he developed the need and the desire to anchor his work in an explicit
ideology, to place it within a framework which would give each separate novel and story the dignity of belonging to a massive, organically
conceived œuvre, a kind of Comédie or Recherche. Thus he named
Freud and Marx as the two thinkers who guided him in his study of
society. This is not the place to examine how and to what extent this
is true. But there can be no doubt that, given the cultural environment
of the postwar era, he chose well. Freud and Marx are so firmly em-
bedded in contemporary intellectual and pseudo-intellectual life that by
naming them, Moravia could be sure of finding broad and well established sympathies for his position.
    This is essentially why I take issue with him. His intellectual dis-
coveries are pseudo-discoveries. With Agostino and Luca, he brought
his contribution to the European novel of adolescence which had had its
heyday several decades earlier. With The Woman of Rome and especially with Two Women and the Roman Tales, he "went toward the
people", thus imitating and following in the footsteps of the neorealists.

With The Conformist, he added his indictment of the Fascist mentality to works like Pratolini's A Hero of Our Time. With Conjugal Love and A Ghost at Noon, he joined in the belated discovery of psychoanalysis by the Italian upper classes. With The Empty Canvas and The Fetish, he wrote his own commentary on alienation and existentialism. With The Lie, he joined forces with those writers and critics who claim that the traditional novel is dead because analysis has taken the place of spontaneous inventiveness, because the writer can no longer be sure that his perception of reality is authentic, and not falsified by his subjective feelings, his mental world.

That leaves the early works. For many Italians, who have a clearer view of Moravia's development than foreigners who came to know him avec retard, he continues to be primarily the author of The Time of Indifference, and it is with that work that he is considered to have won his place in the literary Pantheon. Yet, if you press his admirers for a statement of the merits of The Time of Indifference, they will be able to tell you little more than that it was a forerunner, written long before it became the accepted thing to speak with scathing hardness about the inner decay of the middle class. Of course, even this claim is not quite true, for if no one else, then surely Pirandello had portrayed the crumbling values of the bourgeois world earlier, and had done so with greater poignancy and absoluteness than Moravia would ever be capable of.

In short, I feel that in spite of his success in terms of market value and notoriety, Moravia's case has not yet been proved. It is not an easy case, for his work which is traditional in structure and unimaginative in language will never benefit from the prestige-giving attention of "close" reading. Nor do his own dogmatic statements help, for they underline rather than mitigate its shortcomings. Moravia has by and large been unable to renew himself. In avoiding an answer to the question cited at the beginning of this article, he was unintentionally implying just that. But because it is a difficult insight for a writer to come to terms with - and Moravia is a writer, a born storyteller - he has often been tempted to find the new direction of which the interviewers spoke, in retrospect.

(1968)

NOTES

(1) Alberto Moravia, The Lie, trans. Angus Davidson (New York, 1966) and The Fetish and Other Stories, trans. Angus Davidson (New York, 1965).
(2) In this respect Moravia returns to a subject long identified with Gide, whose Les Faux-Monnayeurs (with the complementary Journal

des Faux-Monnayeurs) is called to mind by The Lie.
(3) Davidson translates "il nulla", applied here to the sex act, as "a nullity" (20), a restriction of Moravia's meaning which I find it difficult to justify.
(4) I have translated this passage myself rather than use Davidson's translation because the latter is a classic example of the unintentional deformation of meaning brought about by the substitution of one metaphor for another. Davidson's translation reads: "A novel? And what sort of novel is it?" "It's the story of a man who, all of a sudden, decides to become involved." "To become involved in what?" "In what's happening under his nose." . . . . "And what does he do then?" "He does nothing." "How do you mean?" "Nothing. He is content to look on." "To look on at what?" "To look on at the things he sees." "But looking on isn't enough." "Why isn't it enough?" "Because a character in a novel has to act." "My character doesn't wish to act." "Why doesn't he wish to act?" "Because he has no reason to act, whereas he has many reasons for looking on." (261-262) It is obvious that the idea of "becoming involved" which in the translation replaces the idea of "paying attention" brings with it the need for a number of additional adjustments. But the most fascinating revelation of this passage is that Davidson had to omit entirely the exchange (immediately following what has been quoted) which refers to the title of the book. It was obviously impossible to introduce the concept of the novelist as liar into this very crucial description of the novelist as looker.
(5) A translation of The Time of Indifference, under the title The Indifferent Ones, had been published by Dutton in 1932; Arthur Livingston's translation of Mistaken Ambitions had been published under the title Wheel of Fortune by Viking in 1937.

GADDA, PASOLINI, AND EXPERIMENTALISM: FORM OR IDEOLOGY?

The subject of this essay is threefold – threefold precisely in the sense which the title implies in simply juxtaposing the names of two writers and a concept rather than relating them more closely at a deeper level. To do full justice to the complex development of Carlo Emilio Gadda, to the equally complex but entirely different development of Pier Paolo Pasolini, and to the multiple aspects of linguistic and structural experimentation in modern Italian literature, three distinct and quite extensive studies would be required.

The connection between Gadda and Pasolini is not genetic. Although to the hasty reader the two are united by their rejection of the traditional literary language and their tapping of the dialect resources of Italy, it cannot truly be maintained that the older writer is a necessary premise for the younger, as Virgil was for Dante, Mallarmé for Valéry or Shakespeare for Manzoni. Pasolini's work, which ranges from lyric to philosophical poetry, from political to literary journalism, from travel reports to film scenarios, is not patterned on the example – the Italians would say "the lesson" – of Gadda, who made his debut in 1926 in the pages of the review Solaria with literary essays and narrative fragments that owe much to the hermeticism of that time.

But though the connection is not a genetic one, it exists. And it exists primarily by virtue of the concept of experimentalism. The term was first used by the Romance philologist Gianfranco Contini in his studies of early Italian literature. (1) It was then chosen by Pasolini to describe an important, and to him determining, aspect of the poetic production of the fifties. And finally it was adopted by the new avant-garde, the so-called Gruppo 63. This group of writers – this "new literary generation", as their mentor Luciano Anceschi called them – first gathered together in 1963 at a noisy literary congress in Palermo which reminded many of the participants of the fuss and fanfare raised half a century earlier by the futurists. The writers of Gruppo 63 were convinced that, as one of their exponents put it, the literature of the future would be marked by experimentation with form and not with subject matter, that is, by a new use of the means of expression rather than by raising to literary dignity – as was done in naturalism, for instance – subjects that had formerly been avoided. Angelo Guglielmi, one of the theoreticians of the group, wrote:

Up to now language has tried to reflect reality as in a mirror. Henceforth language must take its place at the very heart of reality and instead of being a mirror must become a faithful recording machine. Or, as a second solution, language must

remain outside and look in at reality as through a filter, so
that objects will appear in distorted, surrealistic, or halluci-
natory images and forms, and thus once again be capable of
revealing their hidden meanings. (2)

In the new literature, then, and in the experimental novel, as it was
soon to be called, language would no longer state and describe, but
mimic and express. Pasolini made a similar distinction in the 1956
article "Il neo-sperimentalismo" referred to above, when he opposed
the "stylistic syndrome of the new 'committed' writers" to "pathological, expressionistic neo-experimentalism". (3) But while both uses of
language, the mimetic and the expressionistic, appear true and revolutionary innovations with respect to its conventional use in narrative to reflect the chronology of events in terms of logical discourse,
only the second, the expressionistic, actually represents a total subversion of the accepted social and psychological structures. Only the
expressionistic use of language concerns itself, in the words of another critic, with "the perceptual level, with the way in which time
and space are conceived, how objects are seen, how feelings are
recognized and designated, how syntax is articulated". (4) Or to return
to the connection between Gadda and Pasolini, only Gadda - for reasons
that I hope will become clear in the course of this essay - is recognized
by the new avant-garde, whether it thinks of itself as politically committed or uncommitted, as a true and authentic forerunner.

There are certain obvious differences between Gadda and Pasolini, a
consideration of which will, I believe, place the discussion of their
work in a better perspective. The first - and it is no mean one - concerns the generation to which each belongs. Gadda was born in 1893;
Pasolini, in 1922. Both, upon reaching manhood, found themselves on
the threshold of war. But though some historians like to link the two
World Wars, seeing in the second merely a continuation of the first,
they were in fact quite dissimilar, both in the manner of fighting and
in the changes which each brought to the social environment. Gadda
fought in the First World War; he was captured and spent a long time
in a prison camp made famous in the history of Italian literature because he had as barracks mates Ugo Betti, destined to become Italy's
most important playwright after Pirandello, and Bonaventura Tecchi,
who became a writer and scholar of repute and held the chair of
German literature at the University of Rome until his death in 1968.
During his early years Gadda witnessed and lived through that collapse
of old and well-established values which characterizes the transition
period between the nineteenth and early twentieth centuries. The world
that is reflected in most of his works is that of the stable fin de siècle
bourgeoisie, specifically of the Milanese upper classes - whose children were taken to play in the park of the Castello; who were con-

cerned with keeping their houses in immaculate order; who built summer
villas among the hills of the Brianza, the gentle countryside north of
Milan immortalized by Manzoni; and whose family memories included
the still vivid recollections of Hapsburg rule, felt not so much finished
and done with as simply removed in time.

Pasolini, instead, spent his childhood following his army officer
father from one military post in northern Italy to another. In 1943
while he was studying at the University of Bologna, he was evacuated,
as were thousands of other civilians all over Europe. He was sent to
Casarsa, the village in the Friuli from which his mother came. There,
in that northeastern corner of Italy close to the Yugoslav border, he
watched the Partisan warfare, which was as distinctive of the later
years of the Second World War in occupied Europe as trench warfare
had been of the First. Pasolini's earliest works were poems in Friulian,
inspired by his love for the simple, instinctive peasant life of a rural
region that progress had bypassed, the same region that a century
earlier served as the setting for Nievo's wonderful contes champêtres.
But Pasolini's interest in dialect poetry was not limited to his practice
of it. A number of essays attest to his broader view, and in 1955 he
published an important anthology of Italian dialect poetry, Canzoniere
italiano. Its long introductory essay combines scholarly competence
with a Marxian interpretation of the relationship of folk and art poetry,
dwelling on the reasons for the progressive disappearance of folk poetry
in the awakening class consciousness of the backward peasant popu-
lations on their way to urban proletariat status. Marxism, of course,
is a doctrine that played no role in the formation of Gadda, whose whole
orientation was away from the political and economic problems of society and toward those of the individual and collective psyche. Indeed,
in the figures of Freud and Marx, we have as good symbols as any to
epitomize the historico-cultural differences in the situation we have
been discussing.

The second difference between Gadda and Pasolini concerns their
temperaments. There seems to be something eternally young in Pasolini, and this impression is borne out by his restless seeking for always
new avenues of expression: from poetry to militant journalism, from
the novel to cinema. Gadda, by contrast, was born old, old and weary,
with a tendency to pessimism, to bitter humor, to foreseeing catas-
trophes and therefore treading lightly. In the self-portrait which Pasolini contributed in 1960 to a volume of autobiographies by contemporary
Italian writers, he speaks of his daily routine, and especially of his
tireless wanderings through Rome, the city to which he moved in 1950:

> I spend the greater part of my life beyond the edges of the city,
> or as a bad neorealist poet imitating the hermetics would say,
> beyond the city's end-stations. I love life with such violence
> and such intensity that no good can come of it. I am speaking

of the physical side of life: the sun, the grass, youth. It is an addiction more terrible than cocaine. It doesn't cost anything, and it is available in boundless quantites. I devour it ravenously . . . . How it will all end, I don't know . . . . (5)

In his contribution to the same volume, Gadda wrote:

By temperament I am rather inclined to solitude, incapable as I am of chattering vivaciously, uninterested in mundane social life. I approach my fellow men and associate with them with a certain amount of difficulty and hesitation; the hesitation and difficulty increase, the more virtuous they are. In the presence of another human being I feel like a student at an examination. Instead, in my leisure hours I take pleasure in clarifying some "algebra" to myself. This tires me less than a drawing-room conversation where I am forced to appear witty and intelligent without being either. (6)

The juxtaposition of the two passages suggests that we are dealing with two personalities that would have manifested opposite characteristics even if the external circumstances of their lives had been identical. Gadda and Pasolini were not only born into different historical times; they were born as two completely different psychological types. The two facts that psychoanalytically inclined critics would pounce on and magnify – that Gadda and Pasolini both lost a dearly loved and not easily forgotten older brother through war, and that each had a typically ambivalent relation to his parents – turn out to be insignificant and nondetermining in the light of the broad attitudes toward life which make the one man a misanthrope and the other – if I may be permitted to give the word its etymological meaning – a philanthrope. This divergence in basic personality traits is of necessity reflected in the manner in which each faces his task as a writer.

During one of his trips to the United States, the novelist Italo Calvino told of a radio talk on the building industry which Gadda was once asked to give. It seems that he spoke first, with scientific precision, of houses built of reinforced concrete and how it is impossible to insulate them against noise. He then went on to the physiological effects of noise on the nervous system. And finally in a display of verbal fireworks he burst forth against the noises of city life themselves. (7) A similar mounting progression is recalled by Gadda in the self-portrait from which I quoted earlier. He speaks there of the many "philosophical meditations", all written in excellent prose (i.e., conventional style), which he has stored away at home and which are survivals of a time when he had not yet devoted himself to narrative writing. He then mentions the effects the experience of the war had on him: how because of it he turned from philosophy to the vicissitudes of human life and found himself torn between a strong predisposition to give expression exclusively to his lyric and satirical veins and an equally strong desire to understand his fellow men by ''noting down events''. Finally he acknowledges that for him writing is often a means of "seeking vengeance" for the injuries inflicted on men by fate: "So that my storytelling often manifests the resentful tone of the person who speaks while holding back his wrath, his indignation." The anecdote and the self-analysis reveal that Gadda did not choose the narrative style which is most closely associated with his name because he was incapable of expressing himself in any other way. Rather he chose it – or it chose him, a formulation closer, as we shall see, to his view of the polarization of tensions which determines the relationship between the writer and his subject – because it alone could give shape to the nouminous reality, that "algebra" of the universe, which he pursues. On this last point, it might be fruitful to consider carefully the answer Gadda gave when in 1950 he was asked for his opinion on the then triumphant school of neorealism. He voiced his lack of sympathy for its basic assumptions in these terms:

> It is all well and good to tell me that a volley of machine gun fire is reality. But what I expect from the novel is that behind those seven ounces of lead there be some tragic tension, some consecution at work, a mystery, perhaps the reason for the fact, or the absence of reasons . . . . The fact by itself, the object by itself, is but the dead body of reality, the – pardon the expression – fecal residue of history. I would therefore want the poetics of neorealism to be extended to include a nouminous dimension. (8)

The search for the nouminous dimension is what gives its peculiar form to Eros e Priapo (Da furore a cenere) (1967). In spite of what the jacket blurb claims, this is not an antinovel – except if we are ready to make of this expression a catchall for everything that we cannot define otherwise; nor is it a piece of historical writing, history being the complement to fiction as a narrative mode. Eros e Priapo, an indictment of the Fascist era, might be called a psychoanalysis of history, conceived as a scientific research problem with theorems and propositions, but conducted with a virulence and an emotional involvement which allow for no other conclusion than the one already implied in the premise. Specifically, it is an exposé of the pathology of exhibitionistic narcissism and its effects on an audience (in this case the Italian people under Fascism), seen with the devastating clarity and single-mindedness of an individual who could never be a consenting and participating member of that audience. Early in the book Gadda states that his purpose in writing it is to induce self-

knowledge, for "only an act of knowledge can bring about the resurrection of the Italian people, if indeed resurrection can even be at-
tempted from so horrendous a ruin".

The two novels of Gadda's I am about to discuss also deal with knowledge. The first is a detective novel manqué, which means that the
quest for the specific knowledge which is its objective is eventually
foiled. The second proclaims by its very title that knowledge is its
subject, and it is in fact a meditation on anguish and not the drama-
tization of that feeling through a story. Both novels can also be said
to deal with ruin, "frenzy and ashes". In the first, crime upsets the
social order and allows all the baseness and vileness that usually lie
hidden under the mantle of convention to rise to the surface. In the
second, it is mental disease, il male oscuro (the dark evil), which
muddies the waters and breaches that moral order which appeases the
savage drives in man and makes civilized living possible. In neither
novel do we reach the stage of "resurrection", that is, of catharsis.
They are both unfinished, perhaps unfinishable.

The German avant-garde writer, Günter Grass, has described Quer
pasticciaccio brutto de via Merulana (1957) as "the only crime novel I
enjoyed and admired". Although I consider the book less interesting
and powerful than Gadda's other novel, La cognizione del dolore (1963),
I shall discuss it first and at greater length because its setting is Rome,
a city which is familiar to the foreigner and which can thus serve as a
point of orientation in an otherwise labyrinthine and surreal representation of a particular social reality.

As I have already said, Quer pasticciaccio is a murder mystery
whose author fails to give the reader the satisfaction of telling him
what really happened and of identifying the criminal. Actually there
are two crimes involved: a jewelry theft, which is the occasion for
high comedy, and a horrible murder, which opens the gates to the
nether world, represented simultaneously as the social underworld
and the psychological abyss of uncontrolled passion. The two crimes
are related externally because they both take place on the same third-
floor landing of the apartment house at 219 via Merulana, a building
which is known to the neighbouring proletariat (and try translating
even as simple a phrase as "la gente der popolo" without losing its
full flavor!) as the palace of gold. The internal connection between
the crimes is that they both lead to the same group of suspects. These
individuals, all mysteriously associated with one another, belong to
the rural population of Latium, the countryside of Sabine fame sur-
rounding Rome, a unique kind of suburbia which appears in the opening
pages of the book as the luxuriant home of a prolific people and is seen
in the final pages as a gray landscape of abject hovels housing the
lowest kind of vice and deception.

There is no central character in the novel, although readers in
search of the accustomed "hero" may think they discern him in

Francesco Ingravallo, familiarly known as Don Ciccio. Ingravallo, a
police officer assigned to the homicide squad, is on hand in the first
and last scenes of the book and is otherwise omnipresent as the man
in charge of the investigation. But on closer scrutiny it becomes apparent that though Gadda represents him in all his human complexity,
he is actually using him as a screen through which his own, Gadda's,
observations and ideas are filtered. The information we are given
about Ingravallo's background and inner life, although revealed in a
kind of running inner monologue which taps the depth of his consciousness, is of the most generic sort. His idolization of Liliana Balducci,
for instance, the murdered woman whom he had known, is no more
than the respect felt by the social inferior for gentility of manner and
of being. His gift for intuition is the indispensable detective's flair
for discovering what is hidden. His sensual appreciation of the physical attractions of the Balduccis' bevy of "nieces" and maids is the
typical reaction of a youngish man of thirty-five living amid the sensual seductions of Rome. Like the "new" French novelists, Gadda
eschews psychological analysis, while he dwells on the "atoms" of
mental activity. Much of the action of Quer pasticciaccio is seen
through the eyes of Ingravallo - a familiar procedure in the modern
novel - but Ingravallo himself is not an object of observation for the
author. His portrait and his story are never finished. He is essentially
a filtering consciousness, an instrument of knowledge.
   The instrumental use of the principal character and its importance
for the structure of the book become even clearer in the light of two
statements made by Gadda in two very different contexts. The first is
an exposition of Ingravallo's theory of crime. It comes at the beginning of the novel, but only in retrospect do we realize how strategical-
ly it is placed, for only in retrospect do we see it as the necessary, if
camouflaged, direction signal that it is:

> He [Ingravallo] sustained among other things that unforeseen
> catastrophes are never the consequence or the effect, if you
> prefer, of a single motive, of a cause singular; but they are
> rather like a whirlpool, a cyclonic point of depression in the
> consciousness of the world, towards which a whole multitude
> of converging causes has contributed. He also used words
> like knot or tangle or muddle, or gnommero, which in Roman
> dialect means skein.

The second passage deals with the personality in general and Gadda's
personality as a writer in particular. It occurs in an article, "Come
lavoro", which Gadda contributed to a literary periodical in 1950 and
which is now part of his important collection of essays, I viaggi la
morte (1958). Expressing himself in terms which are curiously reminiscent of and at times identical with those of the passage above,

Gadda writes:

> Each of us seems to me to be a lump or knot or tangle of
> physical and metaphysical relationships (the distinction is
> merely operational). Every relationship is kept suspended
> and in equipoise, within the "field" that is proper to it, by
> a polarity of tensions . . . . The act of self-expression - of
> writing - is the result, or better the sympton of that polar-
> ization which occurs between the "I" that judges and the thing
> judged, between the "I" that represents and the thing rep-
> resented.

It is obvious on the strength of the passages just quoted that Gadda rejects both the traditional notion of the logical coherence of the personality and the equally traditional (Romantic) image of the artist as a
creator. The result of this position is that in telling his story Gadda
cannot pursue an overall linear development in which events are related to one another consecutively and logically. Instead, he will pursue
each event in depth, each one being, as he has said, a juncture of
causes which are in their turn tangles of other causes, large and small,
whose relative significance it is impossible to extricate. Thus Commen-
datore Angeloni's preference in food - the hams, marinated herring,
or jellied chicken mold he has delivered to his door - assumes at one
point the same importance as Signora Balducci's ambiguous attachment
to the girls she befriends or her equally ambiguous relationship to her
nephew, or so at least the latter seems to the suspicious Ingravallo.
But how can we, readers who are outside the story, determine here
and elsewhere how much of what Ingravallo "observes" is actually a
fabrication of his "intuition" and how much of what Gadda tells us is
actually essential to the plot - if plot indeed there is? In Quer pasticciaccio, though the reader is never directly addressed, he is constantly drawn into the story as a participant. Over and over again, the
pieces of the puzzle are placed in his hands and he is left to do with
them what he can. If only he were able to free himself of the inveterate
habit of "reading on", of letting scenes passively unroll before him!
For what he should be doing at every turn is "sink into" the page,
pursuing each fact, each phenomenon through all the associations
available to him, just as the author is doing on his part and Ingravallo
(standing for the whole corps of detectives) is doing in exemplary
fashion on his. It can readily be seen that no subject is better suited to
this kind of storytelling than the murder mystery. The green scarf of
the delivery boy (but was he a delivery boy?), the punched tram ticket
(when and by whom was it lost?) seem to urge the plot on. But the investigation bogs down and the plot breaks off. Tired, hungry, and
stupefied, Ingravallo sits at police headquarters, sunk in his musings.
The "mystery" is all about us. Gadda, being a scientist (he worked for

many years as an electrical engineer), belonging to the race of post-metaphysical man, rejects the mystical and the supernatural. But the irrational, the subnatural or supernatural, takes its revenge and presents him with an epistemological problem. And so he creates Ingravallo, a detective whose business it is to ferret out knowledge and whose fate it is to remain ignorant.

It is legitimate at this point to ask whether Quer pasticciaccio, in addition to being read as a metaphor - a giant emblem for the human condition, similar in this to the Divine Comedy, for instance - also lends itself to a naturalistic reading as the depiction of a particular society at a well-established moment in history. The book's ready success, its translations in spite of the linguistic difficulties posed by its stylistic texture, would appear to point in the direction of an affirmative answer. There is no doubt, for instance, that the setting is conceived realistically, even though as in The Magic Mountain, for example, it can easily be turned into symbol. In Quer pasticciaccio we are in Rome, in February 1927, amid the nouveau riche created by the First World War. The financial success of these "sharks", to use a favorite expression of that time, has whet the appetite of the lower classes, who, as in the building at 219 via Merulana, surround and enviously watch them. Every once in a while a choice morsel falls from the tables of the rich: Liliana Balducci's childlessness (a fault in nature) leads her to heap gifts on the young and healthy who can be presumed to bear children. We are in Rome also because we recognize the familiar landmarks: the basilica of Santa Maria Maggiore, the elephant on Piazza della Minerva, the open-air market in Piazza Vittorio, the Collegio Romano, the Villa Borghese . . . and on and on. There is hardly a page without a place name; although we must note that because Gadda does not favor description, these words remain ends in themselves, evocative simply because words are magic formulas, incantations. We are in Rome because of the peculiar quality of its air, its luminous sky, the strolling of its citizens at dusk, the marketing housewives with their bulging shopping bags - how delighted Gadda is by the leafy celery and the broccoli that stick out of them! The humble, everyday life of the Urbs, quite unique in the world. And finally we are in the Rome that is the paradise of bureaucracy, ruled over by the hated "Lantern Jaw, the bowler-hatted Death's Head, the Emir with black fez, and with plume", - by Mussolini in short, to note only a few of the epithets with which Gadda heaps scorn on him.

Much has been made of the violence of Gadda's attacks on Mussolini, of the ferocious inventiveness with which he fixes on always new features of the Duce's personality. This is taken to be an indication of the book's firm location in a definite political environment. I do not question Gadda's anti-Fascism, but am inclined to attribute it, more than to political idealism and thereby applicable to a specific historical setting, to the reactions of a highly individualistic, self-centered man, who feels his jealously guarded inner life <u>constantly</u> in danger of being impinged upon. It is this fear, which often reaches the proportions of a persecution complex, that triggers passages such as the three-page footnote in the original version of the novel (later omitted), where Gadda lashes out at the regime's desire to see everyone married and busy contributing to the demographic campaign. With an explosion of historical, often very amusing, references to famous men who remained bachelors (Beethoven, Petrarch, Saint Augustine, Stendhal, Kant - he names at least fifty) and to other equally famous men who married to their discomfiture and eternal regret (Agamemnon, Napoleon, Shakespeare, Stalin, Peter Petrovich, who was strangled on orders from his wife Catherine the Great, etc., etc.), Gadda makes his plea for being permitted to remain what he elsewhere calls "a solitary glutton, unmarried and melancholy, and subject to fits of cyclothymia".

We are back then where we started. For all its being rooted in historical and geographical reality, <u>Quer pasticciaccio</u> is a novel that has left naturalism behind. Not that Gadda's imagination is not nature-bound, as is attested by his strongly concrete and sensual vocabulary. As a matter of fact, he seems to take contact with the world almost exclusively through the senses. His verbal ingenuity, his creative facility, remind one often of the physical pleasure of "mouthing" words, an extension of the joys of the palate, of his self-confessed gluttony. There is a magnificent passage, an unforgettable episode in <u>La cognizione del dolore</u> which shows the principal character gorging himself on an enormous lobster. It is carried off with such Rabelaisean gusto that it reveals the hand of the man both attracted and repelled, but essentially fascinated, by "oral" excess. Excess of this kind leads inevitably to deformation, and the world Gadda writes about is deformed by his singular, eccentric - I am tempted to say, in this connection, esthetic as opposed to moralistic - vision. In this sense Gadda has gone well beyond naturalism in its literary-historical definition. Like the expressionists in the very years when he began to write, he must have felt at one time that it was senseless to set about "reproducing" the world as it is, that it was indeed impossible to do so, given the absence of any permanent rapport between the individual and reality.

Much of what we have said about <u>Quer pasticciaccio</u> also holds true for <u>La cognizione</u>, but generally to a more concentrated degree. <u>Quer pasticciaccio</u> is an unfinished work; <u>La cognizione</u> is not only unfinished but also fragmentary. In <u>Quer pasticciaccio</u> the creation of suspense inherent in the detective story is constantly undercut by the author's pursuit of the verbal and other associations that come his way. In <u>La cognizione</u> the story line at one point breaks down completely. (It is taken up again in Part Two, both parts of the book dealing with the same subject matter in a manner somewhat reminiscent of Faulkner's

The Sound and the Fury.) Quer pasticciaccio goes deep into the amalgam of petty crime, violence, and unspoken wrongs; La cognizione adds to these the horror of unresolved guilt. In Quer pasticciaccio the setting is not only recognizable as Rome, it actually is Rome; in La cognizione the setting is recognizable as Lombardy, but is actually, within the fiction of the book, the imaginary South American country of Maradagàl. In Quer pasticciaccio the principal character, who is searching for the nouminous reality of life, is a stand-in for the author; in La cognizione the principal character is even closer to being the author himself (he is a war veteran, has lost a brother in the war, and suffers from a mysterious malady which renders life bitter and unendurable), although he hides under the fictional identity of Gonzalo Pirobutirro d'Eltino, hidalgo and engineer of Maradagàl. La cognizione has one quality which Quer pasticciaccio lacks: it is a book about suffering, and its vehemence is therefore frequently softened to elegy. It is a more human book, built around a truly tragic if monstrous character.

More even than Quer pasticciaccio it is a book for connoisseurs, with hardly a word in it that is not intended to call to mind another word, to refer to some cultural or literary experience of Italian history. While the ordinary reader can approach the Rome of Quer pasticciaccio, find his way in it, and move among familiar monuments, only a learned and sophisticated reader will be able to identify in the landscape of Maradagàl not merely the landscape of the Brianza, but the landscape of the Brianza as seen in Manzoni's I promessi sposi. Failure to note connections such as this one would seriously impede not only the comprehension but the enjoyment of the book. It is essential, for instance, that in the passage which describes the mountain Serruchòn(9) the reader be able to detect beneath Gadda's words the counterpoint of Manzoni's description of the same – or is it another? – mountain, the Resegone. Gadda plants an open clue by referring to the Resegone by name; but it is not sufficient to recognize the source intellectually, it must also be savored esthetically by "close" and expert reading. La cognizione del dolore is a book that clamors for an annotated edition, to make explicit its wonderful richness of references, its extraordinary abundance. The English translator of Quer pasticciaccio, William Weaver, has done something of this in his edition of That Awful Mess. Unfortunately, his explanatory notes are limited almost exclusively to historical and political references, thus magnifying the element of anti-Fascist satire which is present in the book, but which by this treatment receives undue emphasis at the expense of the subtler, more literary aspects of the work of this most literary, most idiosyncratic and socially alienated of contemporary Italian writers.

In reviewing Quer pasticciaccio in 1958, (10) Pasolini recognized in it

a stylistic versatility which, he said, would make a critic like Spitzer
as exhilarated - and the comparison is his - as a mouse in a hunk of
cheese. Pasolini analyzed briefly four basically different uses of dialect in the book; pointed to the extraordinary range of its syntactical
forms, even coining the word hypertaxis to place beside the more
usual parataxis and hypotaxis for describing Gadda's "monstrous
syntactical jungle"; and compared Manzoni's and Gadda's use of tenses
as keys to their respective narrative techniques. As can be seen, his
is a most competent and expert approach, a far cry from the run-of-
the-mill practice of journalistic reviewing, which looks for little more
than a novel's relationship to everyday reality. As a reader of Gadda,
Pasolini certainly ranks with the best. In an earlier review of a collection of Gadda short stories, Novelle dal Ducato in fiamme, (11) he
had surveyed, again with economy and concentration, the nineteenth-
and twentieth-century literary precedents to which Gadda owes aspects
of his style: the "art prose" movement of the twenties, which treated
prose as though it were poetry and against which specifically the neorealists reacted; Verga's "narrated interior monologue"; Manzoni's
continuing orientation to the Lombard components of his culture, even
under the surface aspiration to national unity; the social satire and
irony of the Roman dialect poet Belli; and the post-Romantic avant-
garde movement of the Piedmontese and Lombard scapigliati, whose
truly revolutionary experimentation with linguistic and literary forms
is barely beginning to be studied. In view of the breadth and depth of
Pasolini's understanding of Gadda and of his admiration for what he
calls "that very great mind and heart", it is all the more interesting
to note his formulation of the latter's shortcomings. I pass here from
the context of esthetics and literary craftsmanship to that of ideology
and from the novelist Gadda to the novelist Pasolini.

Speaking of Pasolini earlier, I referred briefly to the role played
by the Partisan movement in the formation of his basic sympathies
and convictions. The struggle for liberation from Fascism during the
later stages of the War was felt by the more idealistic and committed
of its exponents as the beginning of a new era in Italian history, the
harbinger of a social revolution which would finally wipe out all class
and regional inequalities. This feeling of buoyancy persisted in spite
of many disappointments and delays until roughly the time of the
Hungarian uprising, an event which seriously shook confidence in the
Communist solution to Italy's problems. Pasolini's political optimism,
nurtured in the successful defeat of Fascism, combined with his personal responsiveness to others and his acceptance of Marxism as a
unifying ideological structure for judging progress, enabled him to
focus on what he sees as the reactionary side of Gadda's position. In
the review of Quer pasticciaccio already mentioned, Pasolini presents
Gadda as simultaneously accepting and rejecting the social reality of
Italy as created by the middle classes in the wake of the Risorgimento.

The resultant ambivalence caused that feeling of despondent anguish and that "tragically mixed and obsessive style" which are the marks of Gadda's helpless and ever renewed fury at finding institutions which are potentially good turned into organizations which are actually bad. "Gadda belongs to an historical time", Pasolini concludes, "when it was impossible to see the world - this magma of disorder, corruption, hypocrisy, stupidity, and injustice - in a perspective of hope".

The full significance of this statement becomes apparent when we examine Pasolini's two novels, Ragazzi di vita (1955) and Una vita violenta (1959). In both Pasolini would like to see the world "in a perspective of hope" but both fall short of being true documents, the first of the "magma of disorder . . . and injustice" which must be destroyed, the second of the awakening of the social consciousness through which this destruction will be effected.

Ragazzi di vita is a novel because it deals with a group of fictional characters, the course of whose life we follow during a determined period of time. But it could just as easily be conceived of as a series of vignettes or episodes only loosely related to one another, whose main function is the representation of a milieu rather than the construction and revelation of a character. Ragazzi di vita came out at the height of the neorealistic vogue and was read at first as a document of the desperate conditions of the Roman subproletariat in the disconsolate slums springing up with unbelievable rapidity on the outskirts of the city.

The documentary aspect of the book appeared to be underlined by the glossary of dialect terms and underworld jargon which Pasolini provides at the end. To some readers the list seems incomplete and insufficient, although it is true, as Pasolini claims in his covering note, that comprehension of the story or of any one episode of it is not really impeded by the inability to translate into standard Italian every one of the rude, vulgar, obscene expressions which occur in the speech of its protagonists. Pasolini feels that no reader coming upon these words for the first time could fail to grasp their meaning through intuition of the context in which they are used. And indeed the dialogue which makes up so much of the book is little more than a string of curses, cries, expletives, urgings, exclamations - the typical "conversational" exchanges which occur when people do not speak to one another but simply, almost by the accident of propinquity, share common experiences.

Dialogue in novels has often been used to discuss important philosophical problems or to introduce the author's personal convictions. Nothing could be further from Pasolini's practice. His message is never entrusted to the words of his characters. Rather it is implicit in his representation of selected conditions, or, in some rare cases, in his own narrated third-person comment on what he is telling. Thus, for instance, there is an episode toward the end of Ragazzi di vita in which one of the protagonists returns to the factory area which had figured in the opening pages. Almost everything is changed: the buildings and grounds are now shining with cleanliness and order, and a new, unbroken wire fence surrounds them. Only the watchman's hut is still the same: it continues to be used as an abusive public latrine. "That was the only spot that Riccetto found familiar", Pasolini unobtrusively comments, "exactly as it was when the war had just ended".

The time span covered by Ragazzi di vita goes from the liberation of Rome in 1944 to the early fifties. Riccetto, who might be considered the principal character if for no other reason than that he is most frequently on stage, lives through the years of his adolescence: he is eleven and receiving his first communion when the story begins, eighteen and having served a three-year term in jail when it ends. In noting with precision the exact limits of the historical situation which serves as background, Pasolini is fulfilling one of the desiderata of the esthetics of neorealism, which calls for the concrete rooting of fiction in a definite and verifiable reality. But Ragazzi di vita is in no sense an historical novel. It has nothing of Pratolini's Metello (1956) where historical events are made part of the plot. Nor do historical events shape its story as they do, in however muted a manner, in Verga's I Malavoglia, for instance. Ragazzi di vita gives back the "colour" of a time only in an episodic, allusive manner. Thus we have in the early pages of the book the description of the pilfering of food and other necessities characteristic of day-to-day existence in occupied Rome. There is reference to the emergency housing of the homeless and the destitute - as a matter of fact, Riccetto's mother is killed in the collapse of an old school building which had been turned to this use. And there is the endless stream of "things", objects of all sorts from sewer lids to automobile tires to articles of furniture, which at one time or another fetched a good price on the market of stolen goods. We have, in other words, the landscape made familiar by films such as Bicycle Thief (1948), but without the underlying ethic of that film which dealt with a man's effort to make good, to find his place in society through his work. The protagonists of Ragazzi di vita do, from time to time, work. They somethimes have money, not necessarily honestly come by. And that money quickly slips out of their fingers again, for they do not consider it as a means of insuring security, of building a place for themselves in society - witness the amusing episode at Ostia, where the fifty thousand lire that Riccetto had just stolen from swindlers for whom he was working are with a Boccaccioesque twist in turn stolen from him.

The truth of the matter is that Riccetto and his friends are outsiders, typical juvenile delinquents unable and unwilling to make the compromises necessary to find their way into a social order, and that it is therefore difficult to consider their stories as representative of a

socio-historical condition. Though Ragazzi di vita can be read as a
Marxist indictment of the capitalist society which makes lives such
as it describes possible, it is in no way an example of socialist realism, for it sets up no exemplary hero who through his awareness
of the dynamics of social change can become the potential founder of
a new order. Ragazzi di vita is the representation of a nether world
no less absolute than that of Quer pasticciaccio. No broad and happy
road leads out of this world, toward that triumph of reason which
Marxist writers, mindful of their Enlightenment origins, like to
prognosticate.

But if the vision of the road leading to the transformed society is
missing in Ragazzi di vita, it is not because Pasolini, as we have
seen in his review of Quer pasticciaccio, does not consciously believe
in its existence. It is simply that he has lost sight of it while telling
his story, while exploring with loving attention the teeming life of the
Roman underworld. For that underworld has a vitality for him, a gay
insouciance, a forceful optimistic élan, a joie de vivre, that obscures
its horror. As one of the gang exults, referring to the company that
finds itself associated in petty crime one epic night at the Villa
Borghese: "Two from Tiburtino, one from Acqua Bullicante, two from
Primavalle, one deserter, and Picchio here from Valle dell'Inferno:
why, we could band together and found the League of the Wicked of
the Suburbs of Rome!" One hears echoes of the exploits of the Three
Musketeers, of the Chevaliers de la Table Ronde of ballad fame, of
all the merry bands that have roamed the face of the earth, reckless-
ly following where adventure called.

For the Rome of Ragazzi di vita is the great scenario of adventure,
a new carte du tendre without the tender sentiment of love but with
similarly compulsory stops. To ride the streetcars of Rome, having
just spent your last pennies for a ticket, is the beginning of adventure,
for you do not know with whom you will be rubbing elbows nor with
what you may end up in your pocket. To go for a swim in the yellow
waters of the Tiber is the beginning of adventure, for you do not know
whom you might meet nor what debris the sluggish water may bring
your way – perhaps only a bird on the verge of drowning, which on an
impulse you will save (a truly amazing episode at the end of Chapter
I). To help an old man steal a couple of cauliflowers from a sodden
field is the beginning of adventure, for he may invite you home to
meet his daughters . . . . And over and above it all, the sky of Rome
with its pastel shades at sunset and its brilliant moon at night. Pasolini's landscape descriptions are extraordinary, shocking the reader
as some pre-romantic landscapes do, with their feathery trees, their
majestic ruins, and a ragged beggar half hidden by a broken column:

By now, behind the low wall which overlooks the Tusculanum
neighbourhood like a terrace, beyond tennis fields and troddec

tracts of land, the sun was setting, warm and red, making
the windows shine on the pile of bluish buildings so that they
looked like some Martian landscape. On this side of the wall
against which Alduccio and the others were slouching indecent-
ly, the grounds of San Giovanni with their little flower beds
and trees spread out equally melancholy, touched by the last
rays of the sun which knocked up against the loggias and the
huge statues on the cathedral, giving a border of gold to the
red granite of the obelisk.

The first reviewers of Ragazzi di vita singled out its social nihilism
and its literary estheticism for special criticism. Pasolini's insistence on a monotonous and unrepresentative segment of the Roman
subproletariat seemed to them a deformation and a stylization of reality which went counter to the fundamental documentary intention of
neorealism. Moreover, an episode such as the one in which the
thoughts of a couple of mongrel dogs during a fight are recorded as
though spoken in the same dialect used by the human protagonists of
the book was cited as a clamorous instance of that flight from naturalistic objectivity to decadent self-indulgence which was also underlined by the picaresque aspects of the novel.
    In an essay on Italian dialect poetry which he had written some
years earlier, (12) Pasolini had already implicitly defended his narrative approach in Ragazzi di vita. In speaking of the Roman poet,
Gioacchino Belli, the nineteenth-century interpreter of the feelings
and opinions of the city's unruly populace, he emphasized, as many
other observers have done, the uniqueness of the Roman citizenry,
those descendants of the plebs of antiquity, who in the midst of splen-
did testimonials of their past have always lived and continue to live
outside of history, that is, outside the awareness and the dynamics
of change. For the ideal of progress conceived in terms of social
betterment, these people substitute the excitement of life lived exclusively for the moment, the happy-go-lucky acceptance of whatever
opportunities, however slight and brief, chance offers them. To represent this "aristocratic Roman proletariat" - the expression is
Pasolini's - in their saga of roguish adventure is thus, Pasolini
claimed, to reflect the "real" Rome, the Rome that rebels against
the political and economic structures of bourgeois society not by
taking a conscious position against them but by simply ignoring them.
And to use the Roman dialect to record the inner content of the fictional lives of these people (dialect is used only in the dialogue parts of
the book and in some rare cases of style indirect libre) is to apply
the general rule later formulated by Pasolini in his answer to a questionnaire on the novel sponsored by the periodical Nuovi argomenti:
"If the character and milieu chosen by the novelist are proletariat,
let him use dialect in part or wholly; if they are middle-class, let

him use the koiné. In this way he cannot go wrong. "(13) By koiné
Pasolini means the uniform, nondialect Italian usage of the petite
bourgeoisie as formed by the unification of Italy, or, to use Gramsci's
description, the language of the bureaucrats who effectively united
the new state at the administrative level but left the Italy of regions
and city districts virtually untouched. Ragazzi di vita, it should be
remembered, was written and is set in the period immediately preceding the new levelling and cohesive forces of Italy's "economic
miracle", which were to do so much to destroy the nation's com-
partmentalized subcultures and to turn large segments of its proletariat into a middle class - without, however, the contributions of
Marxism.

Pasolini's second novel, Una vita violenta, is in part an answer to
the more justified objections raised against Ragazzi di vita. Pasolini,
a convinced and avowed Marxist, was especially sensitive to the critics who took him to task for ideological inadequacy, for having escaped into the private world of a kind of eternal adolescence and
primitiveness instead of attempting to represent the awakening social
consciousness of the masses on their way to claim their place in the
sun. Thus Tommasino Puzzilli, the protagonist of Una vita violenta,
is seen as more fully rounded than Riccetto and is made to undergo
a political education which changes his initial heedless spontaneity
into a sense of responsibility toward others. Whether the book for
all its orthodox intentions is as successful as its predecessor is
questionable. My own feeling is that the first part of Una vita violenta
is more effective than the second and that the episodes most strongly
reminiscent of Ragazzi di vita are what saves it from being a completely pedestrian and unimaginative illustration of a thesis.

Tommasino is at the beginning just another Riccetto. He too lives
in a Hooverville on the outskirts of Rome. He too is involved with the
other boys of his district in a number of wild exploits, such as steal-
ing a car and holding up a hapless gas station attendant one night. He
too meets a girl to whom he becomes engaged and with whom he plays
the role of the proper young fiancé: the descriptions of their Sunday
outings are peculiarly and unexpectedly condescending, but I believe
unwittingly so. There are other episodes in the first part of the book
which mark a departure from Ragazzi di vita: Tommasino's participation in a "rumble" staged by a group of Fascist sympathizers, and
the revolt of the women of Pietralata against the police who are
rounding up their suspect husbands and sons. But the most striking
innovation has to do with technique. It is in a flashback at the beginning of Part Two that we are told of the Puzzillis' coming to Rome
as refugees during the war, of how they were forced to leave the
country, where their land and animals and the father's job as care-
taker in the public schools had permitted them to live quite comfort-
ably, much better than they now live in Rome. Still, in the long run

they turn out to be more fortunate than many of their new neighbours, for they are assigned an apartment in the complex of public housing being built in the no-man's-land of Pietralata. It is to this apartment that Tommasino returns after his stint in jail for having stabbed a heckler during a street fight, and it is at this point that the thrust of the narrative changes.

Tommasino appears to have left his adolescence behind him. He finds work and becomes a respectable member of society – so much so that he averts his eyes when he happens upon an ex-companion who has not succeeded as he has, but has become a crippled beggar huddling on a street in Rome. At the beginning of this turning point, however, Pasolini introduces the theme of death. First there is the brief report of the sudden death of Tommasino's two baby brothers, an episode which makes a strong appeal for sympathy from the reader by bringing into view the injustices and deprivations which reduce human life to the level of animal, or even insect, life. Then there are the initial symptoms of Tommasino's tuberculosis, which eventually leads him to a long stay in a city hospital. There he meets and learns to admire and respect a group of Communists who are organizing and supporting the hospital attendants in a strike. Tommasino joins the party upon his release. But the story is now rapidly approaching the end. Tommasino dies in a new tubercular attack, brought on by his trying to save a prostitute during a flood.

As can be seen, Pasolini's intention in Una vita violenta was to write a novel which would follow the classical pattern by being the complete and exemplary story of a central character. In this respect Una vita violenta is not different from the social novels of the nineteenth century, from Zola, for instance. But while Pasolini is excellent at catching the "feeling" of the life of his protagonists, he is less successful with the concreteness of historical background. He leaves the reader with strong sense impressions: unpleasant odours, rough and dirty textures, deformed limbs, blemished skins, rotting clothing, mud, heaps of garbage. But there is little or nothing in the book which will help a future reader to reconstruct the complexity of an epoch. Pasolini's talent is lyrical and sentimental, not narrative and historical. That is why the episode of the "talking" dogs, tucked away in the flow of euphoric slang, is the real clue to the quality of his art.

As I pointed out at the beginning of this essay, Gadda, rather than Pasolini, is the writer recognized by the novelists of the latest avantgarde as their forerunner. But actually, if we compare Gadda's work with that of Sanguineti or Leonetti, for instance (both are antinovelists, experimentalists with a vengeance), we must conclude that the kinship is more symbolic than real. Sanguineti in Il gioco dell'oca (1967) and Leonetti in Tappeto volante (1967) have written novels which have nothing in common with the genre in its familiar forms, except perhaps

the colourful book jackets and the fictitiousness of the world represented. In attempting to speak of works such as these, it becomes
at once painfully evident that the terms commonly used in connection
with the novel of realism, the novel par excellence, are no longer
adequate. Their authors declare Il gioco dell'oca and Tappeto volante
to be novels. Leonetti even adds the usual postscript disavowing any
responsibility should his characters happen to resemble persons
living or dead. He claims, in other words, the same privileges for
the imagination that storytellers and fabulists have done at all times.
But I believe that novels like Sanguineti's and Leonetti's, if they are
novels at all, are so only by a process of elimination. They are obviously not plays, nor poems, nor essays, nor news reports, nor
philosophic treatises, nor driving manuals. At best, they may be
called constructions, shapes, with the same relation to the novel
proper that a mobile in a museum has to a classical statue of antiquity.
This means that in the concept of construction or shape, as applied to
them, there is not the slightest residue of the idea that art is an imi-
tation, however free and personal, of nature. In the novels of both
Gadda and Pasolini, instead, the connection between art and nature is
still solid, even though Pasolini's narrative is almost exclusively
mimetic, while in Gadda there is an added metaphorical dimension,
the work serving not only to depict reality, however apparently deformed, but also to epitomize the process of knowledge.

The "goose game" which gives its name to Il gioco dell'oca is an
old table game in which the players, casting dice, move their wooden
geese from square to square, incurring hazards or gaining advantages.
Sanguineti has made up his own squares, one hundred and eleven of
them, each one with its illustration: newspaper cuttings; advertisments;
pictures of mermaids, of monsters, of Salvador Dali's girl with
mustache; scenes from music halls; fantasies from comic strips; and
so on. A reproduction of the cardboard on which the game is played
appears on each of the endpapers of the book. Paralleling the squares -
also referred to as slots or coffins - are the one hundred and eleven
short chapters which constitute the so-called novel. They tell no co-
herent story; each chapter consists of an anecdote, a comment, a reflection on life, or an explosion of publicity slogans, well known mottos,
and references to the latest gossip. The book is to be read in the same
way as the game is played, by moving from chapter to chapter as the
throw of the dice indicates. In fact, as the dedication at the beginning
states, the book is to be played with rather than read. "Ce n'est que
superpositions d'images de catalogue", Sanguineti concludes.

Tappeto volante represents a different kind of experiment. The first-
person narrator seems at the outset to be really telling a story: he
wakes up from a nightmare and his day begins. After a few sentences,
however, the reader is aware that if story there be, it is a very strange
story, told in an even stranger way. The narrator, whose name is

Shelley, has a wife whose name is Mary. He is by profession a clock-maker, but instead of repairing clocks, he wrecks them in order to resell them to a particularly sophisticated class of Swiss collectors. Shelley is in love with Olivia, an elusive woman who has set up a whole series of signals by which she communicates, or gives the illusion of communicating, with him. Thus, for instance, Shelley and Olivia may be telephoning to one another when they are seized with the desire to meet. She promises to send a taxi to get him. He goes downstairs and picks out the right one from among the many taxis passing by because he discovers an 18 (part of Olivia's telephone number) in the taxi's license plate. But before taking the taxi he must decipher the meaning of the other numbers: does the coded message mean that he is to take the taxi, that he is to telephone Olivia, or that he is to wait for a call from her? The possibilities are almost infinite, and so are the possibilities of error, given the multiplicity of meanings that each gesture, each word, each signal has. The whole novel proceeds with this rhythm. Olivia, the etymology of whose Shakespearean name is at one point given as Oli-via, she who makes the (salad) oil disappear (there is a maid in the Shelley household who has this detestable habit: is she another spy of Olivia's?), is also supposed to stand for a kind of new Beatrice in this new Vita nuova. In the postscript Leonetti promises to set forth elsewhere the theory of the type of novel he has just written.

It does not take much to see how these two experimental novels of the late sixties support my statement that the narrative intents and procedures of Gadda and Pasolini have very little in common with the new experimentalism, which is essentially structural rather than linguistic. In a second meeting of Gruppo 63, which took place in Palermo in 1965, Renato Barilli spoke of a second generation of experimentalists, who went beyond the instrumental use of a vision autre. They recognized, that is, that Robbe-Grillet and Butor, for instance, in their antinovels may not at all have intended primarily to analyze man's psychological reaction to objects as a comment on his reaction to society, but that they may have been concerned instead "with inventing a mechanism which proceeds at a particular pace, at a rhythm consisting of continual advances and retreats and of vast circular trajectories". (14) Similarly Sanguineti and Günter Grass, Barilli continues, may not at all have chosen to rely on dreams (in Sanguineti's other novel, Capriccio italiano) and dwarfs in order to fight ethical and social taboos, but more simply to effect "an ingenious renewal of the picaresque".

Now, while for Gadda one could certainly speak of vision autre (the deformation and excess of a disordered psyche which gives his expression such virulence), there can be no question that for neither Gadda nor Pasolini writing a novel ever became the equivalent to constructing a game. They are both fundamentally earnest and moralistic in their approach to art. They have a message to transmit, easily recognizable in Pasolini, less so in Gadda. The themes they treat undoubtedly present only divergences if we examine them in the context of one another's work. But when we look at Gadda and Pasolini from a certain distance, from the perspective of the new experimentalism, for instance, we can only conclude that the themes they treat are the old ones - crime, guilt, death - and that the feeling of revulsion for the fault in nature that both writers experience derives from the traditional, classic view of man in his relation to other men and to the world about him.

(1969)

NOTES

(1) Gianfranco Contini, "Preliminari sulla lingua del Petrarca", Paragone-Letteratura, 1951, 3-26.
(2) Angelo Guglielmi, "Avanguardia e sperimentalismo", in Gruppo 63 (Milan, 1964), 19. All translations in the essay are mine, with the exception of the passage on page 140, which is quoted from William Weaver's translation of Quer pasticciaccio (That Awful Mess on Via Merulana, New York, 1965).
(3) P. P. Pasolini, "Il neo-sperimentalismo", Officina, February 1956; now in Passione e ideologia (Milan, 1960), 470-83.
(4) Renato Barilli, "'Cahier de doléance' sull'ultima narrativa italiana", Il Verri, 1960; now in La barriera del naturalismo (Milan, 1964), 171.
(5) Elio Filippo Accrocca, Ritratti su misura di scrittori italiani (Venice, 1960), 205.
(6) Ibid., 321.
(7) Italo Calvino, "Main Currents in Italian Fiction Today", Italian Quarterly, IV, 13-14 (1960), 12.
(8) C. E. Gadda, "Un'opinione sul neorealismo", can now be read in I viaggi la morte (Milan, 1958), 252-53.
(9) C. E. Gadda, La cognizione del dolore (Turin, 1963), 48.
(10) This review can now be read in Passione e ideologia, 318-24.
(11) Ibid., 313-18.
(12) "La poesia dialettale del '900", now in Passione e ideologia, especially 61-62.
(13) "Nove domande sul romanzo", Nuovi argomenti, 38-39 (May-August 1959), 48.
(14) Renato Barilli, in Gruppo 63, Il romanzo sperimentale (Milan, 1966), 23.

INDEX AND BIBLIOGRAPHY

Names referred to in both text and notes are listed below. Rather
than forming a separate Bibliography, secondary sources follow
their author's name. Where reference is to a note, this is indicated
by the number of the note in parentheses attached to the number of
the page on which it occurs.

" 'Cahier de doléances' sull'ultima narrativa italiana, " Il Verri,
IV, 1 (1960), 90-111. Now in La barriera del naturalismo (Milan,
1964).
"Le strutture del romanzo, " in Gruppo 63 (Milan, 1964), 25-47.
Gruppo 63, Il romanzo sperimentale (Milan, 1966), 11-26.
Bassani, G., 3, 4, 5, 12, 13, 16, 17, 26 (19, 24), 32 (51)
Prefaz., Giuseppe Tomasi di Lampedusa, Il gattopardo (Milan,
1958).
Beckett, S., 2, 25 (11)
Belli, G., 130, 145, 149
Bellonci, G., 3
Benco, S., 119, 120 (1), 121 (6)
"Italo Svevo, " Pegaso (Florence, January 1929).
Berni, F., 59
Betti, U., 135
Bishop, T., 83, 103 (7)
Pirandello and the French Theater (New York, 1960).
Blackmur, R. P., 28 (27)
Introd., Henry James, The Art of the Novel. Critical Prefaces
(New York, 1934).
Blasucci, L., 22 (4)
"Giuseppe Tomasi di Lampedusa -- Il Gattopardo, " Belfagor, XIV
(1959), 117-121.
Bocelli, A., 26 (23)
"Tomasi di Lampedusa, " Enciclopedia italiana, Appendix III (Rome,
1961), 959-960.
Böhm, D., 50-51, 57 (33)
Zeitlosigkeit und entgleitende Zeit als konstitutive Dialektik im
Werke von Giovanni Verga (Münster/Westfalen, 1967).
Borlenghi, A., 83, 103 (9)
Pirandello o dell'ambiguità (Padua, 1968).
Bragaglia, L., 83, 102 (2), 103 (4), 104 (20)
Interpreti pirandelliani (Rome, 1969).
Briosi, S., 57 (35)
"Sullo stile del Verga, " Lettere italiane, XXI (1969), 200-206.
Butor, M., 2, 153
Buzzi, G., 24 (9)
Invito alla lettura di Tomasi di Lampedusa (Milan, 1972-73).
Byron, G., 7

Calvino, I., 137, 154 (7)
"Main Currents in Italian Fiction Today, " Italian Quarterly, IV,
no. 13-14 (1960), 3-14.
Capuana, L., 60, 69, 80 (37)
Casanova, G., 130
Cassola, C., 3, 12

David, M., 24 (9), 26 (20), 27 (26), 30 (34)
  La psicoanalisi nella cultura italiana (Turin, 1966).
Davidson, A., 123, 132 (1), 133 (3, 4)
  Trans., Alberto Moravia, The Fetish and Other Stories (New York, 1965).
  Trans., Alberto Moravia, The Lie (New York, 1966).
De Bella, N., 105 (22)
  Narrativa e teatro nell'arte di Luigi Pirandello (Messina, 1962).
Debenedetti, G., 27 (26)
  Il romanzo del Novecento (Milan, 1971).
De Filippo, P., 83
Del Ministro, M., 104 (15)
  "Lettura di testi pirandelliani, " Letteratura, no. 94-96 (1968), 728-752.
De Roberto, F., 4, 26 (21, 23)
De Sanctis, F., 60, 82 (58)
  Storia della letteratura italiana, ed. L. Russo (Milan, 1960).
Devoto, G., 35, 54 (10), 55 (27), 81 (47)
  "Giovanni Verga e i 'piani del racconto', " in Nuovi studi di stilistica (Florence, 1962), 202-214.
Dipace, A., 32 (50)
  Questione delle varianti del "Gattopardo" (Latina, 1971).
Di Pietro, A., 76 (6), 78 (21)
  Saggio su Luigi Pirandello (Milan, 1941).
  Pirandello (Milan, 1951).
  "Luigi Pirandello, " in Letteratura italiana. I contemporanei, I (Milan, 1963), 47-80.

Eskin, S. G., 24 (9)
  "Animal Imagery in Il gattopardo, " Italica, 39 (1962), 189-194.
Evans, A. and C., 24 (9)
  "Salina and Svelto: The Symbolism of Change in Il Gattopardo, " Wisconsin Studies in Contemporary Literature, 4 (1963), 298-304.

Farina, S., 66, 68, 81 (41)
Faulkner, W., 143
Felcini, F., 24 (9), 26 (18), 29 (28), 33 (61)
  "Dieci anni del Gattopardo: Bilancio e prospettive, " Cultura e scuola, 25 (1968), 55-66.
  "Giuseppe Tomasi di Lampedusa, " Letteratura italiana. I contemporanei, III (Milan, 1969), 249-266.
Fergusson, F., 73, 82 (59)
  The Idea of a Theatre (1949) (New York, 1953).
Ferrante, L., 79 (25), 83, 102 (2), 103 (8)
  Pirandello (Florence, 1958).

160

Weaver, W.,   144, 154 (2)
 trans., Gadda, C. E.,   That Awful Mess on Via Merulana (New York, 1965).
Wellek, R.,   31 (42)
 With Austin Warren, Theory of Literature (New York, 1942).
Whitfield, J. H.,   105 (22)
 "La metamorfosi della novella, " in Atti del Congresso interna-
 zionale di studi pirandelliani (Florence, 1967), 735-742.
Woolf, V.,   1, 11

Zola, E.,   67